PAPERS ON PLANNING AND
ECONOMIC MANAGEMENT

Ely Devons

PAPERS ON

PLANNING AND ECONOMIC MANAGEMENT

BY ELY DEVONS

EDITED BY SIR ALEC CAIRNCROSS

MANCHESTER UNIVERSITY PRESS

Published by the University of Manchester at
THE UNIVERSITY PRESS
316–324 Oxford Road, Manchester M13 9NR

UK standard book number: 7190 0408 X

Made and Printed in Great Britain by
Butler & Tanner Ltd, Frome and London

Contents

Acknowledgement

The publishers' thanks are extended to the following bodies and journals for their co-operation in enabling articles first published under their aegis to be reproduced here: the BBC and *The Listener*, Cambridge University Press, *The Economist* (and for waiving its rule of author anonymity in this case), *The Guardian*, Lloyds Bank Ltd (*Lloyds Bank Review*), the London School of Economics (*Economica*), Oliver & Boyd Ltd (the *Scottish Journal of Political Economy*), the Royal Statistical Society, Stevens & Sons Ltd (the *Modern Law Review*), and the University of Manchester (*The Manchester School*).

Ely Devons: a memoir

Ely Devons died on 28 December 1967, at the age of fifty-four, after a prolonged and painful illness, the sequel to earlier bouts of illness that struck him down again and again throughout the last dozen years of his life. To those who did not know him personally he was not a particularly significant figure: the author of a book on planning which few troubled to read, a statistician who had written an elementary guide to British statistics, and an economist whose aim seemed to be to debunk both economics and statistics rather than to make original contributions on either subject to the learned journals. But to those who did know him how different the impression he conveyed! Few more formidable in debate on public affairs; few more intellectually stimulating; not given to writing easily but always in command of the relevant facts; never willing to bow to received opinions without question or to accept that what actually went on must be what everybody assumed to go on; and yet possessed of an acute and firm judgment rooted in common sense. He loved debating and was given to paradox and skittishness. This put many people off who failed to notice how often and how embarrassingly his forecasts, even the extravagant ones, turned out to be right. Behind it all there was a rare integrity which gave him at times the aura of a prophet.

Devons was born in Bangor, North Wales, on 29 July 1913. His father, a Jewish minister, was an immigrant from Vilna who arrived in Britain on a Russian passport in July 1902 at the age of twenty-one. His mother, ten years younger than her husband, was born in Belfast (father and son both married Irish girls). They had a family of six, three boys and three girls, Devons being the second eldest. One of his younger brothers, Sam, has also had a distinguished academic career. He has been in turn a Fellow of Trinity College, Cambridge, Langworthy Professor of Physics at Manchester in succession to P. M. S. Blackett, and Professor of Physics at Columbia. For several years the two brothers were on the Senate at Manchester at the same time.

The family moved about a good deal. When Devons was twelve they were in Stoke-on-Trent where his school reports show him consistently first in a class of thirty-two at Hanley High School. From Stoke the family moved to Portsmouth and then to Manchester. There he attended North Manchester Municipal High School before going on to the University in 1931.

He used to say that it was Harold Laski who persuaded him to study economics in the course of a chance encounter in the street. Whatever the reason for his decision, it was a wise one, and he soon showed a gift for the subject, graduating with first-class honours in 1934 shortly before his twenty-first birthday. He was trained in the old Manchester Honours School (dating back before the first world war, a generation before PPE) of Economics, Politics and Modern History, and these were all subjects that he knew and cared about. Among his teachers was L. B. Namier, whose 'Namieresque' tendency to pin him down and talk *at* him when he was an honours student or young graduate Devons used to describe in later years. Namier (contrary to general opinion) was selective about those on whom he bore down, and this contact was a marked compliment to a very young man.

Part of the work he did for his degree survives in a long essay of about forty thousand words on the history of wage theory from Adam Smith to Alfred Marshall. For an undergraduate essay it is an impressive bit of work. The choice of subject may have owed something to his professor, George Daniels, who had just published an article on wage theory in the second number of a new journal, *The Manchester School*, and who is quoted with nicely timed approval on the penultimate page in support of the dictum that 'wage theory only applies in theory'. The preface—for there is one—opens with delightful candour:

> In undertaking this essay I hardly realised the amount of work that had been done on the theory of wages. Consequently, this essay suffers from the inexperience of the writer in never having undertaken before a piece of work of this type.

Unfortunately, Devons never subsequently undertook 'a piece of work of this type'. But if one can judge from his handling of the long succession of writers on wages up to Marshall and J. B. Clark, he could have been an outstanding historian of economic thought. He does not hesitate to take issue with the celebrities, to establish their inconsistencies, or even to dismiss their theories in a footnote.[1] But he is at pains to bring out the continuity of thought underlying past controversies, and there is a freshness and directness in his treatment of each writer that puts it beyond question that he went to the original source for his material.

It is salutary to read this essay and observe how remote it is from current discussion of wages on the one hand and from the world of the early 'thirties on the other. There is not a single figure anywhere in the volume, no reference to large-scale unemployment, and no mention of any twentieth-century work on wages beyond a passing reference to Dobb, Rowe and Hicks almost on the final page.

After graduation, Devons was awarded the Drummond Fraser Research Fellowship and spent a further year at Manchester on research into British production statistics. This was embodied in his M.A. thesis, submitted in September 1935, on *Changes in productivity per unit of labour in British industry, 1924–34*. The thesis was just as thorough and mature as his B.A. essay. It dealt succinctly with the conceptual problems of productivity measurement and turned aside quickly to the complex issues of interpretation of the conflicting statistical series for output and employment, following warily the path trodden by Bowley, Colin Clark and Tolles and Douglas. Most of the thesis was devoted to the coal and steel industries, for which the statistical data were fullest. It brought out the fact of cyclical swings in productivity, pointing out that

> wherever there has been a heavy decline or rise in production, employment has declined or risen, but not to the same extent, with the result that output per head tends to rise in a period of rising output and to fall in a period of declining output.

Devons then went on to attribute this partly to short-time working, but mainly to the fact that

> . . . a substantial percentage of the labour performed in production is an overhead cost in the short period, and that it is impossible and often

[1] Jevons' theory, for example, although it gets several pages, is waved aside as not calling for discussion, since it is 'metaphysical and only has slight connections with a realistic study of wages'.

inadvisable to reduce employment on the same scale as the reduction in production.

This may be a truism now, but it had never before been enunciated so plainly.

His conclusions about longer-term trends were equally new and interesting. In coal mining he was able to establish the rapid spread of mechanisation, the diversity of experience in different areas and the view that 'the controlling factor in increased technique', both in coal and steel, was the profitability of production and the ability to raise capital rather than the spur of declining output. From this he drew the conclusion that trade cycle theory was mistaken in suggesting that the first impulse to recovery came from the introduction of new technical improvements, since these seemed to follow, not precede, an expansion in output. He emphasised that the gap between actual and potential output was much wider than would appear from the unemployment statistics. Finally, he asserted —anticipating critics of the Verdoorn law—that 'there is apparently no tendency for output per head to increase most in industries with increasing or declining output'. The experience of the textile industries contrasted with that of other industries, including coal-mining, in which mechanisation was low or just beginning to develop so that the scope for improvements was much larger. However important are access to finance and the prospect of an adequate return which brings in finance, there must also be new techniques to introduce.

There was a surefootedness about the thesis that marked all Devons' subsequent work. His first aim was to establish the facts, looking carefully for snags in the statistical data; he drew conclusions from the facts cautiously and without striving after originality.

His thesis launched him on a statistical career. He began in 1935 as an Economic Assistant on the staff of the Joint Committee of Cotton Trades Organisations in Manchester, working under the direction of Glyn Hughes and alongside Christopher Saunders, another Manchester graduate. Four years later, at the outbreak of war, all three moved to the Cotton Control, where Devons worked for some months as a statistician until called to London.

A by-product of his thesis was his first published article, which appeared in the *Economic Journal* in September 1935 shortly after his twenty-second birthday.[2] This was followed in 1938 by a paper to the Manchester Statistical Society on 'Production trends in the United Kingdom',[3] attacking both the official index of industrial production and the methods used by one of the leading statisticians, Dr E. C. Rhodes, in a special memorandum issued by the London and Cambridge Economic Service. Devons linked his results with those of Tolles and Douglas to give a continuous series for census of production years from 1907 to 1935. He showed that between 1924 and 1935 industrial production had increased by about 35 per cent—a conclusion sustained twenty years later by Lomax[4]—and that industrial output had been rising at what then appeared the surprisingly high rate of about 3 per cent per annum.

Shortly after war broke out, Devons married. His wife, Estelle Wine, was a concert pianist, a pupil of Solomon. Although she had to abandon her professional career, she continued to give concerts from time to time throughout her married life, much to the pleasure of their many friends. There were three children of the marriage, two boys and a girl.

I first came to know Devons in March 1940 when he joined what was at that time known as the Central Economic Information Service, a small staff in the War Cabinet Office under John Jewkes and Austin Robinson, which came into existence at the end of 1939 to help Lord Stamp's 'Survey of Economic and Financial Planning for the War Effort'. This cumbersome title had been given to an advisory committee consisting of Stamp, Henry Clay and Hubert Henderson, with Francis Hemming as secretary and Piers Debenham as assistant secretary. Its main function was to look at the economic aspects of departmental preparations for the conduct of the war and make suggestions for improving and co-ordinating existing plans. With the outbreak of war shortly after the committee's appointment, this function was soon overtaken by the need for more active planning and co-ordination on a national scale, and it was obvious that such a need could not be discharged by a committee of economists meeting intermittently with no expert staff. In particular, the secret statistics that accumulated in different departments

[2] 'Output per head in Great Britain, 1924–33', *Economic Journal*, September 1935.

[3] Subsequently reproduced in *The Manchester School*, January 1939.

[4] K. S. Lomax, 'Production and productivity movements in the United Kingdom since 1900', *Journal of the Royal Statistical Society*, 1959, vol. 122, part 2.

and controls up and down Whitehall had to be collected, analysed and made available in a form convenient for the central direction of economic policy. This was the job to which Devons devoted himself when called in by his Manchester teachers, John Jewkes and Harry Campion.

He started in a room which he shared with me in the attic of Richmond Terrace, furnished with an empty grate, a bare table, two chairs, a filing cabinet and an ancient calculating machine. After prolonged negotiations with the various Controls—some of them highly suspicious of his capabilities and intentions—the statistics began to flow in, and in due course were printed and circulated. The format and typeface were revolutionary at the time, though common enough nowadays. The use of Gill Sans type was the outcome of much discussion with his colleagues and with the Stationery Office. A much larger page than had previously been used for official statistics was also introduced. The type and format adopted in what were labelled Series A, Series B, Series C and so on still survive in the *Monthly Digest of Statistics* (the lineal descendant of Series B) and many other official publications. But a third innovation, the printing of totals at the top or on the left of the column instead of at the bottom or on the right, had to be abandoned after the Prime Minister had insisted on restoration of the previous practice.

The group of economists in the War Cabinet Office grew steadily throughout 1940, with the arrival, amongst others, of Lionel Robbins, Evan Durbin, James Meade and Richard Stone. There was always a strong Manchester contingent, including John Jewkes, Harry Campion, Norman Chester and Philip Chantler as well as Ely Devons. There was also close contact with Beveridge, who had somehow launched a manpower survey and found room (in the new police building to which the staff moved late in 1940) both for himself and for his assistant, Harold Wilson. In this group Devons was the youngest—apart from Harold Wilson—but one of the most forceful and creative. These were anxious and busy but hilarious days, in which the absurdities of the situation revived one's spirits and life was never weighed down by any sense of normality in the daily round. Devons could nose out fresh extravagancies like truffles from the undergrowth of civil and military bureaucracy surrounding us. Meanwhile he bent his mind, like the rest of us, to the major issues of economic strategy and to marshalling the statistical information needed for intelligent discussion of these issues.

At the end of 1940 the Prime Minister, egged on we suspected by Lord Cherwell, cut the statisticians off from the economists in the War Cabinet Office, and penned them into the Central Statistical Office under Francis Hemming. The other half of the group was re-christened the Economic Section, with John Jewkes as its first Director. By May Jewkes was reporting on the need for a planning staff in the Ministry of Aircraft Production and was being invited to take charge of the staff which, with some hesitation, he concluded to be necessary. When he accepted this invitation Devons was induced after much heart-searching to join him and abandon the Central Statistical Office, where there seemed little scope for innovation. It proved a highly successful move, and in the next few years he grew to be one of the most influential men in the Ministry, taking over from Jewkes in 1944 as head of the Planning Department when still barely thirty.

Devons came to the Ministry as Chief Statistician and at first was largely occupied with the preparation of a monthly statistical bulletin. When he took this in hand there was no document to which one could turn for a comprehensive record of the output of aircraft, aero-engines and components. Indeed, I well remember that at the end of 1941 nobody knew how many propellers were being produced per month, nor even the monthly output of propellers of the same type (i.e. using the same kind of hub). Instead there was a large pile of weekly returns showing, contract by contract, the cumulative delivery position against each contract; and there were usually several contracts for identical propellers, and still more for propellers using a common hub but with different blades. Although propellers were one of the chief bottlenecks, the returns were not subjected to a systematic process of extraction, tabulation and presentation in the form of convenient time series: it was literally impossible to discover the underlying trends in output without considerable research. The statistics for other components were usually no better.

The Ministry had also functioned under the Beaverbrook regime without anything that could reasonably be called an aircraft programme. There was no document summarising the plans to which individual firms were working and available to serve as a basis for the co-ordination of other plans—for component manufacture and delivery on the one hand and squadron formation on the other. The main reason for this was that the Ministry was not organised to operate a series of carefully co-ordinated programmes: it had been brought into existence to deal with an emergency and relied on a mixture of improvisation and grab. But there was also some feeling of the kind Devons had encountered earlier, that highly secret statistics and programmes should not be too widely circulated even if it meant preventing people from doing their job properly by keeping them in the dark. After 1940 this feeling subsided and the circulation of the *Monthly Statistical Bulletin* and the programmes for airframes and main aircraft components reached nearly 200 without any subsequent protest on grounds of security. All these documents were printed; Devons had early come to appreciate that the printed text, if well presented and expensive enough, is treated with more respect than mimeographed papers that are otherwise adequate.

The staff of the Planning Department included Frank Paish, David Champernowne, Brian and Marjorie Tew, Walter Hagenbuch and others who later occupied chairs in economics or held important positions in business and government. But it was Devons who was the life and soul of the place. He was always abreast of what was going on, alive to the choices that had to be made, and able to foresee the next move before anybody else. He lacked the analytical interests of Frank Paish and the verbal dexterity of John Jewkes. There was also a certain brashness and ruthlessness about him that did not recommend him to everyone: he spoke what he saw even if it hurt or if it was not understood, and he sometimes seemed to speak in riddles because of his love of paradox. But he commanded respect from everyone and was particularly liked by his subordinates of both sexes.

From the start Devons took an interest in the planning side of the work. This grew as time went on, and in 1944, when Jewkes left to go to the Ministry of Reconstruction, Devons was appointed to succeed him. It was, above all, his experience during this final year of the war that he drew on in his subsequent writings about the Ministry of Aircraft Production.[5] The ideas in these writings had not been fully developed when he left the Ministry of Aircraft Production—indeed, he showed no inclination to analyse his exper-

[5] *Planning in practice* (Cambridge University Press, 1950); 'The Problem of co-ordination in aircraft production' in *Lessons of the British War Economy*, ed. D. N. Chester, 1951; 'Economic planning in war and peace', paper read to the Manchester Statistical Society, November 1947, and reprinted in *Essays in Economics*, 1961.

ience in writing at that time and seemed to take it for granted that the job was more in my line than in his. But in after life he turned back constantly to his days in the Ministry of Aircraft Production as a kind of magnifying glass through which to view current controversies.

He also reverted frequently to his association with Sir Wilfred Freeman, who was Chief Executive in the Ministry of Aircraft Production almost throughout Devons' period there, and was very much the dominant personality in the Ministry. For Devons he symbolised the ideal combination of intelligence and judgment, and his appeal was heightened by force of character and by a certain impishness.[6] Freeman, on his side, took to Devons—I can remember his saying, rather to my surprise, soon after Jewkes' departure, that he found it easier to work with Devons than with Jewkes. But no doubt what Devons saw in Freeman, Freeman saw in Devons—and perhaps with more reason.

When the war was over Freeman tried unsuccessfully to get Devons to join him in Courtauld's. Devons was tempted but eventually decided on an academic career and accepted a post as Robert Ottley Reader in Applied Economics at Manchester. This was one of the first appointments in Britain specifically described as in applied economics. It meant, of course, a big drop in salary: in those days a reader earned no more than £750 per annum. Three years later the appointment was raised to a Chair, which Devons held for the next eleven years.

Nearly all Devons' written work was composed during his years at Manchester. Yet he was never able to give more than a small part of his time to writing. For much of his time in the Chair—1949–59—he was Dean of the Faculty of Economic and Social Studies (or had to prop up someone else as dean) and this, while it gave him authority, also limited the time he could give to research. The Faculty was one of considerable distinction—including, for example, Sir Arthur Lewis, Harry Johnson, Michael Polanyi, Max Gluckman and Bill Mackenzie—but it was Devons who contributed most to what Harry Johnson describes as 'a Faculty ethos in which economists, political scientists, public administration experts, social

[6] On one occasion which Devons long remembered, Freeman persuaded him to play truant and the two stole out of Thames House unobserved to go and sit in the sun by the riverside and talk of anything except aircraft. Not a word was said by Freeman on his return in explanation of his absence.

work specialists, anthropologists and sociologists freely exchanged ideas and discussed concepts to their great mutual benefit'.

His colleagues were fond of travelling, but Devons, who had to 'mind the shop', rarely moved far from Manchester. In the summer of 1950 I persuaded him to come to Paris for a month or so to lend a hand in preparing the new statistical bulletins that OEEC began to issue later in the year. This was a job much along the lines of his previous efforts to assemble and present key indicators in convenient form during the war. Thanks largely to him, the bulletins were prepared with great speed. They have undergone remarkably little change in the past twenty years, although the footnotes which he made a point of omitting have crept back in.

In the summer of 1954 Devons went to the Merrill Center (at Southampton, Long Island) for several weeks and was brought into contact with many of the leading American economists. Throughout the 'fifties he gave occasional lectures abroad, for example to the NATO Defence College (on manpower) and to the Centre d'Études Industrielles in Geneva (a series of three lectures on 'Some aspects of administratively directed and price system economies'). He was also a frequent lecturer at conferences in Britain, especially those held by the Association of University Teachers of Economics, at which he was a fairly regular attender. Most of his lectures on these occasions were unscripted (although carefully prepared, as his surviving notes show) but quite a number were written out in full and one or two were published.

An example of the latter is the talk he gave in 1949 to the Cotton Board conference in Harrogate,[7] when he challenged the view that the installation of automatic looms would transform the economic prospects of the cotton industry, and that only short-sightedness by the cotton weavers stood in the way. He directed attention to a different variable: the number of (automatic) looms per worker. Devons' analysis, as is usual on those occasions, created quite a stir, received no support, was never refuted and was soon conveniently forgotten.

While his output during the 'fifties was limited by his teaching and administrative responsibilities, it included two books—*Planning in Practice* (1950) and *Introduction to British Economic Statistics* (1956)—each of them on a subject of the deepest interest to him and

[7] 'The future of prices and costs in the cotton industry', Cotton Board Conference reprint, 1949.

of which he had made himself a master. But in a sense they looked back to an earlier period in his career when he had been first an economic statistician and then a planner. The broadening of his interests in the 'fifties is more fully reflected in his third book—*Essays in Economics*—which, although not published until 1961, consists entirely of work done at Manchester, some of it as far back as 1947, and much of it in 1953–4 for delivery as the Newmarch lectures. Although planning and statistics remain important themes in this volume, there is a growing preoccupation with more philosophical issues and with the limitations for policy making of economic analysis narrowly conceived. Devons felt increasingly the need to take a broad view of social science, to concentrate attention on how economic systems really work, and to link economic analysis with other approaches to the study of decision taking in business and government.

This was a feeling to which he gave expression in a series of talks and essays (many of them reproduced here) and in the staff seminar which he and Arthur Lewis conducted. 'For many years,' Harry Johnson has written, this was 'the most devastatingly critical forum in the country into which a careless economist could blunder.'

Devons took part regularly in other seminars, including those in the departments of Government and of Social Anthropology and Sociology. In these seminars he exercised a great influence on the thinking of his colleagues and on their bright young men, many of whom now hold Chairs in Britain and overseas. He also helped Max Gluckman to organise a series of seminars on how analysts of economic, social and behavioural systems operate when they reach the limits of competence in their discipline. Later he published with Gluckman an introduction and a long analytic conclusion to a volume of papers raising these issues under the title *Closed Systems and Open Minds: the limits of naivety in social anthropology* (1964).

Bill Mackenzie, who held the (new) Chair of Government and Administration at Manchester from 1948 until long after Devons' departure, gives a vivid description of these years:

'I came to Manchester at the beginning of 1949: Arthur Lewis had arrived in 1948. Meantime, a readership in Social Anthropology was on the books: we interviewed Max Gluckman early in 1949, and the committee (including a lot of elderly Arts Faculty cynics) forcibly and unanimously asked that he be offered a chair.

'Hence a Faculty of Economic and Social Studies, very new in the world, with five professors; one of them Michael Polanyi, a "marvellous boy" in his sixties, and four of us forty or younger. We were in fact very mature. But an old university thought us young: a remark by a very old and boorish professor of English about "young whippersnappers" (made before I arrived) was remembered, repeated, resented and became a driving force.

'I suspect that even then Ely was not a professional economist, but a very able man who could talk economic language but could not in that language say all he wanted to say. His book *Planning in Practice* is a book not about economics but about administration, and I hope it will keep its place there as a classic—a naive classic, in that Ely had not followed the development of administrative theory (indeed, had never heard of it), but still a classic.

'I suppose I contributed something, in that I shared with Ely a Whitehall language and a university language, for which Cornford's *Microcosmographia* is the code book; and I had an analogous problem, in my case that of making relevant sense of political doctrine.

'But the catalyst was Max, added to Manchester United and (in a secondary role) to the Manchester University staff golfing society. Structure–function was then in its prime; we learnt from Max, and the key worked in some locks. But not in all, and there was fruitful running debate (Dorothy Emmet helped here) about what on earth a function could be if it were not a purpose. And so on . . .

'We were not (thank God) a movement: there was no question of a quest for unified social science. We were all too busy with our own top priority stuff, and this included our individual efforts to create and sustain working groups of individuals. But we had two things in common, at least; we were inquisitive and reflective about society in action, and we did not care very much about the boundaries of academic disciplines, if they stood in the way of following the argument wherever it might lead. In this Ely was a leader not only in the faculty but in the university. Manchester University meant a great deal to him symbolically; indeed, it was in its symbolic form one of the few things which he treated with deference. The quirks of university politics gave him as much sport as those of Whitehall politics, and he was in no sense the leader of a reform caucus. But he thought naturally in university terms, not simply in those of discipline or department; and his voice, quiet but insistent, carried great weight in many different spheres of university life.'

In 1959, after much heart-searching, Devons accepted the chair in Commerce at the London School of Economics vacated by James Meade. It was an appointment that did not escape criticism, and Devons himself felt a little uncomfortable at his entry into a field of study in which he could not profess to be an expert. He was also disturbed to find how inadequate the literature appeared to be on matters of fact, such as the methods by which trade was financed, and how elaborate it was on matters of pure theory without, however, matching the intricacy and complexity of the real world or providing satisfactory explanations of the main features of international trade.[8]

Nonetheless, he equipped himself manfully for his new responsibilities, as his surviving lecture notes show, and he published several articles on world trade.[9] He continued to lecture on international trade right up to 1966–7. But he had no special interest in the subject, and when the opportunity arose of removing from the title of his Chair any reference to commerce he was rather glad to take it.

His move to London in 1959 coincided with his appointment as a member of the Local Government Commission—a considerable added burden. As the years went by, he became increasingly sceptical of the value of evidence from local councillors and officials without accompanying research. He was out of sympathy with his chairman, unimpressed by the local authorities and their concentration on party advantage to the total exclusion of key issues such as roads and traffic, and finally dismayed by the obvious intention of the government to disregard and eventually disband the commission. He got in first and resigned in 1965, some months before the government did as he had predicted and dismissed his colleagues.

Devons was also acting as a part-time government consultant

[8] See his inaugural lecture, 'Understanding international trade', *Economica*, November 1961.

[9] Apart from his inaugural lecture he wrote an important article on 'World trade in invisibles' for *Lloyds' Bank Review*, April 1961, and another on 'The end of the dollar problem' for the *Irish Banking Review*, June 1960, as well as a number of newspaper articles and reviews. He had also published articles on international trade problems in 1951–2.

from about 1962 onwards, first to the Ministry of Aviation and later to the Ministry of Defence. This did not involve much more than participation in the work of named committees, making *ad hoc* suggestions and comments at the meetings, but not submitting anything in writing. In 1962 he was asked to join the Monopolies Commission but felt unable to combine this with his duties on the Local Government Commission. When approached again in 1966 he agreed to serve, but ill-health prevented him from playing any real part in the work of the commission.

He began to travel abroad more frequently. In April 1961 he visited Moscow with other British economists (following a visit by Soviet economists to the London School of Economics during the previous autumn). In 1962 he was in Turkey advising the Turkish government on planning on behalf of OECD. In the spring of 1963 he went to Cyprus to advise the government there on economic development. The following year he spent several months in the United States as Harkness Visiting Professor at Johns Hopkins University.

Neither government assignments nor foreign travel prevented him from playing a major part in the work of the London School of Economics. Although critical of the administration of the School, to quote Harry Johnson again:

> he inevitably became Convener of the Economics Department, and in that capacity did much to reform and democratise the Department's decision-taking structure, as well as to improve the administration of the School generally. He had the capacity, extremely rare among economists or academics at large, to think and plan in terms of the institution as a whole and its relation to the outside world, rather than in terms of the department within the institution; as an administrator he was exceptionally able, his chief fault being a tendency to assume that others were as clear-minded and far-sighted as he. As Convener, he was also largely responsible for the institution of the M.Sc. degrees in Economics and Econometrics, an innovation whose success he helped to ensure by initiating a campaign to raise money for graduate fellowships from private sources; but perhaps his greatest contribution was to inspire his colleagues, and especially those recently appointed to professorships from outside the School, with his own vision of the potentialities of the School as an international centre for economics teaching and research.

In September 1965 he had just delivered the first of a series of four broadcast talks when he was taken ill and the rest of the series had to be cancelled. From then on, with only short intervals, he was an invalid, nursed devotedly by his wife, and it seemed impossible that he could survive for long. In fact it was over two years before he finally succumbed. Throughout that time (and in fact for many years before) he had remarkably little sleep: much of his reading was done at night. He lost weight, looked increasingly cadaverous and his voice sank to a whisper so that at times he could hardly make himself heard. But his mind was as alert as ever, his insight as remarkable, his judgment as shrewd and penetrating. When I saw him a few days before his death, he still made the running in our conversation and had spotted with evident satisfaction an error in the press about some incident in my earlier career.

Devons gave as his recreations in *Who's who* 'Fell-walking, tree felling, disputing, looking at pictures.' Of these, most people were conscious only of the third. He enjoyed 'disputing', in the sense of trying to sort things out intellectually in argument with others. Although he did not suffer fools gladly and was conscious—sometimes painfully conscious—that this was so, he was not emotionally engaged in winning the argument or anxious to discomfit the loser. He hated arrogance, dogmatism and—most of all—humbug. In his dealings with students he was kindness itself, and went to endless trouble on their account. With colleagues he had a natural gift of leadership, helped by his eye for the weakness of an argument and for the workable solution to a problem. It was only with the pseudo-expert, the stuffed shirt, the intellectually slovenly and the offensively pretentious that he lost patience.

One of his Manchester colleagues, Bill Mackenzie, saw Ely Devons as 'a man who acted ably in any situation in which he was placed: more strikingly, he had a continuous, intense and conscious "feedback" from the situation as he acted on it. In a sense, therefore, he was not a "man of action", still less a "leader of men"; but he had a superb understanding of the "managerial situation", and his only limitation as managerial "gamesman" was that he would insist on explaining how he did it. Most of us conceal our "ploys"; Ely never, and this made for great influence in the long run, in that unexpected people rallied to him in the end as "very clever but an honest man".'

There is no doubt in my mind that Devons had the elements of greatness in him to a degree not reflected in his career or in his writings. He had a rare combination of administrative skill and intellectual power, and to these was added an impressive firmness of character that gave to his personal life an integrity and incorruptibility even in small matters. In other circumstances a career begun so promisingly might have led much further. But he lacked ambition and perhaps also a sense of engagement. It was a sense that might have been aroused, as to some extent it was in Manchester. But economics did not excite him; it appealed too exclusively to the intellectual side of his nature. By 1960 he was writing in a fit of depression—'I *dislike* economics'—and some years later when in Baltimore he confessed to feeling 'increasingly like a fish out of water in current academic economics'. In part, this was a reaction against the narrowness of technical economic analysis and the neglect of wider social and political factors inseparable from economic issues; in part it reflected exhaustion and ill-health and the *anomie* that went with it. Yet there was also perhaps in the disenchantment which he sometimes expressed in his later years a feeling that he had not found himself, that the larger purpose of which he was in quest had eluded him and that he had not succeeded in finding secular expression for the religious energies stoked up in him in his youth. Whatever he may have felt, he underrated his own achievements. For he left behind lasting memorials in all he did in Whitehall, Manchester and London, and in the ideas that he sowed so fruitfully in the minds of his friends.

A.C.

Introduction

Nearly all the papers included in this volume fall under three broad headings. First come a number of pieces on planning: either on planning in war-time and in the period after the war, or on the relationship between central planning and economic organisation and growth. These are succeeded by a series of short essays—many of them originally broadcast talks—on various aspects of government. The emphasis in these essays changes from the ideological and political to the administrative and organisational, with a growing concentration on what goes on in Whitehall and in particular in the Treasury. This interest is also reflected in the papers dealing with the role of the economist in government and the way in which economic issues appear to the public. The third group of papers consists of evidence given to the Robbins Committee on University Education in 1962, supplemented by two other papers on university problems. Finally, a couple of lighter pieces have been added in order to give a more rounded impression of Devons' personality: one on his experiences as a juryman (delivered as one of the John Hinkley Memorial Lectures at Johns Hopkins University) and one on a game he liked to play to make attendance at conferences less tedious.

The first two sections hang together as an expression of Devons' view on what may be called, for short, 'economic administration'. This is not a subject easily treated systematically or reducible to textbook form. If it was ever his intention—which I doubt—Devons never had the leisure to put together in a single volume a connected theory of economic administration, but preferred to make excursions into the subject in a series of commentaries on particular themes. These commentaries have to be read in the context of the historical situation at the time, and the reader may therefore find it useful to be reminded of some of the background to their composition.

(1) *Planning*

Devons' experience of planning included a spell in the War Cabinet Office in the critical year 1940–1, when the adaptation of the economy to the conduct of the war was at its height. This gave him a sense of the strategy of decision making at the centre, and of the limitations imposed on this strategy by administrative pressures—for example, the absence of up-to-date, reliable and consistent information; the shortage of time and staff for making the most of the information available; the importance of personalities and current notions in the conflicts of opinion and will inseparable from decision taking; the difficulty of adequate communication in all large organisations between centre and periphery. But, of course, his interest was never limited to the constraints on economic strategy: he was also interested in the strategy actually adopted, and he had an eye, like any good economist, for inconsistencies in its different elements.

A much deeper insight into planning problems came from his four years in the Ministry of Aircraft Production. Here he found that what was dignified as planning proved in practice to be little more than one step onwards from improvisation: muddle qualified by efforts to co-ordinate with imperfect foresight. The lesson that planning was essentially a technique of grappling with uncertainty, and that it rested on readiness to re-plan, was quickly grasped, although it eluded (and still eludes) public and politicians alike. It grew to be believed outside the Ministry of Aircraft Production that war production—and especially aircraft production—had been brilliantly planned and that war-time experience was a triumphant demonstration of the power of governments to plan and control economic life. Planning was identified with control, and both with the achievement of certainty: the ability so to organise that the government could impose its will on the economy by setting and achieving fixed goals. Devons believed that his experience in the Ministry of Aircraft Production pointed in quite the opposite direction: to the need to avoid the construction of rigid plans and organise the economy in ways that made use of market mechanisms as an instrument of co-ordination. He regarded the war-time situation as exceptional and calling for a degree of centralisation inappropriate in peace-time.

It was to provide a plain account of what planning was really like that Devons wrote his first book, *Planning in Practice.* It did not appear until the end of 1950, by which time some of the post-war illusions about planning had been dispelled. But in the meantime Devons had published one essay analysing the fundamental differences between planning in war and peace.[1] Another (reproduced as the first in the present collection) on the special characteristics of co-ordination in aircraft production in war-time appeared soon afterwards.[2] This second essay, perhaps because it used the word 'co-ordination' instead of the word 'planning', has been largely overlooked by economists. I regard it as a classic in the literature of economic planning; and it has the great merit that although it is about aircraft production it calls for no understanding of aircraft manufacture and dispenses with the detail that makes *Planning in Practice* hard going for the general reader. It ought to be prescribed reading in schools of business management and public administration, since the logic of the essay applies to all efforts to achieve co-ordination through the use of production programmes.

Devons was in the meantime commenting on post-war efforts at planning in a series of articles in *The Manchester School.* These have now lost most of their interest, except to historians of the post-war period, who might otherwise accept the myths in which most of the public debate on planning was wrapped. But an article in 1952 on 'Planning by economic survey' (the third essay in this volume) is still topical as a critique of the ideas about planning expressed in post-war government publications. From 1947 onwards the government issued an annual *Economic Survey* which contained forecasts and plans for the coming year and was professedly what is now called 'a planning document'. The issue for 1947 contained the first and only explanation of what planning was supposed to do. Later issues progressively abandoned the plans, and in due course also the forecasts, until in 1963 the *Economic Survey* was replaced by an *Economic Report* which contented itself with an analysis of the past year and did not attempt to predict or plan the year ahead.

In the mid-'fifties, when talk of planning died out (and people even began to forget that Britain had had any experience of

1 'Economic planning in war and peace', paper read to the Manchester Statistical Society, November 1947, and reprinted in *Essays in Economics*, 1961.

2 'The problem of co-ordination in aircraft production' in *Lessons of the British War Economy*, ed. D. N. Chester, 1951.

planning) Devons turned to other matters. But he liked to draw on his war-time experience in seeking to understand what was happening in Communist countries. This led to a succession of articles: first a broadcast in 1957 on planning in the USSR, then a paper on 'Planning in the West and in the Communist world' which he read in Moscow in 1961 as a member of a visiting group of economists, and finally a more analytic treatment for a seminar in 1962 on the difference between economic systems relying on the price mechanism and on administrative controls. Devons also wrote a number of reviews of books dealing with economic planning, and two of them are reproduced in the following pages.

(2) *Economic management*

Planning has come to stand for one approach to economic organisation, as the price mechanism stands for another. But one has to think in wider terms in order to make sense of a mixed economy in which planning already presupposes pricing, and the fundamental problem is the right balance between centralised and decentralised decision taking. After the war it was only a matter of time before people woke up to the limitations of administrative action and the convenience—indeed indispensability—of relying on market forces in a complex industrial system. As they did so, they came increasingly to speak of 'management' rather than 'planning', and the change was more than one of terminology. Already by the mid-'fifties, as Devons pointed out in his address to the Congress for Cultural Freedom in Milan in September 1955, the ideological dispute over planning was almost a dead issue. Governments had come to accept much enlarged functions, involving conscious responsibility for managing the economy; but they no longer equated this with central planning.

The managerial functions of government make it even more difficult than in the past to consider economic policy in terms of traditional economic theory. On the one hand, it is not possible to abstract from the process of government and write about what governments ought or ought not to do as if they were mere mathematical symbols. Governments make use of a complex administrative apparatus with well developed characteristics which need to be studied by anyone concerned with economic policy. At the same time, it is not possible to divorce economic analysis from its social and political context without running the risk of reducing it to a series of platitudes or irrelevancies. It also goes without saying that policy making is a political operation, and policies can be put into operation only if they command political support. If economists aim at contributing to policy making, therefore, they need to reflect on political as well as on economic behaviour, and on the way in which their conclusions will appear when viewed from the angle of political conflict. It is no doubt because these considerations are so obvious that they are consistently overlooked. But they were never overlooked by Devons, who spent much of his time studying and reflecting on the way in which debate on economic policy is conducted and decisions on economic affairs are reached.

His views on this range of issues are summarised in the papers included in Part II of this volume. Perhaps the most important of these papers are the second and third (on 'The role of the myth in politics' and 'Government on the inner circle') and the sixth (on 'Economists and the public'). The first of these sketches a theory of ideology and is a rejoinder to the 'realists' who reduce political behaviour to the interaction between pressure groups and treat the activities of governments as no more than an effort to reconcile these interests. Devons had already emphasised the significance of pressure groups at the end of his paper on 'Changing economic ideologies', where he drew attention to the strengthening of organised groups and to the threat to political freedom which this posed. The trend as he saw it at that time was towards government becoming 'largely an exercise in the adjustment of group conflicts and arbitration between them'. As he reflected further on this, he asked himself how far the argument should be pushed when it seemed equally legitimate to claim that governments pursued wider social interests. Was this pursuit a myth or was it not in fact—in the form of a recognised principle of action that could be appealed to in debate—just as real as the group interests that dominated political life?

Devons argued that there was a dichotomy in all institutions, political, social and economic, from the Cabinet at one end to the local gardening club at the other, between the governing principle or idea and the everyday reality: between 'the constitutional, formal, mythical way of doing things and the real, informal organisation'. In a rather lengthier exposition of his views before the broadcast talk, he gave four reasons to a Manchester University seminar for the co-existence of the 'mythical' and the 'real' in political life.

First he cited contradictory elements in the behaviour and attitudes of human beings: the setting of standards to which we hope to conform and the failure to reach those standards because of familiar shortcomings. Politics may be a dirty game; but the ideal of statesmanship has to be publicly upheld.

> The myth serves to express, safeguard and reiterate the view that although in practice we may descend to dirty politics yet we have ideals of behaviour, ideals of how the political system should work which we strive after; and these ideals themselves may restrain the full operation of real forces of which we are in a sense ashamed.

Next, there is the very complexity of life, which makes it impossible to provide in advance for all the situations that are likely to arise and for the varying and changing personalities of those who operate the system. In the case of the Civil Service, for example, it is not possible to make a sharp distinction between the responsibility of the Minister for policy and of the official for administration without assuming a quite unreal separability of policy from administration and unlimited expenditure of time by Ministers in taking policy decisions.

> The Civil Service have in fact, day by day, to take policy decisions without the authority of the Minister, and the Minister can take part in only certain issues of policy, depending on his zeal, personality, intellect and interest.

So we deal with the complexity of real life by sticking simultaneously to the myth of Ministerial responsibility and the reality of day-to-day government by the Civil Service.

Exactly the same happens on boards of directors, which must often be less well informed than the men at operating level about what is going on. There is, therefore, a danger that the instructions and policy decisions of the board may be regularly ignored, or alternatively that the board insists rigidly on obedience to its directives by detailed administrative control and a high degree of centralisation. How is it possible, Devons asks, 'to combine the need to allow autonomy, even disobedience, at the operating level in some circumstances with respect for the decisions and views of the supreme authority in others?' In his view, the answer to this familiar riddle lies in the permeation of the organisation by the myth of the superior wisdom of the central authority ('the spirit of the business'), combined with a certain laxity in practice in allowing the operating units to decide issues for themselves.

Finally, the myth is a safeguard for peculiar or extreme circumstances. So long as things go well, affairs can be left to be conducted by their informal day-to-day pattern. But whenever some major issue of principle or the correction of some abuse is in question, the constitutional or mythical side comes into its own. If the annual general meeting were always more than a rubber stamp it would become an intolerable nuisance; but if it were *never* more than a rubber stamp and could not vote the existing committee out of office, it would not only be a waste of time but would be failing its members.

There may, of course, be circumstances in which

the myth is dysfunctional—where its reassertion is such hypocrisy that the continued pretence that it operates may impede the readjustment which is needed to improve the working of the system. And the theory of the working of the reality can on occasions itself become the myth and also prevent necessary readjustment . . . The reality that nobody ever raises matters of importance or argues about the findings of a Committee in Senate could easily become the myth of how the University works and make it difficult for Senate as a body to operate even on crucial occasions. The maintenance of the balance between the two—the myth and the reality—is the secret to the successful working of the system.

I have quoted these passages in elaboration of the broadcast talk partly because the ideas in the talk are highly compressed and partly because they were never subsequently elaborated in any of Devons' published work. Yet they underlay much of his thinking about organisations of all kinds: universities, business firms, government departments, voluntary societies. This is true also of the ideas expressed in his talks on 'Government on the inner circle'. Here his theme is secrecy, and the arguments in defence of secrecy in a democratic country. It is strange how little literature has been devoted to this issue in the United Kingdom since Devons' talk was delivered, well over ten years ago.[3] I doubt whether anything written or said over that period would dispose him to change much of the text. Perhaps he would be less inclined to look to the 'American, French, or Swiss press' rather than the British press as

[3] See also his letters in *The Times*, 27 August and 4 September, 1959, on the same subject 'Need there be so much secrecy?'

sources for 'the arguments going on inside British government circles'. Perhaps also he would spare a paragraph or two for the peculiar problem of 'the leak'. But he would still be able to point to a remarkable degree of secrecy on matters of high public importance and to an equally remarkable absence of any coherent published defence of such secrecy.

The next paper—on the Bank Rate Tribunal case following the rise in Bank rate from 5 per cent to 7 per cent on 19 September 1957—is a useful illustration of the theme developed in 'Government on the inner circle'. An entire volume has recently been devoted to the light this case sheds on decision making in British finance[4] but it is doubtful whether it adds much to what Devons deduced within a few months of the case.[5] The comments which he offers are fair and modest in comparison with some of the more pretentious and strident conclusions drawn elsewhere—indeed, in the very issue of *The Manchester School* in which they appeared. What he had to say remains of current interest in relation to the way in which changes in Bank rate are decided. He points out, for example, how little weight the City appeared to give to Bank rate as an instrument of policy, the absence of prior consultation with those Bank directors who were likely to be concerned over the effect of a large rise in Bank rate on the domestic economic situation, the minor role played by members of the Cabinet other than the Chancellor and the Prime Minister, and the curious absence of any reference by witnesses to the comparatively healthy state of the current balance of payments throughout 1957. He also showed his usual sharp eye for non-events: the non-appearance before the tribunal of the Economic Advisor to the Government, and the non-disclosure of 'the kind of discussion or analysis that went on inside the Treasury or among the Bank's staff, which led to the final recommendations'. The fact is that the case revealed very little indeed about how decisions on Bank rate are taken, who takes the initiative, and how the debate leading up to the decisions proceeds. In these respects the secrecy surrounding 'the inner circle' remained intact.

In the next two papers Devons turns to the role of the economist and economic theory in policy making. This is a subject that

[4] R. A. Chapman, *Decision-making: a case study of the decision to raise the Bank rate in September 1957*.

[5] As often happened, he did not publish all that he had to say and made extensive manuscript notes before embarking on the article.

occupied him a good deal, particularly in the late 'fifties, when he wrote the essays on 'Applied economics—the application of what?' and 'The rôle of the economist in public affairs'.[6] Much earlier, in 1952, he had read a paper at Nottingham on 'Economic theory and economic policy', which has been included here because it states his views in a comparatively unsophisticated way. It may be true, he argues in this paper

> that the particular technique of economic theory cannot cope with the activities of government, since essentially that theory must assume an element of rationality and consistency in action. But . . . a theory that continues to be based virtually on the assumption that the government does not exist or merely has the ring-holding function cannot hope to give us much understanding of the real world in which government action plays such an important part.

It is even less helpful if theory is cast in terms of imperfections and maladjustments which government action can automatically remove and no account is taken of the imperfections and maladjustments *introduced* by the very fact of Government action.

Here and in his John Hinckley Memorial Lecture in November 1964 on 'Economists and the public' Devons insists on the limitations of economic theory, just as he frequently insisted on the limitations of economists (whether inside government or outside); the risk that they might claim to know more than they did; their reliance for policy purposes on comparatively simple, almost platitudinous, propositions; their proneness to oversimplify even to the point of assuming away political conflict. In 'Economists and the public' he takes this a stage further and looks at economists in a mood more of pity than anger as the victims of public impatience and perplexity. Economic issues, he suggests, assume political importance precisely when they cannot be resolved by scientific evidence and a decision has to be taken in comparative ignorance. This does not prevent economists from advancing theories and showing that the greater their zeal the less they know with certainty. These theories are naturally used by politicians in the hope of gratifying the public appetite for rationality and the disputes between economists 'begin to acquire the character of theological disputation'.

[6] Both included in his *Essays in Economics* (Allen & Unwin, 1961). See also his essay on 'Statistics as a basis for policy', especially the passage on statistical magic, pp. 135–6.

This thesis, which harks back to 'The role of the myth in politics' and forward to 'Decisions in ignorance', occupies only a small part of the lecture. But he almost certainly had it in mind to extend it. I recall that shortly before he died he expounded a similar thesis in relation to advertising, pointing out that advertising outlay is usually heaviest where the difference between the competing products is either slight or not easily detected.

The change of government in 1964 concentrated public attention on the place of the economist in policy making and, still more, on the dominant role of the Treasury. It is hardly too much to say that the Treasury, more perhaps than the economic policy of the outgoing government, was one of the major issues at the 1964 election. Devons' interest in the Treasury, unlike that of some of its critics, was based on a study of the published information. He gave a number of seminars on Treasury control, basing himself mainly on the evidence to the Select Committee on the Estimates,[7] Lord Bridges' book in the Whitehall series,[8] and some papers relating to the reorganisation of the Treasury in 1962. He also gave two broadcast talks shortly before the election and published two articles in *The Guardian* after the election. All of these are included below.[9]

Devons' plea in the first of the articles for a freer interchange of staff between the administrative and professional, especially the scientific, branches of the Civil Service was echoed by the Fulton Committee.[10] He also argued for the introduction into the Civil Service from industry and business of 'promising men at the age of thirty or outstanding men at the age of forty' and for some interchange with the nationalised industries. In the second article his theme is the managerial as opposed to administrative function of modern government, and he goes on to make another recommendation echoed by the Fulton committee: the splitting off from the Treasury of the Pay and Management divisions, to form a separate department. But in none of these recommendations is he saying exactly what the Fulton committee said. For example, he wanted a

[7] Reports of the Select Committee on the Estimates, 1955, 1958 and 1963: 'Treasury control', 'Treasury control of expenditure' and 'Treasury control of establishments'.

[8] Lord Bridges, *The Treasury* (Allen & Unwin, 1964).

[9] 'Intelligent laymen in Whitehall', 'Economic management in Whitehall', 'Inflated economists in Whitehall' and 'A Plan for economists'.

[10] Report of the (Fulton) Committee on the Civil Service, 1968, Cmnd 3638.

separate department largely because the Treasury showed too little interest in 'the structure and organisation of departments' and did not take nearly enough time and trouble 'to find out how problems of structure are dealt with in business and whether anything useful is to be learnt from academic studies of management'. Similarly he was content with a single service at Assistant Secretary level and above rather than a single, unified structure. He also went beyond Fulton in arguing for a strengthening of the other departments dealing with economic affairs, with the Treasury confining itself to looking after the general level of economic activity and the balance of payments.

All this seems to me to be a defensible point of view, and a great deal more sensible than what was being written by anybody else for publication in 1964. I have less sympathy with the suggestion that the Economic Section of the Treasury could more appropriately be moved to the Cabinet Office where it began. As Devons conceded, the Treasury would still need a strong staff of economists (where would they have come from in 1964?), and the Economic Section, while technically available for the Cabinet, would work in practice for the 'overlord in charge of economic affairs', i.e. either the Chancellor himself or someone duplicating his most important functions. In 1964 the head of the Economic Section was in any event technically available to the Cabinet as a whole, although rarely consulted in that capacity by other Ministers.

By the time the articles in *The Guardian* appeared, the 1964 election had taken place and major changes in Whitehall were in progress. The Department of Economic Affairs had come into existence, absorbing most of the economists on the staff of the National Economic Development Council as well as a number of professional economists from elsewhere. Four other new government departments were created simultaneously, including the Ministry of Overseas Development, and this put a considerable strain on the entire administrative machine. It was difficult to find staff for the new departments without seriously weakening others, including the Treasury, and the fact that the staff requirements included a large number of economists did not make matters easier.

What annoyed Devons about the importation of economists into Whitehall—and the tone of his articles is one of distinct annoyance—was that this additional demand was not counterbalanced by corresponding efforts to increase the supply of trained economists. He had been trying at the LSE to raise money from industry for postgraduate training, but had received no direct support from the government, nor was any additional support forthcoming after 1964, either through the University Grants Committee (one of Devons' *bêtes noires*) or from government funds. On the contrary, the LSE, with quite inadequate physical facilities, was left to build up by itself graduate teaching in the social sciences on a scale and on a standard that stood out in comparison with efforts elsewhere. In attracting teachers of the highest calibre and in obtaining money from private sources to provide graduate studentships, Devons played a crucial part: at one stage he even contributed in complete secrecy out of his own limited funds. He felt that an opportunity had been neglected not only by the government but also by industry. For in the process of raising money it became clear to him that the purposes which the highly expensive new business schools were intended to serve could have been met at far less expense and probably to far better effect by developing postgraduate teaching—not study, *teaching*—at the LSE and other existing centres.

Those who read the second *Guardian* article should be reminded that it appeared within the first five months of the return to power of the Labour government: the mocking tone was in sharp contrast to the mass of comment then appearing in the press and ensured for it a quite undeserved neglect.[11] I doubt whether, in retrospect, there is a single item in the programme set out in paragraph 3 that does not make good sense, although Devons underrated the difficulty of carrying out some of his suggestions. For example, in my experience university departments are not always eager to embark on 'a broad programme of relevant investigation and research that would be of interest and use to government', even when there is money to be had: they have their own ideas about what needs to be done and often need a good deal of education before they take on board the problems put to them by government economists. I should also argue that Devons makes far too much of the circular mentioned in paragraph 2 advertising six vacancies for young economists. The fact that the government was prepared if necessary to accept one or two graduates without research experience or postgraduate training does not seem to me particularly reprehensible in the light of the subsequent performance of some of those selected.

[11] A letter signed 'Gagged Economist' was published in *The Guardian* on 1 April, 1965 by way of reply. A rejoinder by Devons appeared a week later.

(3) *University affairs*

In the first of the groups of papers on university affairs ('Lotus grove of Academe') Devons indulges his taste for irony. He seeks to justify university life, not in terms of teaching and research but as intellectual leisure for a privileged class. This article was written before the Robbins committee had reported, but Devons was already warning his colleagues that a government that whooped on the universities to expand by offering lavish funds was almost certain to have second thoughts once expansion was well under way, and that the only proper attitude to take in such a situation was one of *timeo danaos*. In his own evidence to the Robbins committee he analysed the weakness of existing financial arrangements and attacked the ambiguity and secrecy of the UGC system. Here he was back on familiar themes: government on the inner circle and decisions in ignorance. He wanted to see the universities enjoy greater financial independence and saw the easiest route to this in a big increase in fees so as to allow them to cover true costs.

I forbear to summarise or comment on this evidence, which, although dating back to 1962, is still topical and of interest to anyone studying the future of university education. Devons was constantly urging the importance of more research into the administrative aspects of university education and suggested that the UGC should recruit staff for this purpose. In view of current controversies, it is interesting to see that the questions which he puts forward for such research do not include any reference to student participation. But by 1965 he was writing on this subject and, so far as I can discover, a note headed 'The rebellious society' and dealing with student attitudes was the last piece he ever wrote with an eye to publication.[12]

ALEC CAIRNCROSS
St Peter's College, Oxford

[12] The text is unfortunately incomplete. There are also a number of manuscript notes on problems of university administration (including a critique of the administrative system at the LSE) which I have been tempted to include in this volume but have felt to be too disjointed for publication as they stand.

Bibliography

The published writings of Ely Devons

September 1935. 'Output per head in Great Britain, 1924–33.' *Economic Journal*, vol. xlv, 577–80.

April 1939. 'Production trends in the United Kingdom.' *The Manchester School*, vol. x, no. 1, pp. 55–61.

September 1946. 'The Soviet economic system' (review). *The Manchester School*, vol. xiv, no. 3, pp. 54–9.

January 1947. 'The progress of reconversion.' *The Manchester School*, vol. xv, no. 1, pp. 1–25.

April 1947. (with J. Jewkes) 'The economic survey for 1947.' *Lloyds Bank Review*.

November 1947. 'Economic planning in war and peace.' Transactions of the *Manchester Statistical Society*, 1947–8 (reprinted in *The Manchester School*, vol. xvi, no. 1, pp. 1–28, and in *Essays in economics*).

January 1948. 'The British four-year plan?' *The Manchester School*, vol. xvi, no. 1, pp. 94–127.

November 1948. Review of Oxford University Institute of Economics and Statistics, *Studies in War Economics*, *Economica*, vol. xv, pp. 310–13.

March 1949. Review of L. C. Ord, *Politics and poverty*. *Economic Journal*, March 1949, pp. 92–5.

May 1949. 'The economic survey for 1949.' *The Manchester School*, vol. xvii, no. 2, pp. 111–27.

October 1949. 'The future of prices and costs in the cotton industry.' Cotton Board Conference reprint.

January 1950. 'Dollars from investment.' Two articles in the *Manchester Guardian*, 18 and 19 January.

April 1950. 'British industrial production.' *Lloyds Bank Review*.

December 1950. *Planning in practice*. Cambridge University Press.

—1951. 'The problem of co-ordination in aircraft production' in *Lessons of the British war economy*, ed. D. N. Chester, Cambridge University Press.

June 1951. 'Some features of international trade in 1950.' *The Three Banks Review*.

September 1951. Review of J. B. Condliffe, *The commerce of nations*. *Manchester Guardian*, 19 September.

January 1952. Reviews in the *Manchester Guardian* of B. de Jouvenel, *Ethics of redistribution* (11 January), and W. Eucken, *The unsuccessful age* (15 January).

July 1952. 'Some aspects of United Kingdom export trade.' *Lloyds Bank Review*.

August 1952. 'Planning by economic survey.' *Economica*, vol. 19, pp. 237–253.

April 1953. Review of books by Harrod, Hawtrey, Pigou and Robertson. *Manchester Guardian*, 12 April.

May 1953. 'An economist looks at the coal industry.' Conference paper, National Association of Colliery Managers, National Coal Mining Conference, Blackpool.

June 1953. 'Can we too prosper?' *The Listener*, 18 June.

August 1953. Review of M. M. Postan, *British war production*, *Economica*, vol. xx, 279–82.

December 1953. Review of J. Hurstfield, *Control of raw materials*. *Journal of the Royal Statistical Society*, vol. 116, part iv, pp. 466–7.

November 1953. 'Work and wealth.' *London calling*, 26 November.

January 1954. Review of K. Boulding, *Planning and the market system*.

—Review of article by Professor W. Mackenzie on 'Committees in administration'.

February–March 1954. Newmarch lectures. These were subsequently published in amended form in bank reviews or learned journals and were reprinted in *Essays in economics*, nos. 6–8.

July 1954. 'Statistics as a basis for policy.' *Lloyds Bank Review* (reprinted in *Essays in economics*).

August 1954. 'Notes on prolegomena towards a theory of the process of small group economic klarification' (mimeographed). Valedictory Address to Merrill Center Conference.

September 1954. 'Statistics of the UK terms of trade.' *The Manchester School*, vol. xxii, no. 3, pp. 258–75 (reprinted in *Essays in economics*).

September 1955. 'Changing economic ideologies in the United Kingdom.' Conference paper, Congress for Cultural Freedom, Milan, September 1955.

October 1955. 'The case for investment and productivity.' *Lloyds Bank Review* (reprinted in *Essays in economics*).

1956. *Introduction to British economic statistics*. Cambridge University Press.

June 1956. 'The role of the myth in politics.' *The Listener*, 21 June.

July 1956. 'Will the price-pegging policy succeed?' *The Listener*, 5 July.

September 1956. 'The wage–price spiral.' *District Bank Review* (reprinted in *Essays in economics*).

October 1956. Review of R. S. Sayers, *Financial policy in World War II. Manchester Guardian*, 8 October.

August 1957. 'Enigma of the Russian economic system.' *The Listener*, 29 August.

1958. 'The aircraft industry' in *The structure of British Industry*, ed. D. L. Burn, Cambridge University Press.

March 1958. 'Government on the inner circle.' *The Listener*, 27 March.

May 1958. (with R. C. Ogley) 'An index of wage rates by industries.' *The Manchester School*, vol. xxvi, no. 2, pp. 77–115 (reprinted in *Essays in economics*).

December 1958. 'The size of universities and university departments.' *Report of proceedings*, Home Universities Conference, 1958, pp. 82–6.

January 1959. 'An economist's view of the Bank Rate Tribunal evidence.' *The Manchester School*, vol. xxvii, no. 1, pp. 1–16.

February 1959. 'The Restrictive Practices Court in action', 'The Monopolies Court in action' and 'Price rings and the court', *Manchester Guardian*, 26 and 27 February.

April 1959. 'Budget news abroad.' *Manchester Guardian*, 28 April.

May 1959. (with J. R. Crossley) 'The pattern of wage rates: *Manchester Guardian* wage index.' *Manchester Guardian*, 21 May.

June 1959. (with J. R. Crossley) 'The *Manchester Guardian* wage index.' *Manchester Guardian*, 10 June.

July 1959. 'The conference game.' *The Economist*, 4 July.

—'The role of the economist in public affairs.' *Lloyds Bank Review* (reprinted in *Essays in economics*).

August–September 1959. 'Need there be so much secrecy?' Letters to *The Times*, 27 August and 7 September.

October 1959. Review of J. Kornai, *Over-centralisation in economic administration. Manchester Guardian*, 22 October.

May 1960. 'Our place in the shifting pattern of world trade.' *Financial Times* Annual Review, 1960.

June 1960. 'The end of the dollar problem.' *Irish Banking Review.*

December 1960. 'On Professor Polanyi's thesis.' *Soviet Survey*, no. 34.

1961. *Essays in economics.* Allen & Unwin.

March 1961. 'Applied economics—the application of what?' in *The logic of personal knowledge: essays presented to Michael Polanyi* (reprinted in *Essays in economics*).

April 1961. 'World trade in invisibles.' *Lloyds Bank Review.*

July 1961. 'The conference game.' *The Economist*, 4 July.

October 1961 (with J. R. Crossley) '*The Guardian* index of wage rates.' *The Guardian*, 27 October.

November 1961. 'Understanding international trade.' *Economica*, vol. 28, pp. 351–9 (reprinted in Italian in *Mercurio*, May 1963).
May 1962. Review of A. K. Cairncross, *Factors in economic development. The Guardian*, 4 May.
—Evidence to (Robbins) Committee on Higher Education.
June 1962. 'Redbrick headache.' *Time and Tide*, 7 June.
July 1962. 'The reform of university finance.' *The Guardian*, 27 July.
—'The selection of university students.' *The Guardian*, 31 July.
August 1962. 'Graduate schools for universities.' *The Guardian*, 1 August.
March 1963. 'Lotus grove of academe.' *The Listener*, 14 March.
November 1963. 'Programme not panic.' *The Guardian*, 5 November.
—'Emergency plans.' *The Guardian*, 6 November.
1964. Contribution to *Closed systems and open minds*, ed. Max Gluckman.
May 1964. 'Intelligent laymen in Whitehall.' *The Listener*, 21 May.
July 1964. 'Economic management in Whitehall.' *The Listener*, 2 July.
November 1964. Review of S. J. Wells, *British export performance. The Guardian.*
February 1965. Review of T. Wilson, *Planning and growth. Scottish Journal of Political Economy*, vol. xii, pp. 105–9.
March 1965. 'Economising on economists.' *The Guardian*, 12 March.
—'Plan for economists.' *The Guardian*, 26 March.
April 1965. 'A reply to "Gagged Economist" ' (letter). *The Guardian*, 18 April.
July 1965. 'Economists and the public.' *Lloyds Bank Review*, no. 77, pp. 19–29 (reprinted in *Cronache Economiche*, no. 277, 1966).
September 1965. 'Serving as a juryman in Britain.' *Modern Law Review*, vol. 28, pp. 561–70 (one of the John Hinkley Memorial Lectures, delivered in 1964 at the Johns Hopkins University).
—'Decisions in ignorance.' Broadcast talk, 11 September.

PLANNING

[1]

The problem of co-ordination in aircraft production[1]

The need for formal co-ordination

The problem of co-ordination was more important in the Ministry of Aircraft Production than in the other supply departments. For although MAP was responsible for the production of many items, such as bombs and dinghies, supplies of which were not closely interrelated, most of the output which the Department covered was used either directly in aircraft or as spares for aircraft. For each aircraft a large number of components—engines, propellers, undercarriages, turrets, equipment, etc.—had to be made. One of the most difficult tasks in aircraft production was to ensure that the plans for the production of these components fitted in with the plans for final aircraft output and the need for spares.

This problem of co-ordination would have been easily solved if there had been an official of superhuman capacity who could have comprehended fully and realistically in his own mind the whole range of choice open to MAP in deciding what to produce. Such an official would have compiled day by day perfectly co-ordinated programmes for every section of the aircraft industry. But MAP never had an official of this calibre and decisions on the pattern of output had to be delegated to thousands of individuals in MAP and in the firms. The task of co-ordination was to secure that each of these individuals acted in a way which fitted in with what all the others were doing.

In the early years of the war, most planning action in MAP was based on the assumption—an assumption implied but not usually

[1] From *Lessons of the British War Economy*, ed. D. N. Chester, Cambridge University Press, 1951.

recognised—that the necessary co-ordination would be achieved if each directorate in MAP responsible for component or raw material production based its plans on the agreed aircraft programme. The aircraft programme was indeed a vital co-ordinating instrument; yet experience showed that adequate co-ordination was not secured by leaving each directorate to base its plans on what it thought was needed for the aircraft programme. Such a system resulted all too often in the over-supply and waste of some components and desperate shortage of others.

As a result of this experience a special directorate—the Directorate-General of Planning, Programmes and Statistics—was set up, with one of its main functions to ensure that the plans of the individual production directorates fitted in with each other. Looking back on the experience of MAP, it is possible to discover why such special co-ordinating arrangements were necessary, and the limits to the degree of co-ordination that could be achieved even with such special arrangements.

While planning was left to each separate directorate, with the aircraft programme as the only connecting link, it was not the duty of any of the directorates concerned to ensure that the supply of components would be adequate for any given aircraft programme or for any proposed changes in that programme. Had it been possible to formulate an aircraft programme and then instruct each directorate that it was its job to supply the components for the fulfilment of that programme, the problem would have been relatively simple. But this would have implied that airframe capacity was in every case the limiting factor in aircraft production; and that if airframe capacity was considered adequate to meet the programme, components, equipment and raw materials supplies could be made available relatively easily. This was not invariably nor even usually the case.

Final aircraft production itself depended on the volume and type of component, equipment and raw material supply that could be made available; and the principal problem in drawing up the aircraft programme was to decide which combination of aircraft would best meet the needs of the Service departments, taking into account possible expansions in components, equipment and raw material capacity and the various alternative ways in which that capacity could be used. So that any given published aircraft programme represented the completion of the process of choosing between the various alternatives open to MAP in the use not only of airframe capacity, but also of components, equipment and material capacity. It could not, therefore, be regarded as the starting-point from which the individual production directorates could proceed. The decisions as to the uses to which component capacity could and should be put and the plans for further expansion had to be taken before, not after, the aircraft programme had been drawn up. It is true that such decisions were often merely implicit in the agreement to proceed on a given aircraft programme and that executive action was usually taken by the individual component production directorates only after the programme had been issued; but the assurance that such action was possible and would yield the results expected had to be given before and not after the issue of the aircraft programme.

It was often thought, and indeed maintained in argument, that this assurance could be obtained by consulting all the directorates concerned with the supply of components, equipment, materials and labour before issuing the aircraft programme. But this was only possible where the question at issue was such that the directorates could give an unambiguous yes or no in reply. For example, suppose the possibility of making ten more Spitfires a month was being considered. The directorates might be asked whether they could supply the extra engines, engine accessories, propellers, equipment, radio, raw materials, etc., for this additional production. They could give an unequivocal answer to this question only if they based it on the assumption that no other supplies were to be interfered with and that they were not to consider extensions of capacity beyond those already agreed. But it was just these assumptions that those asking the question would usually not wish to be made. They would want to know at what cost, either in terms of sacrifice of supplies to other aircraft in the programme or in terms of extensions to capacity, the additional ten Spitfires could be produced.

As soon as the question was asked in this form it was impossible to answer yes or no, and therefore impossible to obtain the answer by asking the individual directorates. For the cost, in terms of alternative aircraft or spares to be given up or in terms of expansions of capacity, could be expressed in innumerable alternative ways. And it was necessary for someone who appreciated the alternatives in the case of each individual directorate to choose that range of combinations of choices which would be most significant—

to come to the conclusion, for example, that if the Air Ministry would be prepared to see the Stirling programme cut by five aircraft a month and agree to some change in policy as to the fitment of engines to the Beaufighter, it would be possible to build ten extra Spitfires a month without any extensions of raw materials or component capacity. And it was in this form, and not the simple yes or no form, that all changes in the aircraft programme had to be considered. For it was hardly ever true that a proposed change could not be achieved at any cost in terms of sacrificed alternatives.

It was sometimes argued that discussion of the whole range of choices and selection of the most suitable one could be achieved by calling all those concerned to a meeting. But this method hardly ever worked satisfactorily. Production directors were not adept at carrying in their minds the various production possibilities that were open to them and the consequences of each on their plans. In any case, such meetings were confused and inconclusive unless someone had beforehand limited the range of possible choices to the two or three which he thought the most significant and from which he considered the final choice had to be made. It was this limitation of the problem of choice to two or three courses of action which was essentially the function of the co-ordinator.

The problem of choosing between the various possible combinations of aircraft and components was complicated by the fact that components were needed for repair and squadron maintenance as well as for embodiment in complete aircraft. Constitutionally, the Service departments were responsible for deciding what supplies should be ordered to meet spares needs, even though in most cases the spares orders were placed through MAP. From the point of view of the provisioning sections of the Service departments, these spares could be calculated unequivocally according to rules laid down for them, and the final result gave an unqualified figure of the volume required. Normally, however, these demands and those for complete aircraft could not all be met in full. But there was no regular machinery by which the conflict between these two demands could be resolved. The provisioning sections of the Service departments thought of their needs as absolute and had no means of balancing them against the needs of new aircraft. The production directorates in MAP did not usually know the basis on which these spares demands were calculated and therefore could not assess the importance of meeting them as compared with the demands for new aircraft. In addition, the production directorates were not concerned with the allocation between various uses of the components produced; they considered their job completed—and quite rightly—when the component supplies left the factory. And yet every issue of the aircraft and component programmes implied a resolution of this conflict between the demands for spare components and those for new aircraft. Whenever a component was in short supply, it had to be decided how far the shortage could be met by cutting the supplies for spares and how far by reducing new aircraft output.

The need to have some body of officials concerned with these issues, outside the production directorates and the provisioning branches of the Services, was strengthened by distrust of the methods used by the Services in making their calculations and the ponderous machinery involved in their revision. Every change in the aircraft programme involved some revision of the plans for squadron formation, and this in turn should have resulted in a revision of the demands for spare components. But the Service departments had a fairly rigid system of reviewing their demands for spares only once in every six months. Since each review took many months to complete, the results were often related to out-of-date aircraft and squadron formation plans. In revising and keeping up to date production programmes for major components, such as engines, propellers, undercarriages, etc., enormous waste and difficulties in production would have resulted if MAP had taken these estimates of the Service departments as the basis for their production planning.

Further, in the later years of the war when the labour force available to MAP was strictly limited, every major revision in the aircraft programme had to be followed immediately by revisions in the components programme if the required labour was to be released. In these circumstances it was impossible to wait for revised spares calculations from the Service departments. Someone in MAP had to assess what should be allowed for spares so that revised component production programmes could be issued speedily. And this was a

The function of co-ordination had to be performed continuously,
competent to undertake.
task which the production directorates were neither willing nor
not merely when an entirely new aircraft programme was under consideration. For the factors influencing the relation between aircraft and components supply were changing daily. This was not

merely because the Services were continually changing their demands, but also because the prospects of fulfilment of individual aircraft, component and equipment programmes fluctuated from day to day. A continuous struggle was waged in planning between the realistic and target principles,[2] and the programmes for every aircraft and component represented a compromise between the two opposing forces. The degree of realism of target was, of course, never the same in all programmes at any given time. To have planned the relationship between the various programmes at their full face value in each case would have resulted in waste and repeated breakdowns in production. It was dangerous to leave each director-general to allow for this factor in his own programme. For each would have insisted that all other programmes should be 100 per cent realistic, but that he should be allowed to have any target element in his own programme which he thought necessary. This meant that some officials who had no vested interest in any individual programme except the final aircraft programme had to allow for this factor. Someone had to decide what risks should be taken in the light of possible future changes in Service demands and of the likely fulfilment of the various aircraft, component and equipment programmes.

This task was complicated by the inefficiency of the production directorates in assessing the likely fulfilment of the promises put forward by the firms. Many of the production directors learned little from production experience and continued throughout the period of the war to accept almost without question the optimistic estimates of the firms. Criticism of these estimates had, therefore, in many cases to come from somebody outside the production directorates although that was not essentially a co-ordinating function.

There was also the risk that where the planning and the allocation of capacity were left to each directorate, with the aircraft programme

[2] 'Target planning' was based on the assumption that firms would do their best only if the programmes gave them a target a little in excess of what they could really achieve. 'Realistic planning' argued that planning on such a target basis would inevitably lead to waste and lack of balance in component supplies; and that maximum output would be achieved if all programmes were based on a sober estimate of what it was really expected the firms would produce. For a full treatment of the relative merits of target and realistic planning, see my book *Planning in Practice* (Cambridge University Press, 1950), especially chapter II.

as the sole co-ordinating instrument, deficiencies in production would be concealed by each directorate for as long as possible. And by the time disclosure could no longer be avoided it was often too late to make the changes in the aircraft programme which would have been made if the deficiency in components supply had been revealed when it was first known to the production directorate concerned. The tendency to conceal any possible fall-down on programmes were common, because such a deficiency nearly always brought a flood of criticism which never redounded to the good reputation of the directorate responsible. The production director was tempted to conceal the deficiency until the last moment in the hope that its disclosure could be avoided altogether, either through some change in the aircraft programme which would reduce the demand for the component, or because the production of some other item would fall short to an even greater extent than the one for which he was responsible. It was vital, therefore, to have some officials without such a vested interest in concealment watching the progress of the production of each component in relation to the requirements for aircraft and spares.

There was one other important reason why leaving the process of co-ordination to the individual production directorates led to waste and confusion. For every change in the aircraft programme which was put into effect, many were considered and rejected. If each production director had been aware of all the proposed changes he would have been working all the time on shifting sands. He would be tempted to take into account in his day-to-day decisions the latest proposal which was under consideration, for he would have no means of knowing which of the proposals was likely to be accepted and which rejected. It was essential, therefore, that discussion of proposals at the preliminary stage should be confined to a group of officials who, while they were not taking day-to-day decisions, could yet assess from their knowledge of the plans for components and equipment supply whether the changes were likely to be acceptable to MAP. They would be in a position to decide which proposals should be rejected forthwith and which should be given further consideration. In the latter cases they could also decide whether any of MAP's major proposals for changes in production capacity for components or equipment would be seriously affected by the proposed change in the aircraft programme. The co-ordinators could in this way act as a barrier preventing the many fantastic proposals for modifying the programme spreading throughout MAP and causing alarm and panic.

Establishment of the planning directorate

It would be wrong to conclude that all the above arguments were in the minds of those in MAP who decided to set up a Directorate of Programmes, Planning and Statistics. They were, however, the main justification for its existence and played an important part in influencing the scope of its activities once it had been established. When it was first started in 1941 the Directorate confined its activities to looking after the issue and revision of the aircraft programme and the collection of statistics indicating the actual progress of production. It soon discovered, however, that it could not exercise the function of issuing a realistic aircraft programme and calling attention when necessary to the desirability of amending that programme, unless it could be sure that component production had been planned on a scale adequate to meet aircraft and spares needs. But it could not obtain this assurance from the production directorates for some of the most important components, because there were no long-period programmes showing what was to be produced. For example, in the case of aero-engines there was merely a short-period forecast showing output only three months ahead. In the case of propellers and propeller equipment even this meagre information was not available. This was partly because the officials in the production directorates did not realise the importance of drawing up programmes, and partly because they lacked the necessary information on what would be required to meet the needs for spares. They worked, therefore, on a hand-to-mouth basis. In such circumstances planning decisions were taken by default rather than by carefully and consciously considered choices from various possible courses of action.

The planning directorate felt compelled to persuade the production directorates to draw up programmes showing expected production of each type of component by each firm over a period of two years ahead. The planning directorate assumed joint responsibility with the production directorates for these programmes and they were issued as official MAP plans. The first to be drawn up was for aero-engines. At that stage the central directorate was still learning the technique of programming and working out methods of allowing for spares needs without depending on the provisioning branches of the Air Ministry. But once acquired, the same technique could be applied to other components, and within a short time programmes were issued regularly for engines, power plants, radiators, carburettors and magnetos; propellers, constant-speed units and spinners; undercarriages, wheels and tyres; turrets, aircraft guns and bombs; and for certain items of radio equipment. In drawing up these programmes the Directorate had to satisfy itself both that supplies would be adequate to meet requirements and that they could be achieved within the limits of existing capacity or new capacity planned to come into operation at some time in the future.

A substantial part of the total supply of some of these components was due to come from the United States and Canada. The rate of supply expected from these sources had to be fitted in with the plans for production in the United Kingdom. As the central directorate assumed responsibility for programming home production, it found it necessary to draw up comparable programmes for supplies from overseas. In consultation with the British Air Commission in Washington a programme for North American supplies was therefore drawn up. The planning directorate took on the responsibility for ensuring that this programme was revised in accordance with changing United Kingdom requirements and production and allocation expectations in the United States. It thus became the main channel of communication with the BAC on programme matters.

As the planning directorate assumed important programme responsibilities it had to be closely associated with all discussions that took place on the total manpower to be allocated to MAP, and the effects on the aircraft programme of changes in these allocations. Eventually it took over the duty of calculating the labour needed for any given programme, and of assessing the cuts that would have to be made in the programmes if effect was to be given to the manpower allocations.

Statistics of production, employment and stocks were essential in fulfilling these planning and co-ordinating functions. A large part of the time of the directorate was spent in collecting this information and ensuring its accuracy and consistency, so that it could be used without too much hesitation as a basis for planning future production or allocating components in short supply. Regular comparison of production and programmes was also the best way of calling attention to deficiencies. To this end the Directorate compiled and circulated throughout the department regular statistical bulletins, with a commentary calling particular attention to those items where things seemed to be going wrong.

The limits of co-ordination

The exercise of these planning and co-ordinating functions gave rise to innumerable problems. Of these the most important was the question how far the Directorate should extend its activities. All the efforts made by MAP to deal with the problem of co-ordination demonstrated that planning must be a compromise between two inevitably opposing tendencies. The effective planning of any given component demanded that the official concerned should be familiar in great detail with the production problems of that section. The more he knew of the detail of these production problems the better able he was to judge what capacity would be needed for a given programme, what output could be obtained from a given capacity, and which of the requested changes in programme could be met and at what cost. But the more expert he became in the problems of this particular section the less he knew about the other sections of the industry and, therefore, the less able he was to take account of the effects on his own section of what was happening elsewhere. As a result, he might be an efficient planner in the sense that he could assess fairly accurately how much labour, materials and factory space were needed to achieve a certain production of the item with which he was concerned. Yet, because he was unaware of what was happening in other sections, he might make bad mistakes in deciding what was needed from his own section and might arrange for production which would give the wrong quantities and selection of items.

On the other hand, officials who spent most of their time trying to ensure that the plans of the individual sections fitted in with each other had to know something about every section of the industry, and therefore could not know in detail the production problems and possibilities of any particular section. As a result, the plans they drew up might be perfectly co-ordinated, in the sense that if the production laid down by them for each section were achieved, the right supply of components and spares would come forward for the aircraft that were being made; and yet their plans might be rendered nugatory because they were not related to production possibilities.

Every official in the central directorate was continually being faced with this dilemma. He knew that if he was to draw up a realistic programme for the component which he was looking after, he ought to know nearly as much about production possibilities as the production directorate. Yet he also knew that if he spent his time becoming a specialist in that field he would have little or no time to find out what was happening to related components or to the prospects and production plans for the aircraft to which his component was to be fitted.

Take, for example, the field or responsibility of the official in the central directorate responsible for the propeller programme. He had to assess the reliability of the estimates of production capacity put forward by the firms and the production directorate. He had to be aware of the progress of propeller production so as to give ample warning in advance of any short-fall that was likely to affect the aircraft programme or supplies for spares. He had to know what supplies could be expected from the United States; whether these would have to be modified before they could be fitted to British aircraft, and, if so, at what rate that modification could be done. He had to be able to calculate at short notice whether the propeller programme could be adapted to meet some proposed change in the aircraft programme; and, if this necessitated an expansion of capacity, whether such an expansion was possible and, if so, at what cost. He had to know something of the progress of propeller development to ensure that the latest types were included in the production programme at the earliest date possible.

In addition to all this he had to know what was happening in the spheres for which his colleagues were responsible. He had to be aware of the likely fulfilment of the programmes for each aircraft type, so as to take account of any short-fall or excess over programme in planning propeller production. He had to be familiar with any discussions of prospective alterations in the aircraft programme, and had himself to decide whether to take the risk of allowing for these in any changes he was then making to the propeller programme. He had to watch progress in components related to his—for example, the power plant and constant-speed unit—so as to have warning as early as possible of any change which would require an alteration to propeller production. He had to allow for spares requirements, for although constitutionally the decision on this issue rested with the Service departments, experience soon showed that he could not accept their estimates without question. The resolution of conflict between spares and new aircraft requirements was largely his responsibility, and when quick changes had to be made in the programme—and this was the usual and not the exceptional case—he would have to make his own estimates of what to allow for spares. In making such estimates he had to take account of supplies that would be forthcoming from repaired components.

If he was to cover this wide range of problems, a senior official of the planning directorate could not take charge of more than one major component and one or two minor ones associated with it. And if he was to take action in line with that of his colleagues in the planning directorate, the total field covered had to be limited.

The need to limit the field of the central directorate can be seen most clearly when one considers the duties of the head of that directorate. His main function was to co-ordinate the activities of his colleagues and act as the main spokesman of the directorate. He had to draw the attention of the Chief Executive to the need for revising the aircraft programme and had to advise him on the possibility of providing supplies to meet any changes in the programmes proposed by the Service department. Sometimes he was given time to consult his staff, but often—particularly when various possibilities were discussed at a meeting with the Service departments—he had to give a view on the spot. This meant that he had to know nearly as much as each of his senior colleagues about component production and plans, and the possibility of modifying these plans. Also, that he had to keep his senior colleagues fully informed of the latest proposed changes in the aircraft programme so that they could decide whether these should be allowed for in their component planning, and so that they, in turn, could draw his attention to any important effects on components planning which he had overlooked. For this to be done successfully, the total staff had to be small enough for him to see them all practically every day to discuss the latest developments.

Although it was necessary for these reasons to limit the field over which co-ordination was attempted, it would, of course, be a mistake to overlook the errors in planning which were bound to result from such a limitation. It was implicit in the methods used by the planning directorate that a change in the aircraft programme would be adopted if it considered that the major components for which it issued programmes could and would be made available. It was thus assumed that the plans for all the unprogrammed items would somehow or other be adapted to the change. Obviously, such an assumption often proved unwarranted.

The central planning directorate was all the time torn between the desire to extend its activities to more and more components in order to secure a greater measure of co-ordination in MAP's production activities, and the fear that if it took on too much either its plans would become unrealistic or it would become so big that its own activities would need co-ordinating. The exact sphere which it could on balance cover most efficiently was not worked out from first principles, but had to be discovered by trial and error in actual practice. The field which could be covered depended on three major factors: the brainpower and co-ordinating ability of the officials concerned; the variables that had to be taken into account and the rate at which these variables changed; and the speed with which action had to be taken. The less able the officials concerned, the more numerous the variations in the factors which they had to take into account; and the greater the speed with which decisions had to be taken, the smaller the sphere of activity which they could usefully attempt to co-ordinate. The more able the officials, the more stable the variables and the longer the period which could be allowed for co-ordination before taking action, the more extensive the field over which co-ordination could usefully be attempted.

Now, these three major factors—ability of the officials, number and degree of changes in the variables, and the time allowed in which to take a decision—were, of course, continually changing throughout the war. There were some periods when the whole aircraft programme was under discussion and quick advice had to be given on the desirability of choosing one of the many different courses of action. On these occasions the need for co-ordination was at its greatest, but the task of co-ordination most difficult. The head of the planning and programmes division was so occupied attending meetings where prospective programme changes were being discussed that he had little time to see even his senior colleagues. In consequence they knew little of what was going on and he lost touch with important developments in components production. Such was the multiplicity of changes being discussed and the speed with which he had to give answers, that the most he could achieve was to take account of the effects of any proposed change on the most important component—engines—and in these circumstances co-ordination was limited to the engine–aircraft relationship. At the other extreme, when a new aircraft programme had been issued and all subsidiary programmes had been adjusted to it, there was usually a period of relative quiet when co-ordination was comparatively easy. It was on such occasions that the staff complained of lack of work and were tempted to extend their co-ordinating activities to new spheres. But they learned by experience that such periods of quiet never lasted long and that the temptation to take on more programmes had to be resisted. Indeed, one of the main features of the task of co-ordination was that it was easiest when least needed, i.e. when conditions were fairly stable, and most difficult when it was most necessary, i.e. when conditions were changing rapidly.

It was often asserted that lack of statistics set a limit to the extent of co-ordination; that if one only had complete and accurate statistics about all the variables to be taken into account, perfect planning and co-ordination would have been possible. This was a complete fallacy; for although adequate statistics were necessary, it was the limitation in the number of interrelated variables that could be comprehended by one brain that was the effective limiting factor. When decisions had to be taken quickly, which was the usual case, there was not even time to examine in detail the statistics which were in fact available; the decision had to be taken on the basis of the rough-and-ready orders of magnitude that the co-ordinators carried in their minds. Perfect co-ordination could have been achieved only by supermen.

Implementation of the programme

There was another major factor, apart from these intellectual difficulties, which limited the sphere of co-ordination which the planning directorate could undertake. This was the enormous amount of time and energy which had to be spent by its officials in arguments and discussions as to what the correct programme should be and whether the programme, once laid down, should be implemented. These disputes arose because the central directorate did not always possess the power to ensure that its views were enforced. As a co-ordinating directorate, it inevitably overlapped with the activities of other directorates and departments. Every function which it undertook impinged on the activities of some other directorate. In drawing up the undercarriage programme, for example, it was in theory the responsibility of the undercarriage directorate to say what could be produced and of the provisioning branches of the Service departments to say what was required. Inevitably, in trying to close any gap between these two, the planning directorate had to take a view of the reliability of the estimates put forward by each side. But it had no executive power to override the view of either side. It merely acted as an advisory body to the Chief Executive in MAP and could recommend to him the programme that should be issued, pointing out in what respects its proposals met neither the wishes of the Service departments nor the view of the production directorate.

For the machinery to work smoothly, it was necessary that only a small number of major issues of dispute should be put to the Chief Executive, and that all others should be solved without asking for his intervention. Even when it was generally recognised that the planning directorate had the support of the Chief Executive and that he would adopt their advice if the issues were put up to him—and this was not always the case—the resolution of these conflicts absorbed an enormous amount of time and energy. On many occasions, in order to secure the issue of a programme, the planning directorate had to adopt the views of the production directorates or the Service departments, even though they felt these were grossly mistaken.

The influence of the planning directorate was most powerful in the engine programme, largely because it was generally recognised that the relationship between the engine and aircraft programmes was so complex that it could be appreciated only by the officials who understood the main features of both. It was least powerful in the case of radio and undercarriage equipment. In these cases the programmes issued by the planning directorate to a large extent merely reflected the views of the production directorates or the Service departments, and the planning directorate could only hope that as the course of events proved these views wrong the planning process would be improved.

The stage of dispute and argument did not finish with the issue of the programme. Only aircraft and engine contracts were automatically placed in accordance with the programme. The provisioning and finance divisions of the Service departments and of MAP did not feel bound to alter their contracts to accord with revisions in other programmes. The officials of the planning directorate had therefore to spend much time persuading them so to alter their contracts. If they did not succeed, as often happened, they would then try to persuade the production directorates, and through them the firms, to arrange their production in accordance with the official programme and not in accordance with the contracts they had received.

These disputes inevitably gave rise to confusion and exaggerated the difficulties of securing co-ordination between various sections of the industry. They also absorbed much of the time of the officials of the planning directorate and limited the field over which they could extend their activities.

Importance of informal contacts

As has been explained earlier, in drawing up and discussing revisions of programmes the planning directorate had to assess the reliability of production estimates put forward by the firms, and to be on the look out for any signs indicating that the programme would not be met. Suppose that MAP was discussing with the Air Ministry the possibility of increasing the output of a particular type of aircraft and that this aircraft absorbed all the undercarriages of a particular type which were being produced. Then it was obviously important that those taking part in the discussion should know whether the firm making that particular type of undercarriage was likely to achieve its programme. Similarly, the planning directorate had to gauge the next likely moves in Air Ministry and Admiralty policy, for these had to be taken into account in any revisions of component production plans. For example, suppose that a project to expand propeller capacity to meet existing requirements was being considered in MAP. If it was thought likely that the Air Ministry would request a change in the aircraft programme in the near future which would increase the demand for this propeller, this would be an added reason for proceeding with the project forthwith. On the other hand, if the Air Ministry was expected to reduce its requirements for the aircraft taking this type of propeller, that would be an argument for postponing a decision on the expansion project.

To the newcomer to the problems of co-ordination it seemed easy to ensure that the planning directorate were given this necessary advance information. It merely needed an instruction to the production directors that they should provide the central directorate with the earliest warning of any sign that the programmes for which they were responsible would not be fulfilled. In fact such co-ordination by instruction never worked. The production directorates were not always themselves fully aware of what was happening at the firms. In any case, such an instruction invariably aroused the suspicion in the production directorates that the planning directorate were trying to interfere in matters which did not concern them.

In order to get the information they needed the planning directorate used two main lines of attack. First, they engaged in the most subtle forms of spying they could contrive. The most effective was to find some person in the production directorate who had a grievance, worm one's way into his confidence, and then get him to 'spill the beans' on what was really happening in his directorate. This activity varied in usefulness as the power and influence of the central directorate fluctuated. If it was generally known that that directorate could get things done, officials who were making no headway in trying to get action taken by their own directorates would often provide information to the central directorate and urge them to press for some action to be taken. In these cases it was, of course, always implicitly understood that the central directorate would not divulge its sources of information, for that would have jeopardised the position of the informant and he would be reluctant ever to take such a risk again. The other main line of attack was to discover officials either at MAP, the firms or the Air Ministry who realised the importance of co-ordination and were not over-sensitive about the prestige of their own directorate, cultivate their acquaintance or even friendship where this was possible, and use them as the main instruments of co-ordination, especially in an emergency when quick decisions were necessary.

It was by such channels that the most efficient co-ordination was achieved and yet it would have been quite impossible to bring such a system into being by administrative arrangements. Take, for example, the problem of co-ordination between MAP and the Air Ministry on the aircraft programme. It was clearly of great value to those doing the programming in MAP to know the issues being debated in the Air Ministry which would affect the demand for aircraft, for they would be able to take these into account in their own work. They could also stop the Air Ministry wasting its time considering schemes for which they knew MAP could not provide the aircraft. Similarly, it was of value to the Air Ministry officials responsible for planning the formation of squadrons and equipping them with aircraft to know the latest production developments in MAP, particularly any revisions in the aircraft programme that were being considered for production reasons. Yet it was impossible to arrange formally this interchange of advance information, although it was essential to efficient co-ordination. For each department was unwilling to admit officials of the other to its own secrets. Each feared that information so gathered might be used against it in inter-departmental argument, and wished to guard against premature action being taken by the other on schemes which were still under debate. But such interchange became possible, and did in fact take place regularly, as soon as the officials concerned in MAP and the Air Ministry got to know each other well, found that they could trust each other, and as a result were prepared to divulge secrets which constitutionally they should have kept to themselves. It became common practice, for example, for the head of the planning directorate in MAP to tell his contact in the Air Ministry of any important proposed change in the programme being considered by MAP, both so that he could find out whether the Air Ministry were likely to welcome the change and also so that the Air Ministry official could take account of it in his own work. But the existence of such contacts could not be officially recognised, and depended on each side feeling confident that the other would not give him away or use the advance information in any way to bring criticism on MAP or on the Air Ministry.

The success or failure of the activities of the planning directorate in MAP depended principally on the extent to which they were able to build up such contacts in the Service departments, in the production directorates and at the firms. They were most successful in aircraft engines, propellers and raw materials and least successful in radio equipment. For many reasons the relations between the planning directorate and the radio production directorate were formal and official, and as a consequence the central directorate's attempts at radio planning were never very successful.

Position of the directorate

Although the central directorate had to criticise the plans of the production directorates, it had itself to be above criticism. For it could only maintain its own position and ensure that its programmes and suggestions for revising these programmes were taken seriously if the advice on which they were based was accepted without fear of contradiction. For if it became generally known that the central planning directorate was being compelled to issue plans and programmes with which it did not agree, its word would count for little throughout the department, and the numerous unofficial contacts on which it depended to fulfil its co-ordinating function would gradually wither away. For example, the official in charge of calculating raw material requirements was not likely to consult the planning directorate about future changes in programmes and tell it whether raw materials would be available if he discovered by experience that the changes which that directorate had in mind were regularly being turned down. The prestige of the directorate, therefore, had to be of the highest order.

The prestige of the directorate could be maintained only if it had the support of the head of the production divisions of MAP—known at first as the Controller-General and later as the Chief Executive. It was not only necessary that the planning directorate should be directly responsible to the Chief Executive, but also that the Chief Executive should normally be prepared to accept its advice on programme matters. The usefulness of the planning directorate varied directly with the esteem in which it was held by the Chief Executive. At times its advice was ignored or not even sought on major issues of programme policy, and it was then unable to fulfil any of its functions efficiently. When it was generally known that its activities were being supported and its advice was being taken by the Chief Executive, its power was substantial.

The power of the central directorate was naturally open to abuse. To retain this power, the directorate had to ensure that experience demonstrated that it gave the right advice. To achieve this, it had to be certain that if the plans which it laid down for component production were fulfilled, no aircraft would be held up for lack of components. It was always tempted, therefore, to over-insure against all possible risks, for there was no special motive driving it to keep these insurances to a minimum. True, over-insurance would lead to a surplus and waste of components, but such waste was never very obvious—on the contrary, many officials regarded the presence of large stocks of components as evidence of good planning—while the existence of a single aircraft without some necessary component was always sufficient to excite heated argument and discussion.

Further, since in the last analysis an estimate of whether components would be available for any proposed aircraft programme was largely a matter of judgment, there was always the danger that the officials concerned in making such judgments would be influenced by their own views of the desirability of the objectives which the proposed change was meant to achieve. For example, if an official in the central directorate was asked whether components would be available for an increase in the programme for a particular aircraft, and he felt that such an increase would be a mistake because in his view the usefulness of the aircraft and the purposes to which it was to be put were exaggerated, it was almost inevitable that he would allow himself to be influenced by this view in making his judgment about the availability of components.

Yet another paradox in the successful operation of the co-ordinating directorate was that although it had to have substantial power and be certain that its advice would normally be taken, yet it had to be absolved from responsibility. For technically it was merely advising the Chief Executive on programme matters. Since its function was essentially co-ordinating, it was dealing all the time with matters which were the prime responsibility of other directorates or departments. As has been explained earlier, the production directorate was responsible for assessing capacity, and the provisioning branch of the Air Ministry for calculating requirements. The planning directorate could suggest to the Chief Executive that these estimates were wrong and that others should be used in drawing up the programme, but even if the Chief Executive agreed it had then to proceed to persuade the directorate primarily concerned to alter its estimates.

If it had taken over complete responsibility for ensuring that the programme really represented the production which the firms were capable of achieving, this would have had unfortunate consequences. First, it would have weakened the sense of authority of the production directorates. They would have felt aggrieved because their functions were being usurped, and would also have disclaimed responsibility for the estimates of the central directorate and might, therefore, have refused to be bound by the official programme. It was essential, therefore, that it should appear that the final estimate was theirs, even if the central directorate found it necessary to interfere and criticise. Second, if the central directorate had attempted to assume the major responsibility for assessing productive capacity, it would have found it necessary to argue with the firms concerned. This would have been disastrous, for the central directorate would then have found itself dragged into dealing with the firms on detailed production issues. The discussion and solution of these would have taken so much time that the staff would have had to be enlarged or the more proper tasks of co-ordination would have been neglected. In either case the machinery for co-ordination would have broken down. This is just one more example of the general problem of co-ordination, that of finding the best balance between appreciating in detail the various aspects of one or two of the variable factors in the problem under consideration and that of assessing the significance of a large number of factors concerned but only in general terms. The co-ordinator had to be perpetually on his guard against succumbing to the temptation of becoming a specialist on one particular section, for this could be achieved only at the cost of his ignoring all other issues and so failing to fulfil his essential function as a co-ordinator.

One of the most difficult problems of co-ordination was that of securing staff. For it can be realised that to exercise their functions efficiently they had to be endowed with the most peculiar qualities. The most important capacity was that of being able to think in terms of figures. The co-ordinator had to carry in his mind in quantitative terms the various aspects of the problems with which he was concerned and be prepared to give advice on the basis of this knowledge. For he might be called in to a meeting or discussion at a moment's notice to discuss the practicability of some proposed change in programme. Given that capacity, he possessed enormous power, for anyone at a meeting who could promptly present in quantitative terms the various alternatives that were open and the consequences of each could usually ensure that the course of action which he thought most advisable was adopted. Second, he had to realise that all problems of planning are problems in the choice between alternatives, that a decision to produce more of one product was at the same time a decision to produce less of something else. It was for this reason that those with some training in economics usually made, other things being equal, the best planners. But neither of these capacities was of any use unless the official possessed a manner, character and ability which enabled him to develop friendly relations with the production directorates and Air Ministry divisions with which he was concerned. He had to be able to criticise without irritating, to advise without appearing to interfere, and to worm his way into their secrets and confidence without appearing to spy.

Lastly, he had to realise the full limits of his capacities in relation to the task which he was attempting: that by its very nature perfect planning and co-ordination was impossible and that in the last analysis the advice he gave had to be based on judgment rather than a scientific examination of facts. Those who were best at planning and co-ordination in MAP were those who felt that complete overall planning and co-ordination by one directorate was quite impossible.

[2]
War-time planning

(1) *British war production*[1]

One must admire the way in which Professor Postan has managed to condense a great mass of material; and he has succeeded, without doubt, in producing a readable, even an exciting book. This is mainly because he has not been content merely to tell the story of the development of war production and its problems; at every stage he comments, criticises, perhaps even praises or blames, tries to find out what went wrong and why, and whether things could have been done better. Some readers may protest that there is so much of Professor Postan's views of what might have been that it is difficult to distinguish between the facts and Professor Postan's comments on them. But if this is the price one has to pay for animated and stimulating analytical historical writing, I, for one, think the price well worth while paying. Not that I agree with much of Professor Postan's interpretation of events and comments on them. On the contrary; my copy of the book is peppered with queries, exclamation marks and notes of disagreement, and I think Professor Postan is mistaken in some of his conclusions. It is quite impossible to deal with all the controversial points in a review, and I shall refer to a selection only. Most of these are concerned with the planning and programming of aircraft production. But the reader should be warned that since I worked in MAP during the war, Professor Postan's views of these issues may be more detached than mine.

Professor Postan quite rightly argues at various stages of his study that the most important and difficult problem of munitions planning on the grand scale in war-time is to relate alternative strategies to economic possibilities and costs. There were, in my view, two

[1] This review of Professor M. M. Postan's *British War Production* appeared in *Economica*, August 1953, pp. 279–82. The first few paragraphs have been omitted.

crucial issues where this marrying process was defective and to which I would urge a study of this sort to devote more attention. The first was the worthwhileness of the heavy bomber programme; the second the adequacy of manpower planning.

The expanded heavy bomber programme was put into effect in the autumn of 1941, when the strategy it implied seemed to give the only possible hope of the United Kingdom defeating Germany on her own. What is astonishing is that this strategy was not reconsidered when the United States entered the war and when it was clear that Russia would not be overwhelmed 'in a matter of weeks'. Early in 1942 was the crucial period. It was then not too late to change production plans; the inordinate cost of the bomber programme was already apparent—both in its command over economic resources and in depriving other branches of the Services of urgently needed aircraft; the technical effectiveness of the heavy bomber in damaging the enemy's productive capacity was beginning to be questioned. But heavy bombing was the sacred cow of British strategy, and the programme went on virtually without question. Professor Postan quotes, without comment, the Prime Minister's opinion in the summer of 1943 that 'the failure to increase the supply of bombers was then the greatest danger facing the war effort as a whole' (p. 305). It would be interesting to calculate whether the cost in man-hours of building and equipping the heavy bombers was greater or less than the man-hours they destroyed in German production in 1943 and 1944.

Professor Postan certainly draws attention to the inquiry conducted by the Prime Minister's statistical branch and the Ministry of Production in the middle of 1943, whether it would be cheaper to use Mosquitos instead of heavy bombers for the bombing policy. But the middle of 1943 was much too late, and it is not surprising that the conclusions in favour of the Mosquito 'had little backing in the Air Ministry and MAP'. They would indeed have been quite irresponsible had they agreed to a wholesale changeover of aircraft production at that stage of the war. For it would only have been worth while, even given the superiority of the Mosquito, on the assumption that the war in Europe continued until 1945 and 1946.

The weakness of manpower planning was the failure of the central authorities—especially the Ministry of Production, which according to Professor Postan exercised an increasingly important role in this sphere in the later years of the war—to look ahead more than twelve months. The crucial time was early in 1943. The labour force employed by MAP and the Admiralty was due to expand considerably to the end of the current manpower allocation period —December 1943—and the Ministry of Supply's labour force was to be only slightly reduced. All three supply departments were, therefore, planning new capacity throughout 1943 (see table 56, p. 448, which gives a most valuable set of figures, not available elsewhere, of government expenditure on fixed capital during the period 1936–45), much of which would not come into operation until 1944 or even 1945. And the supply departments carried on with these plans, assuming that they would be allowed to retain throughout 1944 at least the labour force they were due to have at the end of 1943. But to anyone reviewing the manpower position at the centre, with the knowledge that by the middle of 1943 the barrel had been scraped empty, it should have been clear that the supply departments would have to release substantial labour in 1944, if the Services were not to be drastically depleted. Thus the supply departments could and should have been told in the spring of 1943, if not earlier, not to plan for further expansions of capacity in 1944. In fact it was not until late 1943 that the supply departments were told that they would have to release substantial manpower in 1944. By that time the waste of resources had already occurred.

The relation between Service requirements, design, development and production was another difficult war-time planning problem, although not without interesting peace-time parallels in the relation between technical development and production. The difficulties were most intricate in the case of tanks and aircraft, and Professor Postan devotes considerable attention to the latter (see especially pp. 322–45). It is a fascinating but baffling and perplexing task to try to discover why some aircraft failed and others succeeded. Considerable stress is put on the disappointing performance and production delays of most of the new aircraft introduced during the war—the Whirlwind, Typhoon, Tempest, Warwick and nearly all the naval types. Professor Postan examines the circumstances of these failures and tries to come to general conclusions about causes. I find some of the argument unconvincing, and think that more attention should be paid to the circumstances surrounding success before generalising on this difficult subject. Why were the Lancaster and the Mosquito so successful? What peculiar sets of qualities and circumstances enabled Rolls-Royce to do such a remarkable job in technical development and production? To discuss technical development and the quality of aircraft in the second world war without discussing the remarkable Rolls-Royce performance is indeed like Hamlet without the Prince. But perhaps this will be discussed more thoroughly in the volume on the design and development of weapons.

In his discussion of planning at MAP and in the concluding chapter on programmes and planning, Professor Postan shows unmistakably his regret that there was so little attempt by the department to inquire into production arrangements at the factories or by research and analysis to find the most efficient methods of manufacture, and then induce or require(?) the firms to adopt them. He seems to me to refer always nostalgically to the time when Sir Ernest Lemon and his industrial engineers spent at the production division of the Air Ministry. It is impossible to discuss at length the role of 'industrial planning' in a review, but I do not agree with Professor Postan's explanation of the issues and am certain that he has misinterpreted the views of the war-time staff of the Directorate of Statistics and Programmes on this subject.

The standard of statistical interpretation in the book is sadly disappointing. I repeatedly found it quite impossible to reconcile Professor Postan's statements about trends with the evidence of the figures themselves. I give three examples:

> It will thus be seen that, however measured, production of aircraft rose steadily in the first half of 1942, somewhat slowly in the second half of 1942 and the first half of 1943, slumped in the third quarter of 1943 and then rose again towards the end of 1943 and more steeply in 1944 [p. 310].

This completely overlooks the seasonal variations in output due to holidays in July and August (in the third quarter output was always low) and the varying incidence of the weather in holding up flight testing in winter, with consequential low deliveries in November to February and then high deliveries in the spring, when the accumulation was cleared up. Even so, the drop in 1943 from 2,201 in the second quarter to 2,171 in the third was hardly a slump!

> In this story of [aircraft] output failing to expand with the end of 1943 but expanding more rapidly thereafter . . . [p. 311].

In fact, heavy bomber production, the main expanding item, progressed as follows to the end of 1943: January 1941, 17; January 1942, 81; January 1943, 282; December 1943, 420!

> Whereas under the provisional manpower allocation for 1944 MAP was to lose 69,000 workers, the allocations as revised in September 1944 involved a reduction of 189,000. But here again, actual reductions lagged behind original plans [p. 376].

On the contrary, MAP lost over 240,000 from its labour force during 1944 (from 1,712,000 in December 1943 to 1,471,000 in December 1944—see *Statistical Digest of the War*, table 19, p. 17).

There are many other topics on which I should like to comment—the role and effectiveness of the Ministry of Production; the instruments of economic planning, especially allocations, priority and designation, and the function of each; Professor Postan's interesting discussion of whether the Munich breathing space enabled us to catch up with Germany; the interesting and curious tendency in this country to exaggerate German strength in 1940. Indeed, there are innumerable fascinating topics in this book worth discussing and arguing about. But this review is long enough already and I must desist. I hope that I have shown, notwithstanding my criticism, that this is an absorbing book well worth while reading; certainly no economist interested in planning and economic administration can afford to neglect it.

(2) *The control of raw materials*[2]

The war historians face a stupendous and perplexing task. There is a terrifying mass of original documents, and there are thousands of people who actually took part in the performance, each with his own ideas of how, when and why things happened. How to select from all this evidence and condense the selection into a meaningful history which will be worth reading? All the historians so far, including the author of this latest volume in the War Production series, confine themselves to the Whitehall material, so producing histories which are official in more than one sense. But even with this limitation, the material is overwhelming and the task of dealing with it formidable. How much easier it will be for some future historian to rewrite it all when the events can be viewed in dispassionate perspective, when the mice have eaten some of the files, and when none of those who were alive at the time are there to point

[2] This review of J. Hurstfield's *The Control of Raw Materials* appeared in the *Journal of the Royal Statistical Society*, August 1953.

out the distant connection between what was written on the official files and what actually happened.

Mr Hurstfield has had a specially difficult task in writing the history of raw materials. For practically every war-time problem had its raw material aspect: munitions production, import and shipping policy, exports, home production and manpower, civilian supplies and rationing, Anglo-American relations, were all inextricably interwoven with issues of raw materials policy and supply. Mr Hurstfield has attempted to make his task manageable by dealing with this tangle of subjects in four main parts. First, a section on pre-war preparations, including a review of control, both government and private, of raw materials during the inter-war years which is hardly relevant to the remainder of the book. Second, 'The requirements of raw materials', dealing in turn with munitions, export and home civilian needs. Then 'The supply of raw materials', which comprises the main part of the book. Here we have a detailed treatment, for successive periods, of import problems and policy with special attention given to Anglo-American supply relations, followed by a discussion of home supply, conservation, costs and prices. Finally a section headed 'Conclusion: the organisation of control', which is mainly concerned with the manning of the controls, the respective roles and functions of the controls and the raw materials division of the Ministry of Supply, and the relations between them.

Each section is a competent summary, lucidly written and amply peppered with the most important statistics. There are frequent pauses when the reader is asked to sit back and take a general analytical view of some of the problems and issues raised in the mainly narrative sections. Here we get some interesting critical comments on failings in organisation and policy. Altogether a well produced book and well worth reading. Yet I felt there was something missing. I started reading the book hoping to get some understanding of how the system of control really operated, but I was disappointed. All the paraphernalia of planning is there—requirements, allocations, priority, designation, preference, plans, programme, co-ordination, the user principle, etc.—but they all flit across the pages like phantoms. I got no picture of how they all added up to a workable system for obtaining and distributing raw materials supplies as a substitute for a system based on money and prices.

I think that Mr Hurstfield has failed to achieve this—indeed, perhaps he was not trying to do so—because he attempts to deal with practically every material, import programme and statement of requirements. I would have found it much more enlightening if he had taken one material, say steel, for one period and shown in some detail how the statements of requirements and supplies were built up in the departments, the arguments that were used by each department in presenting its case to the Materials Committee, the tussle that went on before an allocation was agreed, and what changes, if any, the departments had to make in their plans when they knew what had been allocated for the coming period. And if one wanted to show how the system changed, developed and improved as the war went on, why not take a case like this in 1940 and then one in 1943 or 1944 and discuss the differences?

Similarly, the story of the complex and ever-changing arrangements for Anglo-American supply left me with little impression of what the combined boards did and how they did it, except that they were all co-ordinating. An explanation in some detail of what one meeting of one of these boards did and what effects their decisions had would have been much more helpful.

I suppose all this amounts to a plea for the use of the case study method when one is attempting to show how an administrative system works. But perhaps it would not be history. If it is not, then the official histories are all going to by-pass one of the most interesting and fascinating aspects of war-time economic experience.

There is one comment I would like to make on the interpretation of events which is common to all the volumes published so far and which Mr Hurstfield follows. This is the great emphasis that is put on how little was achieved between September 1939 and June 1940, the 'phoney war' period, and how everything changed after Dunkirk. I begin to wonder whether the argument is not overdone. In the civilian field one must not forget that resistance to clothes rationing in the highest quarters lasted well after Dunkirk. If Mr Hurstfield had included the figures for 1940 in his table of *per capita* consumption in the United Kingdom (p. 125), the reader would have been able to see that by far the biggest proportionate reduction in consumption took place between 1939 and 1940, and he might have found this a little surprising in view of what is said in the text. The official historians' view of the phoney war period is undoubtedly the fashionable one, but it is not just the kind of fashionable interpretation which historians themselves delight in upsetting? Is not Mr Hurstfield overdoing it when he refers to the general attitude during the early months of the war as 'the first fine careless rapture of that sunny autumn' (p. 116)?

[3]

Planning by economic survey[1]

In the *Economic Survey* for 1947—the first of the series—there was a general introductory chapter on 'Economic planning' explaining 'The kind of plan' the government had in mind, and 'How the plan is made'. This gives the main official indication of how the authors of the *Survey* thought, or wished the public to think, that planning would proceed. It is interesting to look back now at this exposition and examine how these ideas have developed in successive *Economic Surveys*. Unfortunately, no later *Economic Survey* contains a similar introductory chapter—it would indeed be of great interest to read what the authors of the *Surveys* would have written on 'economic planning' as a preface to the 1952 *Survey*, after the lessons of the last five years. In the absence of this, one has to proceed by a process of detection. By examining how the treatment of various aspects of planning has changed from *Survey* to *Survey*, it might be possible to assess how the present system of planning compares with the exposition given in 1947. It is not my intention to examine in detail the accuracy and reliability of the various plans and forecasts that have been made year by year, fascinating though this might be. I am concerned rather to outline the changing content and methods of the plans given in the *Economic Surveys*.

I

In the *Economic Survey* for 1947 three sets of plans were envisaged. First, plans for individual industries; second, economic 'budgets' for manpower and national income and expenditure; and third, analyses of particular problems, such as foreign exchange, investment, fuel and power, steel, timber and other scarce materials.

[1] From *Economica*, August 1952, pp. 237–53. The annual *Economic Survey*, first issued by the Government in 1947, was discontinued in 1963 and replaced by an *Economic Report* from which forecasts and plans were absent.

The main plans for individual industries were to be related to what were called 'basic' industries.

There are a number of basic industries and services—coal, power, steel, agriculture, transport, building—the efficient development of which is fundamental to our entire productive employment. A long-term plan is being developed for each of these industries. It must be one of the chief aims of the Government's economic plan to see that these plans are pressed forward as fast as possible and kept in proper relationship with each other and with the rest of the economy. [1947:11][2]

The economic 'budgets' for manpower and national income and expenditure were to set out resources and requirements.

The man-power budget compares the estimated future working population with the number of workers required industry by industry. The national income and expenditure budget compares the estimated value of the national production of goods and services with the value of all the goods and services required. [1947:15]

These economic 'budgets' are prepared by a central staff, working with representatives of the Government departments concerned under an official committee. On the resources side the Ministry of Labour forecasts the working population, and an estimate is made on the best evidence available about the prospective value of output. In regard to requirements, the position is less simple. Some, such as the man-power for the Armed Forces, originate within the Government machine. Others originate outside the areas of Government control, but are sponsored by Government departments . . . others again, where no Government control operates, are estimates of what the market will claim. [1947:16]

There is no discussion of the significance of a statement of the relationship between supplies and requirements for the national product as a whole, where the requirements figure contains a large element 'of what the market will claim'. It is indeed difficult to discover what the authors had in mind when they refer to 'the value of all the goods and services required'.

The plans for particular sectors or commodities were to supplement these two general economic 'budgets'.

The foreign exchange statement compares our import requirements with our prospective income from exports, visible and invisible. Con-

[2] The references are, throughout, to the numbered paragraphs in particular *Economic Surveys*.

sideration of this statement, in relation to the rate at which we can afford to spend the United States and Canadian credits, provides the basis for deciding on the one hand the import programme, and on the other the export target. The latter is a claim on the man-power 'budget'. [1947:18].

The investment statement compares the estimate of what is required to be spent on capital equipment and maintenance with the labour and materials available for the industries which produce equipment, such as building and engineering.

It is also necessary to make sure that the plans under this head are consistent with the funds which are estimated to become available for financing capital work, which is an item in the national income 'budget'. [1947:19]

The statements for fuel and power, steel and other scarce materials show the effect on the whole economy of shortages of these basic supplies. [1947:20]

The authors of the 1947 *Survey* explained that when these separate budgets had been drawn up they had to be made to fit. It would not be sufficient to allocate supplies between the various requirements so that the totals agreed for each budget; each budget had also to be reconciled with the rest, so that the budgets as a whole gave a consistent basis for planning for the coming year. There is little discussion of how this—the most difficult problem of planning—was to be achieved. The only indication of how the co-ordination of the individual plans was to be secured is given in the following paragraph:

Planning the allocation of resources between the various national requirements is at present a task of deciding which out of a number of claimants must go short—in other words, which are the most important national priorities. It is precisely the same problem, only on a national scale, as the housewife has to solve every week. On the one side are the resources which we have to spend, on the other side are the things upon which we want to spend them. The two must be made to match. After full examination of possible means of attaining a balance, the official committee submits to Ministers a report on what measures should be taken and their decisions form the basis for subsequent action. [1947:25]

II

These extracts from the *Economic Survey* for 1947 show the authors' views at the time of the theoretical structure of planning. Even then there were expressions of doubt and hesitation about the significance and usefulness of such plans, and especially about the difficulties of implementing them. But remarkably little was said about the intrinsic difficulty of drawing up correct and consistent plans; the emphasis was rather on the difficulty of implementation because the government wished to proceed by 'democratic' rather than 'totalitarian' methods.

> The apparatus of Government controls is used to guide the economy in the direction which is indicated by the plan. This control apparatus, taken as a whole, can have a substantial effect upon the course of the national economy. But the controls cannot by themselves bring about very rapid changes or make fine adjustments in the economic structure. To do this, they would have to be much more detailed in their application and more drastic in their scope. Indeed, the task of directing by democratic methods an economic system as large and complex as ours is far beyond the power of any Government machine working by itself, no matter how efficient it may be. Events can be directed in the way that is desired in the national interest only if the Government, both sides of industry and the people accept the objectives and then work together to achieve this end. [1947:27]

How the *Economic Survey* helps the individual or the firm to decide what he should do to make the plan succeed, assuming that he is anxious for its success, is left a mystery. Beyond the knowledge that he should work hard (or should he really do this if he is in an unessential industry?), not press for higher wages, salaries or profits, and save a lot, he is given no criteria to guide him in deciding what to do to make the plan succeed. This view of the plan as a framework drawn up by the government which requires everyone to do voluntarily what is necessary for its success, remains a rather nebulous one.

III

The *Economic Survey* for 1947 did not in fact give all the budgets and plans which were discussed in the introductory chapter on the system of planning. Specific output plans were given only for coal, electricity (generating plant), shipbuilding and building. There were also general budgets for foreign trade and labour. But on capital investment and national income and expenditure—which became the central features of some of the later *Surveys*—only summary information was provided. This merely gave the percentage distribution of fixed capital investment during the coming years between various activities, and the distribution of the national output between consumption, public expenditure, capital investment, and overseas trade. In no sense could these have been called budgets, showing the relationship between requirements and resources; they were merely forecasts of what was expected to happen, and then not in a very helpful form.

The full flowering of the 1947 *Survey* system of planning did not come until the *Surveys* for 1948 and 1949. In the *Survey* for 1948 detailed production plans were given for a wide range of specific commodities, import and export programmes were given in some detail, and there were summary estimates for capital investment and manpower distribution. But the most important innovation was the introduction of an analysis of national income and expenditure and a detailed discussion of the problem of inflation.[3] The national income and expenditure plans were presented in three stages. First, an estimate of national output, the foreign balance and the total of resources available for home use, the latter being sub-divided between personal consumption, government expenditure and home investment. Then a statement of expected current public expenditure and revenue on the basis of existing rates of taxation, from which was derived a figure of the prospective public authorities' surplus or deficit. And lastly, an analysis of the national capital account which compared expected total investment with the sources available to finance it. In this statement at first private savings, and later personal savings, were treated as the residual item, and the question was asked whether this level of savings could be expected to occur voluntarily. It was around the situation as portrayed by these tables that the problem of inflation was discussed in the *Surveys* for 1948 and later years.

IV

It is now proposed to examine what happened to these various plans and programmes in later *Surveys*; to see what remained in the

[3] Although the 1947 *Survey* was full of statements indicating that our resources were not enough for everything that we wanted to do, this was not treated as a symptom of an inflationary situation. Indeed, the word inflation was not mentioned.

later *Surveys* of the theoretical structure outlined in the *Surveys* for 1947 and 1948.

(1) *Plans for individual industries*

In the *Survey* for 1948 individual production or capacity targets were given for coal, mining machinery, electricity, oil, steel, transport (locomotives, wagons and carriages, track laying, commercial and public service vehicles and shipbuilding), textiles (cotton, wool and rayon), and agriculture. In 1949 the targets for transport and oil had disappeared, but estimates of the expected consumption of a wide range of raw materials were added. These were continued in the 1950 *Survey* but in the 1951 *Survey* the raw material figures related only to actual and not to expected consumption, and no targets were given for textile production. So that by 1951 specific industry targets had been narrowed down to figures for coal, steel and agricultural production. Even more significant than the narrowing down of the planned figures given is the change in the way in which the plans for individual industries were discussed. The major part of chapter II of the *Survey* for 1951, which deals with individual industries and products, is concerned with reviewing the recent events and existing problems of industry—coal, electricity, steel, raw material supplies, building, textiles and agriculture. The glimpses into the future are brief, tentative and hesitant, and even where figures are suggested for the coming year they are hedged about with numerous qualifications. A typical example of the vagueness of the plans, even when figures were given, is the following statement about the steel plan in the *Survey* for 1949.

> It is accordingly possible to arrive at a variety of views on the probable steel output—from the pessimistic, which would assess the figure at less than the 1948 output, to the highly optimistic, based on full capacity of the furnaces. The objective is the maximum output the industry can achieve with the materials it can obtain. In the most favourable circumstances this should be 15¼–15½ million tons of ingot steel. [1949:27]

By 1951 this section of the *Survey* was much more a review of the recent past than a plan for the future.

(2) *The manpower budget*

The manpower budget was one of the first casualties as the *Surveys* progressed; indeed, it hardly ever came to life. The *Survey* for 1947 had explained that the budget would 'compare the estimated future working population with the number of workers required industry by industry'. A budget of this kind was not in fact given in any of the *Surveys*. In the *Survey* for 1947 there was an estimate of the total working population at the end of the year and its distribution by the main industrial groups. But it was explained that

> this is neither an ideal distribution nor a forecast of what will happen; it represents the approximate distribution which is needed to carry out the objectives in paragraph 18 and which the Government considers can be achieved if the nation as a whole sets itself to achieve them. [1947:128]

Similar figures of the total labour force and its distribution by industries were given in the *Survey* for 1948, but the explanation of the significance of these 'forecasts' was now rather different:

> Any projected distribution (of man-power) is therefore largely a forecast of the results of other factors and if some figures turn out differently it is not necessarily in every case a matter of regret.[4] But the labour forces proposed for coal, agriculture and textiles are targets in the full sense. [1948:186]

The figures of manpower distribution by the end of the year were given again in the 1949 *Survey*, but now 'a target in the full sense' was given only for coal-mining. For although increases of 11,000 in cotton and 6,000 in wool are shown in the table, the *Survey* states that 'an improvement on these figures would be desirable' [1949:91]. The table giving a forecast of manpower distribution reappeared in the *Survey* for 1950, but all reference to targets for specific industries had disappeared. And by 1951 this general table was also omitted. The omission went almost unnoticed and no regret was expressed by the authors of the *Survey* at this rather sorry ending of the attempts to include a manpower budget as an essential element in the plan.

Manpower issues were not ignored in the 1951 *Survey*. The discussion centred round the problems of obtaining the manpower needed for the rearmament programme. Although some estimates of the labour force required for this were given, the treatment was largely qualitative, and no attempt was made to show in a manpower budget where the labour for armament production was to come from.

[4] We are not told in which cases it would not be a matter for regret if the figures turned out differently.

(3) *Foreign trade and the balance of payments*

Since the beginning of the series, events have forced discussion of problems of foreign trade and the balance of payments into a central position in all the *Economic Surveys*. Yet the difficulty of forecasting the foreign trade situation for any length of time ahead was recognised at a very early stage. The pattern of trade that would be necessary in the long run could be sketched in broad outline, and a reasonably reliable detailed estimate could be made of the balance of payments for a few months ahead; but to forecast the foreign trade situation for the intermediate period of a year to eighteen months ahead implied an assessment of the timing of fluctuations in international trade which proved quite impossible. The sections on foreign trade became more and more a detailed review of the nature of the United Kingdom and sterling area balance of payments problems, with general suggestions as to how these should be tackled, than anything in the nature of the firm programme for foreign trade envisaged in the *Survey* for 1947. Even on the import side, where the government exercised a substantial measure of control, it proved impossible to lay down a firm programme for more than a very short period ahead.

Such attempts as were made in the *Economic Surveys* to draw up foreign trade programmes showed also that the spring of each year—when the *Surveys* were issued—was not a particularly appropriate time to take planning decisions in this field. International events, such as the grant of ERP, the devaluation of non-dollar currencies, or a change in the economic situation in the United States, paid little respect to the calendar, and thus it was impossible to reserve for the *Economic Survey* discussion of the major decisions in foreign trade policy. Nor did the review of the foreign trade situation in the *Economic Surveys* enable the planners to foresee, let alone anticipate, some of the major changes in international trade which affected the external position of the United Kingdom. The mounting hesitations with which estimates for the future were put forward can be seen from the following brief account of the foreign trade statements in successive *Surveys*. In the *Survey* for 1947 estimates of imports, net invisible income, planned borrowing, and exports—as a residual—were put forward for the whole of the coming year. In the *Survey* for 1948 even more detailed export targets were given for groups of industries and markets, but an import programme was given for the first half of 1948 only. 'Import programmes for the second half of 1948 have not yet been finally decided. These must inevitably depend on decisions about the European Recovery Programme' [1948:31]. Even the figures for the overseas balance for the first half of the year derived from these import and export programmes were put forward with great hesitation:

> These estimates are, however, subject to a considerable margin of error. It is not possible to predict with great accuracy either the difference between total payments and receipts, or the distribution of exports between the sterling area and the rest of the world. [1948:70]

In the *Survey* for 1949 estimates, although in considerable detail, were again given only for the first half of the year. The reason given on this occasion was also the uncertainty of the volume of ERP aid. In the *Survey* for 1950 all detailed estimates of export targets, imports and the foreign balance for the coming year had disappeared. There was a long detailed discussion of the course of events in 1949, and of the proposals put forward in the Long-term Programme submitted to OEEC for bringing the sterling area external accounts into balance by 1952–53; but very little about 1950:

> It is particularly difficult to forecast how much progress will be made in 1950 because the devaluation of last September has profoundly affected every aspect of the balance of payments, and until more time has elapsed it is impossible to disentangle the short-term from the more permanent effects. Any attempt to do so now in the form of apparently precise statistics would be seriously misleading. [1950:46]

Further factors quoted by the authors as making the future especially uncertain were the dependence of the future course of raw material prices on the course of United States activity and the liberalisation of trade between this country and the other members of OEEC.

The *Economic Survey* for 1951 also avoided giving any detailed foreign trade programmes. It was argued that because of

> the discussions which are now proceeding in NATO in order to provide for an equitable distribution of the economic burden of defence, . . . and because of the rapid changes which are now in progress, it is impossible to make detailed forecasts of the development of our external position in 1951 and subsequent years. [1951:87]

The general character of the problems before us can, however, be clearly indicated. [1951:87]

As a consequence of the events of 1950 there was much more discussion in the *Survey* for 1951 than in earlier *Surveys* of the importance of movements in the terms of trade. This issue had been avoided in earlier *Surveys* by assuming the terms of trade to remain unchanged, but such an assumption was no longer possible. Any precise forecasting of the terms of trade was, however, avoided by working out a figure for the required value of total exports in 1951, but not indicating how far this was to be met by an increase in prices and how far by an increase in volume.

The events of 1951 have demonstrated perhaps even more conclusively than those of earlier years the great difficulty of forecasting our changing overseas fortunes. Although the 1951 *Survey* portrayed the overseas position as critical, there was no inkling even of the possibility of the disastrous change in the balance of payments which took place in the second half of the year.

(4) *Capital investment*

The attempts at capital investment planning in the early *Economic Surveys* were dogged by misfortune. Presumably two purposes were to be served in drawing up a capital investment plan. A detailed programme would apportion capital investment according to 'social priorities', and a plan for investment in total was necessary as an essential part of the national income and expenditure accounts. A detailed statement of proposals for capital investment in a wide range of industries was given in the White Paper on capital investment in 1948 (Cmd. 7268), issued at the end of 1947. Similar statements appeared in appendixes to the *Surveys* for 1949 and 1950. In spite of this detail, however, it was never made clear—perhaps it is not possible to make clear—by what criteria the choice of investment projects was made. In most cases there was just a statement of the amount of investment in the particular industry which the government proposed to allow. These proposals seemed to be based on *ad hoc* decisions in each case. In the event, the individual investment plans bore little relation to what actually happened. Usually the sectors where investment was planned to increase increased less than the plan; and where reductions were called for, the reduction did not fully materialise.

It is doubtful whether the publication of the detailed plans served any useful purpose except to show the basis on which the estimate for total investment was arrived at. This is recognised by implication in the following comment on the detailed plans given in the *Survey* for 1949.

> The sum of these estimates suggests an increase of some £120 million in 1949. But past experience has shown that, however carefully the estimates for work to be undertaken may be drawn up, the investment actually achieved will be less than the programme as a result of unforeseen difficulties and delays. It is impossible to say in advance which programmes will be effected. . . . [1949:45]

In any event, the detailed statement of investment plans was discontinued after the *Survey* for 1950.

The total of all the specific programmes did not add to the total of investment which had to be allowed for in the national income and expenditure estimates, since there were important fields of capital investment which were not covered in the detailed statements. The amount of investment in fields outside the planned items was grossly underestimated in the *Survey* for 1948, partly through ignorance of the volume of work done on repair and maintenance. The *Survey* for 1948 gave £1,420 million as the amount of fixed investment planned for the coming year, in ignorance assumed that this covered the whole field of fixed investment, and merely added another £380 million to cover the expected rise in prices, stocks, and work in progress.[5] This gave a total of £1,800 million for home investment—the figure used in drawing up the capital account in the national income and expenditure statement. In fact, investment in 1948 turned out to be £2,352 million.[6] This substantial difference was only partly due to the fact that fixed investment increased even though the plan called for some reduction and because prices rose more than had been allowed for. A good deal of the discrepancy arose from the fact that the plan did not cover the whole field of investment.[7]

This gross error was remedied in the 1949 *Survey*, when £370

[5] The figure of £380 million also covered the increase in exports not yet paid for, since at the time this was included in 'home investment'.

[6] This is the figure given in the 1948 national income White Paper. It was revised to £2,590 million in the White Paper for 1949.

[7] That this was so can be seen clearly by comparing the estimate of actual fixed investment in 1947 given in the *Survey* for 1948—£1,550 million—with

million was included to cover miscellaneous items of investment not specified in detail. As a consequence the total of fixed investment which materialised in 1949 was much closer to the *Survey* estimate. Yet if one added to this miscellaneous item the estimate which had to be made for stocks and work in progress—admittedly one of the shakiest estimates in the *Survey*[8]—the proportion of the total of investment which could be estimated with any pretensions to precision was not much more than half the total. Thus in the *Economic Survey* for 1949 programmed investment accounted for £1,755 million out of a total estimated home investment of £2,330 million. In the *Survey* for 1950 planned fixed investment was still discussed in some detail, but there was no indication of how the authors had proceeded from the figure of £1,786 million for this item to the £2,435 million given for 'gross capital formation' in the national income tables. It was not possible to discover what had been assumed about the movement of miscellaneous investment, price changes, and the movement of stocks and work in progress. As has already been mentioned, no detail figures of prospective fixed investment were given in the 1951 *Survey*; but the figure given in the national income forecasts showed fixed investment and the increase in stocks and work in progress separately for the first time. But this attempt to allow more precisely for stock changes was not particularly successful. This is hardly surprising in view of the paucity of information about actual stock changes and the unpredictable nature of stock movements. Indeed, it is very doubtful whether stock movements, which are highly sensitive to changes in prices and the general economic climate, can ever be 'planned' in advance. And yet such movements may form an important element in the total of home investment.

---

the figure for 1947—£1,800 million—published a few weeks later in the national income White Paper for 1947.

[8] It is not merely the forecasts of the movements in this item which were subject to a wide margin of error, but also the estimates of what had actually happened after the event. This can be seen from the following figures for this item from the national income White Papers for 1949 to 1951:

Figures given in national income White Papers for	*Value of physical increase in stocks and work in progress (£ million)*			
	1948	1949	1950	1951
1949	75	150	—	—
1950	200	215	115	—
1951	280	325	204	370

The experience of attempts to plan the total of home investment has also shown the difficulty of estimating at all precisely in terms of a calendar year the effect of government measures to encourage or discourage investment. Much investment has to proceed on a long-term basis and the rate at which it takes place cannot easily be changed at short notice. This is clearly recognised in the following comment on prospective building investment in the *Survey* for 1951:

The planning and execution of most building works take a considerable period, and to be effective the control of investment programmes must look far ahead. The investment programme for 1951 was prepared and approved in 1950, and account was then taken of the probable increase in the total output of the building and civil engineering industries. Much of the work allowed for in this programme, particularly that to be carried out in the early part of 1951, was licensed and, in some cases, even begun during 1950. Some of the other work may, however, have to be deferred in order to give priority to specific defence projects where this is necessary to avoid overburdening local building resources. At the same time it will be necessary to reduce the total programmes of civil investment in 1951 and 1952 in order to make room for further defence building work. These are being re-examined and until the examination is completed it will be impossible to say how large the cuts in civil investment will be, or where they will fall. [1951:76]

(5) *National income and expenditure*

National income and expenditure accounts were used for the first time in the *Survey* for 1948 as a method of portraying the general economic situation in the coming year. The calculations made in that *Survey* proceeded on the assumption that by drawing up such a system of accounts it was possible to discover whether the situation was likely to continue to be inflationary, and if so the magnitude of the inflationary gap.

It is now possible to build up an estimate of the total national income and expenditure. From this we can judge whether the total of what we are attempting is or is not within the limits of our overall resources and whether any measures are necessary to limit some of the expenditure, and reduce it to a better balance with the expected output from available resources. [1948:97]

The *Survey* posed the problem of the inflationary gap in terms of a hypothetical balance sheet of capital expenditure and the sources available to finance it, with personal savings as a residual item. The authors then asked whether this required level of personal savings was likely to occur. As an aid to answering this question, the required personal savings were calculated as a percentage of total disposable income, and this was compared with similar percentages for 1946 and 1947, and 1938. It was then concluded that

> when allowance is made for these factors,[9] which did not prevail to anything like the same extent in 1938, it is unlikely that, without a radical change in the willingness of individuals to save, the total of net saving in 1948, in the absence of inflation, will reach the necessary figure.

Leaving on one side the extremely tenuous basis on which these figures are calculated—it is recognised in the *Surveys* that they involve estimates which are little more than guesswork—it is worth while enquiring whether in principle calculations of this sort can in fact tell us whether the future economic situation is going to be inflationary or not. In my view it is a complete misunderstanding of the nature of these estimates to expect them to yield forecasts of this sort. In making the estimates themselves one has to make implicit assumptions as to the continuance of inflation; and it is not surprising that if inflationary assumptions are made in these individual estimates, the resulting accounts will portray an inflationary situation. Thus if one starts with an inflationary situation and assumes that investment will be at a high level in the coming year and will be limited only by physical controls, if one assumes that the pressure of consumer expenditure will be such that it will need to be restrained by rationing, and if one assumes that increased government expenditure will not be matched by higher rates of taxation, it is hardly surprising that a system of national accounts drawn up on these assumptions results in a residual figure of personal savings which is not likely to be forthcoming voluntarily. The judgment about the degree of inflationary pressure which is likely is part of the calculating process—it is implied in the assumptions made about the level of investment, consumption and government expenditure; it does not emerge as the final result of the whole exercise. In any case, when the situation was clearly inflationary, as in 1948 and 1951, the calculations added little to our information;

[9] 'The desire of many persons to use their past savings to re-equip themselves with durable consumption goods' . . . and also to use 'past savings to maintain standards of expenditure greater than present taxed income will permit'.

and when the future economic climate seemed to be doubtful, as in 1950 and 1952, the national income accounts appeared to give practically no help in deciding which way the scales were likely to tip. It is when we are on this razor edge, with some forces still inflationary but others working in a deflationary direction, that it would be most useful to know what is going to happen, and yet it is in just such a situation that it is most difficult to make plans or forecasts.

At most the estimates of the national accounts are a useful framework within which to discuss these problems. They make explicit the assumptions that are being made and they may prevent us overlooking some important interrelationships which might otherwise be neglected. But to think that they can provide the basis for deciding how big a budget surplus or deficit the Chancellor should aim for in his budget is grossly to exaggerate their importance. An assessment of the force of inflationary or deflationary tendencies continues to be a most difficult exercise in the examination of all the information—quantitative and qualitative—available about the economic situation, both at home and overseas.

One can trace some degree of recognition of this view in the later *Economic Surveys*. The *Survey* for 1950 states that

> the analysis which follows (of national income and expenditure) is based on a number of stated assumptions. The selection of these is a matter of judgment, and the most important depend on a sense of responsibility shown by the people as a whole to the needs of the situation. With different assumptions, the conclusions would be different. [1950:68]

In assessing the future economic situation, the *Survey* for 1949 paid less attention to the national income accounts, and much more regard was given, in traditional fashion, to the movement of certain key economic indicators. Since 1949 this form of analysis has been extended, and in 1951 reference was made to the level of unemployment, the movement of prices and stocks, the level of bank advances and the rate of interest in assessing the extent to which inflationary pressure had been brought under control in the previous year.

Experience has also demonstrated that inflationary pressure which results from a costs/prices spiral cannot be adequately portrayed in a set of national accounts. In the earlier *Economic Surveys* this problem was completely avoided by giving the national income and expenditure estimates in terms of the prices ruling at the end of the previous year. There was, of course, an appeal for restraint in pressing for higher incomes and prices, but no attempt to embody an assessment of the likely degree of success of these appeals in the system of national accounts for the coming year. Yet of course wage/price movements played a crucial part in determining how the allocation of resources in fact turned out in any particular year. Only in the 1951 *Survey* was some attempt made to include income and price movements in the forecast for the coming year, and the basis on which this was done has since proved pitifully incorrect.

V

By the *Survey* for 1951 a good deal of the planning system portrayed in the first *Survey* had disappeared.[10] The manpower budget had gone completely; there were now no details of investment plans; the plans of production in specific industries were limited to a very narrow range; forecasts for foreign trade were given for only a short time ahead, and then in the most hesitant terms. Forecasts of the national income and expenditure still remained, but they were hedged round with numerous qualifications at every stage. Yet it was these accounts which commanded most attention when the *Survey* was published, for they bore on budgetary policy more closely than any other section of the *Survey*.

The result of this gradual whittling away of the forecasts and plans given in the *Survey* was to turn the document more and more into a review of the economic events of the previous year and make it less and less a clear set of plans for the coming year. The *Survey* for 1952 completed this process. Practically all reference in statistical terms to plans for the coming year had disappeared. The major part of the *Survey* was devoted to a review of the changing economic situation since the middle of 1951. The measures which the government had taken or proposed to take to deal with our economic problems were explained, but the effect they were expected to have in the next twelve months was outlined only in the broadest terms. Even the forecast of national income and expenditure was no longer given, although there was some reference to a few crucial figures in the section on 'The balance of the economy in 1952'. The almost

[10] Disappeared from the published documents; some of the plans which are no longer published may, of course, still be constructed and circulated in Whitehall.

complete disappearance of specific programmes for the future in the 1952 *Survey* can perhaps be explained in terms of the political complexion of a new government and its anti-planning philosophy. On the other hand it could be viewed merely as a further stage in learning how difficult it is to put forward precise plans for the future in the spring of each year—a process of learning which has been going on continuously since 1948.

[4]

The enigma of the Russian economic system[1]

The working of the Russian economic system is an enigma. There has been a great deal of theoretical discussion about the nature of the planned economy; much comment on Russian five-year plans; courageous attempts to make sense of Russian statistics; and elaborate scrutiny of the ever-changing rules, regulations, and formal organisation. But there has been little analysis of how the system actually works in practice. Most academic discussion in Russia is written in ideological jargon, full of abstruse argument about dogma, but almost completely unrelated to actual economic behaviour; and the Russian managers and administrators who have been running the economy have written remarkably little about their own methods and experience.

Yet it is of the greatest importance that we should understand how the Russian economy works. Apart from its intrinsic fascination, it is politically important that we should understand how far, and in what respects, Russia and the West are divided by essential differences in the way in which they run their economic affairs; and those countries which think of taking the Russian system as their model should appreciate more realistically what it is they are copying. For them to assume that Russian practice corresponds closely to the myths and ideology of Russian economic planning may well lead them to disaster.

I am no expert on Russia. All I know about the working of the system is at second-hand. But the more I read and hear about the Soviet economic administration, the more I feel that the essential basis of the system can be understood in terms of our own economic experience. There are many aspects of our own experience which should give us an insight into what goes on in Russia. The way in which our economy was run during the war; the government's

[1] From *The Listener*, 29 August 1957.

attempts to control and co-ordinate investment in peace-time; the administrative problems of running large firms, both privately and publicly owned—all have close parallels in crucial aspects of the working of the Russian economy. We have used this experience far too little in trying to understand Russia. It has been too readily taken for granted that the Russian system is radically different from anything that we have ever known. It has been assumed that, through the surrender of political freedom as we understand it, Russia has been able to run her economy in a way which corresponds closely to the theoretical models of a planned economy.

The basic operational unit in Russia, as in the West, is the firm. When one reads about the behaviour and problems of the firm in Russia, what is striking is the similarity, not the contrast, with the problems and behaviour of firms in England or the United States. The Russian firm may get its finance, especially its finance for expansion, in a different way, and is subject to different and more frequent interventions from outside controlling authorities; but the administrative problems of running the firm itself are much the same as here. The similarities are particularly striking for the large-scale units. The large Russian combines, and firms such as General Motors or United Steel in America, ICI or the nationalised boards in this country, have many problems in common. Ownership makes little difference to the fundamental administrative problem of running large-scale units, as the reports of the Fleck and Herbert committees on the nationalised coal and electricity industries demonstrate. Much of what is written about business administration and organisation in the West has striking parallels in discussion in Russia.

But, it will be argued, the Russian firm is controlled and guided by instructions from higher planning authorities—the Ministries, the Supreme Economic Council, and Gosplan. These authorities, it is said, decide what the firms shall produce, and the firms' activities are largely determined by what is arranged for them in co-ordinated yearly, or longer-term, five-yearly plans. But the way in which this planning and co-ordination works is in my view usually misunderstood. The formal administrative procedures by which these plans are drawn up are often mistakenly taken as providing the clue to the essential working of the system. The usual picture of planning in Russia is roughly as follows. At the beginning of each yearly or five-yearly planning period the supreme authorities lay down the general objectives to be achieved during the next planning period. These general instructions are passed down the administrative hierarchy through the Ministries to the firms, who then draw up their detailed proposals for production with accompanying statements of what they will need in labour, materials, machinery, etc., in order to achieve their targets. The firms' plans are then passed back up the hierarchy, and are progressively amalgamated and co-ordinated at each level until they reach Gosplan and the Supreme Economic Council. Here they are further examined, reconciled, appropriately amended, and given final approval. In this final form they are passed back down the same channels again, to be broken down progressively until they become final plans for the individual firms. The firms then take these as the operative instructions for production during the ensuing period; and contracts are made between Ministries and firms in accordance with these plans.

But in the explanation of this procedure that I have read or heard, no detailed information is given of what this co-ordination, amalgamation and reconciliation consists of, as the plans and counterplans move up and down the administrative hierarchy in this way. Usually there is little more than a statement that the supreme economic authorities decide on what should be the broad division between consumption and investment. But such broad decisions are of little interest to the individual firms, and though of substantial political and social importance, are not significant for the crucial, complex problem of fitting together in a coherent pattern the production plans of thousands of separate units. This is the essential problem of economic administration: how to fit together, for example, in their complex variety of quantity and quality the wide range of goods to be produced by the firms in the metal producing, engineering and machine tool industries. The idea that the plans of the separate firms in each of these industries can be reconciled and appropriately adjusted in detail by passing them once up and down the planning hierarchy is fantastic. We were never able to do anything like this during the war, and there is no shred of evidence that the Russians have discovered some wonderful new analytical and administrative technique for dealing with this problem. The Russians apparently are uninterested in elaborate input–output analysis.

In my view this crucial aspect of co-ordination—the dovetailing of the details of production—is achieved in practice by continuous interaction and negotiation between the producing firms themselves, and between the firms and Ministries and other organisations which place the contracts for the final products, whether for private or government use. There is evidence to support this view in what is written about Russia, and it fits in with our own war-time experience of how a so-called planned system works. There are many stories of how these relations, both legal and illegal, operate between firms in Russia. It is significant that the authorities turn a blind eye to illegal relations, such as black market operations and barter deals, as long as these lead to successful production. The whole complex of these relations is made respectable in the planning jargon by talking of operating on the principle of 'democratic centralism' or combining 'centralised planning' with 'decentralised operational functions'.

In Russia, with no highly-developed market or price system, these interrelations between the activities of different firms proceed in a crude way, and often the individual firm or Ministry tries to escape from the risks of relying on other firms or Ministries by extending its own range of activities. Firms and Ministries set up their own building departments, machine tool shops, etc. This again is a phenomenon familiar to us from the war, and even in peace-time there is a constant temptation for the large firm, especially in times of high overall demand, to try to free itself from the risks of relying on uncertain supplies and services from outside. The great danger is that if this practice becomes widespread the advantages of specialisation are sacrificed. The Russians clearly recognise the danger and have repeatedly criticised the tendency for the mammoth combines and separate Ministries to try to reduce their dependence on the rest of the economy.

It is because the Russian firms over the course of years have spontaneously developed an intricate web of connections, both legal and illegal, with each other, and have set up their own departments for supply and services where the risks of reliance on others seems too great, that the system works. This, rather than the co-ordination of production from a single plannin gcentre, fits the pieces of the jigsaw together.

Wherein, then, consists the planning by the controlling Ministries and other planning authorities? For without doubt there is plenty of interference and control by those authorities. Again interpreting what is written and said about Russia against the background of our own experience, especially during the war, I would pick out the following as the crucial features of this planning and control. The Ministries exercise substantial power over the firms when they place contracts for finished products; clearly the activities of the engineering industry—in Russia perhaps even more than in this country and in the United States—must be determined to a substantial degree by orders for armaments. Projects for major expansion, either in existing firms or entirely new firms, must be closely controlled and progressed by the Ministries and planning authorities. Relations between overall supplies and requirements for basic materials such as coal, steel, electricity, cement, oil and non-ferrous metals receive a great deal of attention. In the Russian planning jargon these are referred to as the key material balances. Lastly, the higher administrative authorities exercise considerable authority through their power to appoint and sack the directors of the firms.

Argument about the direction, scale, financing, and location of new projects, and about the availability of basic material supplies, must go on continuously between the firms (especially the few hundred big ones), the Ministries and the various planning authorities. No doubt this rises to a crescendo when a new five-year plan is being prepared. And at every stage broad statistical pictures are compiled or concocted showing how the various projects and plans fit together, just as they are now in this country in discussions on future plans for coal, electricity, oil and atomic energy. But I suggest that it is a mistake to think of the reconciliation between all these plans and projects as taking place in one grand act of analysis at the highest level. The reconciliation and co-ordination, such as it is, can more realistically be thought of as emerging from the continuous jostling of different Ministries and planning boards, each arguing for its own particular schemes and pressing the needs of the particular sectors for which it is responsible. Planning is a process of continuous negotiation, with readjustment of plans and projects taking place through administrative pressure and counter-pressure.

There is another kind of control and intervention from above. Instructions to improve quality, to adopt improved techniques of production, to economise in the use of scarce materials, to speed up the delivery of priority items seem to descend on the firms in an unending stream from higher administrative organs. And there is a continuous demand for reports and statistics on these and other aspects of the firms' plans and activities. These instructions, demands and inquisitions may come from different levels in the hierarchy, from different Ministries and planning authorities, or from the various party organisations. Consequently they are often contradictory, but the astute director of the firm knows which to ignore and which to take seriously, and realises how important it is to make the right contacts in the Ministries themselves. How familiar all this would be to a British businessman recalling his dealings with Whitehall during the war, or to one in charge of an aircraft firm today!

The Russians have learnt by experience that you cannot have responsible and efficient action at the level of the firm with continuous intervention and instruction from numerous outside authorities. Conflicting instructions from outside give the manager innumerable excuses for failure, and waste and inefficiency may result from a serious attempt to run the firm from a distance. Every argument for delegation, decentralisation and devolution used in discussions about business administration in the West is echoed, although in a different jargon, in Russia. And the case for such devolution has been pressed with increasing emphasis as Russian industry has grown and become more complex. More and more, the Russians are adopting methods which give the firm greater autonomy in its operations. In practice this means giving greater scope to prices and costs and less emphasis on detailed administrative control; judging performance more in terms of profits instead of physical indicators. Russian planners would no doubt claim that prices, costs, and profits have a different significance in a socialist economy from that in a capitalist one; but when, for example, they argue that the best way to induce firms to produce the more difficult and costly varieties of products is to put up the price and profit margin for these, the argument has a familiar ring to capitalist ears.

The recent Khrushchev reform aiming at regional planning has been widely interpreted as another move towards greater autonomy for the firm. The arguments for regional decentralisation in Russia remind me of the arguments for regional boards in this country during the war. Such a move is just as likely to be a failure in Russia as it was here, if it really expected to result in effective co-ordination and planning on a regional rather than a national basis. I see the Russian system as a complex combination of guided interaction through administrative adjustment and control, and spontaneous interaction through the market and prices.

Where administrative action predominates, as in Russia, there is a feeling at the centre—in the Ministries, the Supreme Economic Council, and the planning boards—of rational control and interrelated planning. Decisions about major ventures are seen in relation to one another, and the development of the economy can be looked at in broad terms. But inevitably these are broad, sweeping decisions, made in ignorance of the complex changing situation facing the individual operating units. In practice they must often be mistaken, vague, delayed and contradictory. The individual firm regards the planning machinery as a crazy, confused, bureaucratic superstructure.

By contrast, in a system such as ours where prices and the pull of the market predominate, everything looks rational and well adjusted at the level of the individual firm. The firm can adjust its production, its sources of supply, its prices, and its methods of production to meet the ever-changing complex of market forces. This fine process of adjustment seems clearly superior and more efficient than anything which could be achieved by working to administrative direction from outside. But if one looks at the economy in its broader, especially developing, aspects, the market economy seems confused and chaotic. For example, each firm appears to pursue its own investment projects without regard to general needs or the likely long-term development of the economy.

A planned system, or what I would prefer to call an administratively directed system, therefore, seems rational at the centre and chaotic at the periphery, whereas a market system appears rational at the periphery but chaotic when viewed from the centre.

In practice, the centrally administered system in Russia has developed towards more and more devolution to the firm, in order to secure rationality at that level, and this has meant giving greater play to adjustment through prices and costs. By contrast, in Western economies, there has been an increasingly marked tendency to take a broader view of the overall development of the economy, especially in considering major investment projects. This is not merely where the government is involved, as in the nationalised industries in this country. Private firms—especially the larger ones—both in this country and the United States seem more and more to consider their investment plans in relation to an assessment of overall trends in the economy and likely developments in related and competing products. The kind of statistical appreciations made before taking decisions about investment in the steel industry in the United States or in ICI or Unilever in this country are not likely to be different in kind from those made in Russian planning offices and Ministries. Indeed, if looking ahead at the overall development of the economy over the next twenty or twenty-five years is one of the outstanding features of planning, then America is probably doing more planning than Russia, and doing it more efficiently.

I do not want to claim that what I have said here provides anything like a comprehensive explanation of the working of the Russian economy. Far from it: for example, I have not mentioned agriculture or the working of the financial system and what I have said bears only indirectly on that highly controversial issue, the extent and causes of growth in Russian production. I have merely been concerned to argue that if we want to understand the Russian system we must pay more attention to how administrative direction works in practice, and how this is interwoven with operation through prices and the market. An appreciation of how these two forms of behaviour are combined is also important in understanding the working of our own economy; and it is of the greatest interest to such countries as Poland and Yugoslavia, who are trying to work out new ways of running their economic affairs.

[5]

A case study in central planning[1]

In the post-war period the countries of eastern Europe under Russian influence engaged in a vast experiment in economic planning. They attempted to put into operation the theory that an economic system could be run in accordance with a centrally designed blueprint laying down the details of production. To the local Communist parties such rigorous central planning was an essential feature of the Russian economic system which they wished to copy. There had been so little honest analysis in Russia of the way in which the country's economy actually worked, or of the lessons of its planning experience, that it was the myth rather than the reality of the Russian system that the satellites set out to copy. Curiously, there is little evidence that Russian economic administrators helped the satellites to develop their planning systems or gave them any warning of the difficulties and problems they were likely to meet. These countries had to learn for themselves, slowly and painfully, the lesson that it is impossible to run an economy in accordance with the planning myth. If the attempt is, however, made, then either the economy develops methods of circumventing the plan and the planners, or the planning leads to a tangle of irrational situations and wasteful inefficiency.

Most of these countries have now departed from rigorous central planning and are attempting, to a greater or lesser degree, to decentralise and to give greater independence to the actual operating units. There is a general recognition that an attempt to run everything in detail from the centre leads to trouble. But the reason why this is so is still not widely understood. It is often too readily assumed that it is because central planning demands the surrender of every vestige of freedom that in the long run it becomes unwork-

[1] This review of Janos Kornai's *Overcentralization in Economic Administration* appeared in the *Manchester Guardian*, 19 October 1959.

able and intolerable. What is overlooked is the fact that, even in the most powerful dictatorship, running a modern economy by administrative fiat and the laying down of detailed production programmes at the centre gives rise to great difficulties. If the painful and dearly bought lesson which these countries have learnt is to have a wider influence, it is important that the exact nature of these difficulties should be appreciated. Mr Kornai's study of planning in Hungarian light industry, now available in an excellent English translation by Mr Knapp, is an outstanding contribution to such understanding. This study was originally published in Hungary in 1957, and is based on the working of light industries during the period 1950–6, when central planning was at its height.

To those experts in the West who are familiar with the details of the development of Russian economic planning there will be nothing strikingly new in Mr Kornai's study, but, coming as it does from the inside, it provides a particularly valuable detailed case study of how centralised planning works in practice. The analysis is refreshingly frank, realistic and free from dogma for a work published behind the Iron Curtain. As Mr Kornai explains,

> There are, of course, dozens of textbooks and collections of notes for use at universities which describe our method of economic administration and planning, our price and wages system, etc. However, all these have a serious fault in common: instead of telling us how our economic mechanism really works, they describe how it *would* work if it worked as their authors would wish.

The difficulties the planners experienced in practice were of three kinds. First, in a changing economy (and if there is no change, planning is unnecessary) the central directorate found it impossible to work out accurately in advance co-ordinated plans for all the operating units in their complex detail, or to arrange for their modification as circumstances changed. Second, there was the difficulty of providing satisfactory criteria of instructions to the producing units and of measuring their efficiency. And lastly, there was the problem of providing the necessary incentive to managers to do their job efficiently.

Even in a highly centralised economy, as Mr Kornai explains, a single authority cannot plan all aspects of the economy in one grand act of co-ordination. A series of departments are involved, and each of these, given the nature of the burden which it carries, must often proceed independently. Time will not stand still while each attempts to reconcile and co-ordinate its actions, ever-changing because circumstances change, with the remainder. In Hungary the plan index numbers, investment, the monetary system, prices, material supplies, foreign trade, the wages fund and the appointment of managerial personnel, all had their own administrative machines, which proceeded to a considerable degree independently of the remainder. As a consequence, the export departments would enter into commitments for exports without these being provided for in the plans for production or raw material supplies. The production plans were often unrealistic because they took little account of the variability and uncertainty in supplies of raw materials. Changes in the general economic plan for Hungary as a whole often came as a complete surprise to the directorate in charge of light industries.

The tangle that develops in an attempt to devise appropriate instructions to operating units and to form reliable measures of efficiency has often been described in relation to Russia, and Mr Kornai's very detailed analysis confirms the picture. Specifying plans in great quantitative detail made the plan too rigid, since it would not allow for the changing needs of customers and in any case implied an amazing depth of knowledge at the centre. If value figures were used instead, there was an incentive to distort production towards items of high value. Similarly, an attempt to keep a check on efficiency by the use of indices of labour productivity acted as a disincentive to producing goods with a high labour content. Indices of planned cost reduction encouraged the sacrifice of quality and the reduction of variety, and inhibited the introduction of new items of production. As the distortion caused by these indices was made apparent, the planners were tempted to introduce further control indices to check the distortion, until there were so many indices that both the planners and the planned were completely baffled as to their significance. And 'as soon as a new index or regulation is adopted, with the intention of putting a stop to one dodge, several new dodges are promptly introduced'.

If these indices are used, as they were in Hungary, to deal with the problem of incentives, by linking pay to the fulfilment of the indices, the temptation to fiddle is reinforced. In the last resort the central planners had to rely to a substantial degree upon the individual units for information about their true production capacity. Incentive payment related to percentage fulfilment of the plan encouraged managers to be secretive about the real capacity of their factories in the hope of getting away with an easy plan, and encouraged a counter-tendency among the planners to assume that all protests against higher plans were merely 'moaning'.

Mr Kornai's study deals in great detail with these problems as well as many others, all documented with actual evidence from Hungarian light industry. It adds up to a damning indictment of detailed central planning. Indeed, as one reads of one inefficiency after another one begins to wonder how the system produced anything at all. And yet, according to figures given by Kornai, production in Hungarian light industry doubled between 1949 and 1955! Would that Mr Kornai had devoted a little more attention to reconciling his criticisms of the system with this high increase in output. Or was output in 1949 so low that doubling it has little significance?

The main lesson which Kornai derives from his study is that central control should be reduced to essentials and that greater discretion and independence should be given to the operating units. But this, as Kornai argues, cannot be achieved by massive propaganda in favour of decentralisation and delegation. A fundamental change is needed. 'Some force must replace the part previously played by instructions coming from the centre.' And the force suggested is profit, supplemented by a more realistic use of prices to balance supply and demand! How tragic that these countries should have to go through this dire experience in order to learn the role profits and prices play in making a decentralised economic system possible.

The planned economies now seem to be pursuing in varying degrees this path of giving greater scope to prices and profits. But property remains in public ownership, and central control over investment, finance, credit and prices, is still quite rigorous. It remains to be seen how such attempts to use the advantages of the price system and at the same time give the planners control over the general direction of the economy, will work in practice. Certainly if more realistic studies of the kind undertaken by Mr Kornai were available, we should all understand more clearly how these economies actually work, instead of being misled by the myths of planning. And the planned economies would be able to learn more from each other's experiences than they have been able to do in the past.

[6]

Planning in the West and in the Communist world

Some lessons and problems[1]

In the last half-century both the West and the Communist world have had considerable experience of economic planning. In the West the economic system was planned by administrative direction in both world wars, and there has been increased intervention and planning by governments in the post-war period compared with pre-war. The growth of large-scale business units, in both the private and public sector, has raised problems of planning at the level of the individual enterprise which were almost completely unknown in the nineteenth century. The Communist world has had great and varied experience of planning, both at the national and enterprise level.

Although a great deal has been written in the West and in the Communist world about particular aspects of this experience, there has been a tendency to treat the experience of the West and the Communist world quite separately, as if the problems common to both are relatively insignificant. I take the view that our experience overlaps at many points, and that we can learn a great deal from each other about how planning works in practice, and the main problems which emerge and for which some solution has to be found.

It would be presumptuous to suggest that in one short discussion one could analyse this experience comprehensively, and all I hope to do is to indicate a few of the important lessons which I think we can learn from our own experience and from our analysis of the development of Russian economic planning. Our view of Russian planning is necessarily that of outside observers, and I hope that in the discussion more light will be thrown on these issues by Russian

[1] A paper read to a conference of British and Soviet economists in Moscow, April 1961.

economists who have knowledge from the inside of how the economic system works.

(1) *Planning in theory and reality*

Theoretical argument and discussion about national planning, both in the West and in the East, has usually proceeded in terms of theoretical models of the economic system, discussing how, if at all, these models can be clothed with statistical reality to give answers about the detailed plans for production, consumption, prices, employment, etc. (For example, when I was a student of economics in the 1930's a great deal of the planning debate in the West was about the system of equations that would need to be solved in a planned economy.) Implicit in this approach is the view that planning would proceed by the solution of such a model and that, without this, planning could not 'work'.

Both Western and Russian experience have demonstrated that this theoretical argument is, at present (and, I would argue, as far as we can see ahead in the future) largely irrelevant to the problems of planning in practice. I am sure that in planning the economic system in England during the first world war no attempt was made to arrive at a plan by attempting to find a solution to a set of equations. And yet it is generally recognised that the system was planned administratively and, notwithstanding many errors and problems, on the whole planned successfully. From all I have read and heard about Russian planning experience the same is true. Indeed, whenever I read about Russian planning methods and problems I am always reminded of similar experience in the English war economy. The similarities are startlingly striking.

While it is easy to state negatively that the theoretical models of planning literature are not used in practice, it is much more difficult to explain how in fact planning proceeds in practice. I give merely the skeleton of some of the important features:

(*a*) Planning in practice proceeds not by solving the economic problems from zero, but by taking the past and present as given and proceeding to get clear what changes and developments one wants to make over the next year, five years or ten years.

(*b*) Since a plan cannot be arrived at by the solution of a model, the plan for the succeeding period has to be worked out by an administrative system. This means giving responsibility for different parts of the economy to separate 'departments', each in control of a group of enterprises, and superimposing on these departments 'co-ordinating departments'. These co-ordinating departments are then largely concerned with (i) seeing that the individual plans are not in conflict with each other, (ii) instructing the departments on new features and policies, decided at the centre, which they wish them to take into account in their planning, (iii) watching the progress of the plan, and taking the necessary action to deal with unexpected change (which always occurs) and to deal with shortages and bottlenecks.

The working out of the plan, both at the stage when a new plan is drawn up and in day to day operations, is thus a continuous process of action and interaction between the central planning division, the departments, and the individual enterprises. Although administratively this may be a hierarchy with the central planning divisions as the pyramid, from the economic point of view it is best thought of as a circular system, with all sections interdependent.

(*c*) The central planning divisions cannot co-ordinate everything done by the departments in detail, nor can the departments co-ordinate and control everything done by the enterprises. The central planners therefore concern themselves with major strategic items—e.g. steel, electricity, cement (and, in the United Kingdom in war-time, with aircraft, finished munitions, etc)—in terms of both immediate and future production, and with instituting instruments for co-ordination, e.g. materials allocation, broad manpower allocations, etc. For the rest—the detail—this has to be left to be adjusted to the main features as well as possible (with intervention from the centre when some bottleneck emerges in practice), with perhaps some attempt to introduce the necessary adjustment through flexible prices, etc.

(2) *Some of the problems of planning*

The major issue in practice is how much to attempt to control and decide at the centre and how much to leave to adjustment between the departments and firms, and by what instruments to obtain this adjustment. The need for co-ordination pushes everything to the centre; the need for realism, quick adjustment and the avoidance of delay through a top-heavy bureaucratic structure pushes for decentralisation. Decentralisation may take different forms—to departments, to firms, to regions, etc. Each has its own advantages and disadvantages. Decentralisation to departments, for example, gives departments an incentive to become self-contained (to have their own building and repair, etc, divisions). Decentralisation to regions leads to an attempt by the regions to be self-contained, and therefore to the loss of the advantages of regional specialisation.

The great danger is the oscillation from centralisation to decentralisation: for example, after a few years of centralisation to be over-impressed by its disadvantages (which one knows from experience) and by the advantages of decentralisation (which are impressive in theory), and vice versa.

Whatever the degree of decentralisation, there must be some incentive to the departments and enterprises to adjust to the changing situation which confronts them in the most efficient way. This can be attempted either by administrative action, such as plans for labour efficiency, capital usage, etc, or through price and profits policies, giving them an incentive to adjust. This raises the whole complex problem of the relationship between administrative action and prices and profits in a planned system. This problem applies not only to the running of the economy as a whole, but also to individual enterprises. Take for example the National Coal Board. There is a need to increase coking coal output, and the Coal Board can arrange with the divisions for plans for increased output. But if at the same time the price of coking coal is set at such a figure that some divisions make a loss on output (this was true a few years ago; I am not sure whether it is true now), then they are asking the divisions to increase their losses by increasing output. It is difficult for those in the divisions to realise that they can be successful in meeting the plan and increase their losses at the same time.

How do the departments and firms decide what to produce? In war-time a substantial part of output is on government account, and most consumers' expenditure is rationed. This is therefore a *relatively* simple problem. But in peace-time, if one wants to give the consumers greater and greater choice, the pattern of final output cannot be decided at the centre but must be continuously adjusted. It may be that through consumers' surveys and enquiries the distributive organisations can find out more and more about what consumers want, but this is not enough unless there is some incentive for distributors to try and meet these wishes, and for producers to try and meet the wishes of distributors.

Where there are sectors of the economy which consist predominantly of a large number of small units—e.g. agriculture and distribution—administrative action from the centre in terms of large lumps (as in steel, etc) is difficult and inefficient, and the need for some decentralised administrative system, or working through prices, is even more important.

In planning investment, great risks have to be taken in assessing the efficiency of different possible new lines of development. If a single decision is taken at the centre, this may be very advantageous if the risk taken turns out to be correct, but it can lead to great waste if it turns out to be wrong. Unless one can assume that the centre always has superior wisdom, there may be an argument for spreading the risk, to allow each department or firm to make its own assessment. In the United Kingdom, for example, a few years ago, a central single decision was taken on the relative future efficiency of atomic energy electricity generation and the traditional generating stations. It is now clear that this decision underestimated the likely cost of atomic energy plants and paid too little regard to the further reductions in cost of traditional generating stations. But the government is now heavily committed in its plans for atomic energy generation. Indeed, planning at the government, department and enterprise level all demonstrate how difficult it is to tell *in advance* the likely cost of major new projects—or, indeed, to know in advance when new technical and economic developments (e.g. cost relationships between materials) are likely to occur in the future. In these circumstances, should risk-taking be centralised in one decision, or spread by allowing decentralised decisions, with different departments and firms each taking their own view of the future? If one spreads risks in this way, for the system to work well those who turn out to have been right must be rewarded, and those who are wrong penalised.

(3) *Monetary and product planning*

I have discussed so far mainly the product aspects of planning. But there is an important interrelation between this and the money flows throughout the economy. The relationship between the two could be substantially ignored in England during the war because of (*a*) price control, (*b*) taxation, (*c*) consumers' rationing (and, therefore, 'compulsory saving' of income above minimum consumption).

But the interrelation cannot be ignored if (*a*) one wants to use prices as an instrument for the functioning of the economy and (*b*) consumers have such an income that fluctuations in their savings are important.

In the Russian system the problem may be different in degree, because so high a proportion of saving is done by the State through turnover tax and returning a substantial part of profits to the central budget. But, to the extent to which this is done, it makes the working of incentives through prices, profit margins and wages much more difficult, and will I think become progressively more difficult as the Russian national income increases.

At present the main contrast between planning in the West and the Communist world is that in the West an attempt is made to plan the overall money flows through monetary and fiscal policy, and—with increasingly important exceptions—to allow the product adjustment to come about through the reaction to changing free prices, and money incomes. In the Communist world, product planning is predominant, and—again with increasingly important exceptions—prices and money incomes are adjusted to fit the product flow. But we in the West are finding that the fiscal and monetary planning needed to plan the money flows have important effects on product flows (for example our system of taxation, it is often argued, has important effects on labour and business mobility and innovation), and product planning is an increasingly important feature of our economy—especially in the large-scale enterprises, both public and private. In Russia the need for decentralisation and the need to adjust to consumer needs and demands as the economy becomes richer and more complex make ever more important the introduction and use in the economy of instruments, such as flexible prices, which will lead to continuous and spontaneous adjustment without administrative direction from the centre.

(4) *Conclusion*

It would be arrogant on my part to suggest that I could draw a specific list of conclusions from this brief and in many ways superficial survey of planning experience in the West and Communist world. But I hope it does at least demonstrate the validity of the point from which I started. Although there may be major dissimilarities between our economic experience, I think that there are more common problems than is usually recognised. We can learn a great deal from each other, not only in the exchange of economic ideas and theories, but also in understanding how our economic systems work in practice.

[7]

Price and administrative economic systems[1]

The development of economics, and particularly of economic theory, in the West has been largely in terms of an economic system in which prices, both of factors of production and of products, play the dominant, if not the only, role, and in which the problems of allocation of resources, co-ordination and adjustment to change take place through the adjustment of prices. The model of the economic system as a 'price mechanism', as it has come to be called, is the standard model used as a basis for understanding and interpreting a Western economy.

It is true that in the first world war this way of running an economy was substantially interfered with, and some monographs were written on how things were done during the war. But this experience had little influence on the development of economics, and there are practically no traces of it in the major works or in the flood of articles on economic theory during the inter-war years.

But there was developing during that period—and indeed the origins go back a long way into the past—an alternative view of the way in which an economic system could and should be run. This view objected to the price system on three grounds: the reliance on profits and variations in prices as the incentive and consequence of change; the inequalities of income to which it gave rise; and its allegedly wasteful inefficiency, mainly through fluctuations in trade and employment. Out of this emerged—and I recognise that I am slurring over a most complex historical development —a view that the economic system should be run by an alternative method, by which the allocation of resources and their interrelation and co-ordination should be decided by administrative action, rather than by allowing individual decisions to act and react on each other

[1] A paper read to various economic seminars (including one at the University of Glasgow) in 1962.

through prices. This view came to be known as 'planning'—which has, however, now acquired so many possible meanings that it tends more to confuse than to clarify the issues involved.

In the 'thirties there was some discussion among economists in the West about the possibility of running a modern economic system through 'administrative action' of this kind. The model they discussed was one in which a central planning authority, apprised of all the possible alternative ways in which economic resources could be used and the ends for which they might be used, solved the economic problem by laying down in detail what should be produced and how. The instrument by which such a system would run was administrative instruction, instead of reaction to price, income and profit. This—which I call the 'superman theory' of an administrative economic system, since it involved the central solution of the most detailed economic behaviour—was shown to be an impossible method for running an economic system, some arguing that it was administratively impossible, others that the technical problems, in terms of the equations to be solved at the centre, were incapable of solution. So it was argued that 'planning' was impossible and that attempts to run a system on this basis would lead to gross inefficiency and eventual breakdown, just as the model of the perfectly competitive price system showed that everything could be solved 'perfectly and efficiently' without any overall administrative action.

But there have since been two major experiences which, in my view, show that this contrast between two economic models—the price mechanism model and the administratively planned model—is a sterile way of attempting to analyse the relative roles and functions of price and administrative behaviour in any economic system and the way in which they may interact with each other. The first is the experience of running the economy during the second world war; the second the experience of Russia, and the growing analysis and understanding by Western economists of the way in which the Russian economic system is run. On the first—the war economy—there is, of course, general agreement that the British economy was planned, and that in that planning administrative action by the government played a major role. By such action I have in mind *not* that there was rationing and price control of consumer demand, but that a major part of the economic decision process at 'intermediate stages' took place not through influencing prices and incomes—

planning through the price mechanism—but by administrative decision, allocation, direction and specific decision what to produce and where. There has—unfortunately, in my view—been singularly little discussion among economists as to how this system worked. It clearly did not work, even in a remote sense, like the 'models' discussed in the planning controversies of the 'thirties. There has been a tendency to dismiss the war-time situation as something distinct and separate—usually on such grounds as that there was a 'general common interest' in war-time, while in peace-time there are a large variety of individual, distinct and different interests, or that direction was politically acceptable in war-time in a way in which it would not be in peace-time. This may be true, but even if it is it leaves unanswered many important questions. Why was it thought that administrative direction and allocation were more efficient in such a system than 'planning through prices'? For which particular problems and issues did the advantages of such administrative action stand out as of major importance? Where, if at all, was the use of the system overdone, and would the use of prices, in the light of later analysis, have yielded better results? And—most difficult of all—what role, if any, did prices continue to play, and how can one explain a system in which prices and administrative behaviour both play a role? There have been many descriptions and monographs of various aspects of the war economy, but we still await an exposition in terms of some general theory of how the system worked from some genius.

Russian experience has raised very similar issues. Unfortunately the Russians themselves have produced little that is worthwhile as a general explanation of how the Soviet economy works. There have been lots of articles and newspaper comments about particular bits, but there is, I believe, no standard work which attempts to explain the working of the economy as a system. Such general expositions as the former are in terms of highly misleading notions of an administrative hierarchy of decision making. As more and more Western economists have paid attention to the Russian system, we are, however, beginning to get more and more understanding. And this has been increased by the tendency in recent years for the Russians themselves to be more open in discussing their economic problems in public.

But this exposition of how the Russian system works has certainly peculiarities about it. It is compounded of three elements: first, an attempt to show, through an analysis of organisation and administration, the process of decision making and the instruments of planning used, how the system operates; second, an exposition of how these techniques and administrative arrangements result in contradictions, anomalies, strains and even ludicrous oddities and chaos; lastly, how many of these oddities and contradictions arise from the irrationality of prices in the Russian system, and how many of them could and would have been avoided if more rational prices were used? Indeed, the Russians themselves, in controversies over the running of their economic affairs in recent years, have tended to argue in terms which imply more and more use of planning through prices. Yet I have the feeling—and I put it no higher than this, since I am by no means conversant with all that has been written—that the central issues have been avoided, just as they have been avoided in analysing the British war economy. Where is administrative action the essential element in the economy, and what are its particular advantages and disadvantages? In what circumstances has action through price behaviour demonstrated itself to be superior, even in the Russian system? Why, if at all, given the superiority of administrative action in the past, should it be thought that a greater use of prices will be made in the future? And, where there is a combination of the two running in parallel, how does one explain a situation which has continuously elements of price and administrative behaviour?

Take an example—say, in capital investment, where administrative decision in terms of the co-ordination of plans and development has played a major role. It is argued frequently both inside and outside Russia that the system of allocation of investment projects would be much improved if more attention were paid to rates of return, and that the use of capital would be more efficient if the users were debited with a charge for its use. Yet it is not argued—at least in Russia—that a system of investment guided solely by rates of return in some kind of artificially created capital market would be superior to what they have now. This is not what they want. Nor is it implied by those Western economists who criticise the way in which the Russians select their capital projects within the context of their planning system. (I mean by this to exclude those economists who think that the Russians should convert themselves to a free enterprise system.) Somehow or other the two are to run together. A substantial element of administrative and political decision, together with some element of the price system apparatus, is to continue. My question is: can one analyse these two elements within some general theoretical framework, or must one deal with them quite distinctly? I do not know what the answer is, but I do feel that we should think about this more than we do. Or take another example: price fixing. Here again, economists in the West give many examples of where apparently irrational price fixing has led to the most weird situations, and there have been plenty of arguments to this effect in the Russian press and in Khrushchev's speeches. Clearly, in many of these situations a more sensible set of prices would have been more successful in achieving the objectives the planners had in mind. But a general set of principles which may throw light on when 'planning through rational prices' rather than 'planning through administrative action' is preferable is still missing. And if there is a mixture of the two, how does one explain the mixture, or think in terms of an economic system which uses both?

While examination and study of the Russian economic system leads more and more to the conclusion that it cannot be explained simply in terms of a model of administrative behaviour, it is to my mind also true that a model of a Western economy largely in terms of a price system leaves out important elements which are essential features of its operation. It does this in two important respects: first, by judging actual elements of price and price behaviour by the criteria of 'perfect price adjustment', and dismissing departures from this as imperfections and aberrations; second, it tends to exclude from its analysis of the system those elements which cannot be explained in terms of prices and price behaviour.

In relation to the first, I have often wondered myself whether an economic system in which all elements adjusted themselves from day to day to price changes would be either a workable or a tolerable system in which to live. Some element of 'stickiness' in prices and incomes seems to be not only an essential element in the way our system works, but also necessary to its reasonable working. And we need a theory of the role of price 'stickiness' as well as a theory of price adjustment, although I am not at all sure how we combine the two in explaining how things operate. Very few prices in our economy now emerge (so to speak) anonymously, through the operation of markets; many of them are settled and fixed by important individual decision—decisions of the government, the trade unions, the banks, the nationalised industries and individual firms.

The analysis of these decisions in terms of costs and demand continues to be an important element explaining what goes on, but it is not sufficient in itself. The behaviour, and consequently the interaction, between sectors of the economy has to be explained in other terms too. Do we dismiss these other elements as aberrations—which economics treats as departures from 'correct economic pricing', the reasons for which should be examined by the student of administration or government—or do we attempt to include them in 'economic theory'? It is clear that their inclusion would modify considerably the existing traditional theoretical basis of economics; it would lose some of its elegance, simplicity and rigour, and it is on these that it prides itself in comparison with the other social sciences.

In dealing with the theory of the firm, economics has drawn a distinction between its internal and external relations, and concentrated on the latter. The external interrelations between firms are thought of mainly in terms of adjustments *via* the price system, while the internal arrangements are governed by administrative decision. Again, I think this distinction is very much overdone; that the internal system contains elements of price interrelations, and the external contains elements of administrative rather than price behaviour. Many large firms now attempt to imitate the 'price system' within their own organisation by giving their constituent units a high degree of independence, and sometimes making constituent units 'buy' from each other or 'compete' with one another. Yet they reserve certain functions for central administrative decision. Similarly, with firms apparently independent and interrelated only through the market system, there are frequently close tie-ups which are decided administratively. I do not have in mind the whole range of restrictive practices, but arrangements between firms and their suppliers or main customers which approximate closely to the administrative arrangements between departments within a large firm.

Economics has, of course, given some attention to these issues in the discussion of the organisation of industry where the reasons for horizontal or vertical integration are examined, but there is a tendency to assume that, so to speak, once the issue is settled the interrelations within the firm are of a quite different character from those outside, and that it is the latter which are the main subject-matter of economics. I am suggesting, first, that each set of interrelations is a mixture, no doubt in different degrees, of price and administrative behaviour; and second, that an understanding and analysis of the system internal to the firm is important in any understanding of its external relations.

One of the striking features that has emerged, for example, from the study of the Russian economy is the similarity between the problems of Russian planning and the problems especially of the large units in the Western economy, say ICI and General Motors. ICI is a planned system, just as elements of the Russian system are, the interrelations between the parts governed primarily by administrative decision, but with an admixture, either real or by imitation, of price elements. To me the fascinating question is what determines the role of the one element compared with the other. As in my questions about Russia, what is the essential nature of the superiority of administrative rather than price co-ordination in certain circumstances, and vice versa?

One can look at the same issue in a different way. In crude terms, the virtues of the price system are decentralised decision making, scope for independent initiative and risk taking, and adjustment to the demands of the market. The virtues of administrative actions are planned co-ordination, attention to the overall view. When do the advantages of one or the other predominate, and in what ways, if at all, can they be combined? This issue is now, of course, being hotly debated, particularly in relation to the long-term growth of the British economy, where the view is gathering strength that an 'overall view' which has to be arranged administratively and planned is necessary. But any explanation of why this is necessary for growth has not been adequately given.

One of the most interesting questions in all this is the speed of adjustment. It is an issue on which economic theory has little to contribute, since, as I said earlier, we have no real analysis of 'stickiness'. I suspect that speed of adjustment through administrative action was one of the features of the war economy which justified 'planning'; that this is also an important element in the Russian system, and the justification for economic activity through the large firm in the West. But there is no general theoretical basis on which one can argue that such speed is more likely through administrative action, or planning, than through a decentralised price system. One has to look at the empirical evidence, which rarely leads to maintainable general propositions of universal validity.

May I sum up a rather inadequate exposition of what I am after.

When we look at reality, as distinct from building theoretical models, any economic system is a mixture of 'price' and 'administrative' behaviour. It is only in terms of both together that we can get an adequate understanding of how the system works. Yet our present apparatus of analysis does not make it possible to do this. We have a 'price' theory, and can show aberrations and departures from the ideal price system. We also have a technique of a kind, although hardly a general theory, for describing administrative behaviour. What I am pleading for is some kind of theoretical framework which will enable us to deal with the admixture of the two together rather than as quite separate aspects of reality. What this framework should be and how one can develop it I fear I do not know. Perhaps I am asking for the impossible.

[8]
Planning and growth[1]

During the last few years problems of economic growth have progressively come to occupy a central place both in academic economics and in discussion of economic policy. Nearly all countries, whether rich or poor, under-developed or advanced, have become concerned—some might say obsessed—with their growth rates and their ranking in international league tables of rates of increase in gross national product per head. It has long been argued that planning has an important role to play in the growth of under-developed countries; but the idea of planning as important for growth in advanced countries is quite recent, and largely the result of French experience. It is this experience, together with disappointment at the continuing recurrence of balance of payments crises, which has led to a resurgence in the United Kingdom of the discussion of the role of planning.

It is particularly valuable, therefore, to have collected together Professor Wilson's essays on this subject, many previously published but some, including the first and longest, after which the book takes its title, reproduced here for the first time. The essays cover a wide range of topics, but there is more of a central theme than is common in collections of this kind.

Professor Wilson discusses the relevance of the experience of Russia, British war-time experience, and French planning to planning in under-developed and advanced economies. In this discussion he draws a distinction between action by the State 'to ensure that the general economic environment is favourable to growth' and the government proposing 'a certain rate of growth for total output . . . and rates of growth for particular industries'. Although action by the State of the first kind is accepted in principle by most econ-

[1] This review of Professor T. Wilson's *Planning and Growth* appeared in the *Scottish Journal of Political Economy*, February 1965, pp. 105–9.

omists, there is by no means agreement on the particular measures desirable. Taxation measures to encourage investment innovation and hard work, more extensive education, improved transport facilities, the encouragement of zones of growth in the older industrial areas (see the essay on 'Regional policies and growth'), assistance in applying scientific research in both industry and agriculture, are all given by Professor Wilson as examples of growth policies under the first heading. But there is room for plenty of disagreement on the relative importance of each of these, and on the way in which they should be implemented. Take taxation, for example. 'Growth will be rapid,' Professor Wilson writes, 'only if adequate incentives are given to those who exert special efforts or incur special risks. It is, therefore, of the utmost importance that taxation should discourage hard work, enterprise and thrift as little as possible' (p. 9). This general proposition would probably command fairly widespread support, but it still leaves room for substantial disagreement about the effect of particular measures of taxation—disagreement which, to some extent at least, reflects our ignorance about the relation between taxation and 'hard work, enterprise and thrift'.

Whatever specific measures may be taken to encourage growth, and altogether they may add up, as Professor Wilson argues, to something sufficiently ambitious to be worth calling a 'growth policy', the question still remains whether there is some additional advantage to be obtained by planning of the second kind through the preparation of targets or programmes for the economy as a whole and for particular industries or sectors.

It is interesting to reflect that growth arguments for planning in the United Kingdom were hardly considered in the literature of the war and early post-war years. The case for planning, either through manipulating the price mechanism or by more direct methods, was based on the alleged deficiencies of the ordinary market mechanism in a static context. Unemployment and instability, inequality, misallocation of resources through monopoly and imperfect competition, divergences between private and social cost, were usually given as the arguments for government intervention and planning. To take but three fairly influential examples: Meade, Durbin and Lewis. In Meade's *Planning and the Price Mechanism* there is no mention of economic growth; Lewis pays a little attention to growth but discusses long-term planning as 'no more than a game'.[2] Durbin does not even regard a slow rate of growth as a deficiency of the capitalist system. On the contrary,

> A new type of capitalism is coming into existence—State-controlled, monopolistic, still predominantly unegalitarian. The case against such an economy, and the weaknesses exhibited by it, are obvious. Its virtues are in the maintenance of a most substantial rate of expansion . . .[3]

Why should it now be thought that, even with specific measures to encourage growth, the economy will not grow as fast as it could, and that the growth rate might be improved by a substantial margin with official targets? In examining this question Professor Wilson goes over British war-time and Russian experience to try and see the effect on growth of programme planning in these two cases, and to see what can be learned from that experience. This is a valiant attempt to deal with a very difficult question in a very brief space. The discussion is stimulating, but I found it, particularly on Russia, tantalisingly inconclusive, especially if read in conjunction with the chapter on 'The profit motive and growth'. This latter chapter stresses the deficiencies and difficulties of running a system on output targets and 'success indicators' for individual factories, and the advantages, which the Russians are now coming to realise, of using profits 'as a valuable administrative device for decentralising certain decisions and permitting managers greater scope for independent action' (p. 107).

A critical step is to allow managers to compete for the factors of production instead of allocating to them inputs that are determined by the

[2] 'One cannot plan very far ahead. A five-year plan cannot be more than a vague indication of aspirations. The national income in five years' time depends first on what happens to productivity. Before the war, productivity in this country increased at about 3 per cent per annum [*sic*]; today it is below the pre-war level, and no one knows whether in five years' time it will be 10 per cent less than pre-war or 30 per cent above pre-war. How can one plan a national income within limits of error so wide that they can swallow up the whole allocation to investment or to public expenditure, or to exports, or to any major industry? Again, the national income in five years' time from now will depend on the terms of trade and the demand for exports, which may affect the balance of payments either way. One must plan five years ahead all those parts of the economy which need five-year plans—afforestation, power stations and so on—and one can usefully plan specific investment projects, but a *general* five-year plan for the whole economy is no more than a game.' W. A. Lewis, *Principles of Economic Planning*, Allen & Unwin, 1949, p. 110.

[3] E. F. M. Durbin, *The Politics of Democratic Socialism*, Routledge & Kegan Paul, 1940, p. 147.

planners. It can be held that if this is done, firms will be run more efficiently, and greater scope for innovation on the initiative of the managers should be strongly favourable to growth. [pp. 107–8]

Is this meant to imply that if the Russians had made greater use of the profit and price systems in the last thirty years the rate of growth would have been faster? This is not made clear. There is a similar inconclusiveness in the earlier discussion of Russian planning in the chapter on 'Planning and growth' (pp. 23–34), although here the balance seems to me to be tilted towards the conclusion that output planning *did* favour growth. Perhaps Professor Wilson takes the view that the relative usefulness of output planning has changed over time, and that with the greater complexity of Russian output and the desire to pay more attention to consumer demand, including variety, there will and should be greater emphasis on prices and profits as guides to output and methods of production. If so, it would have been useful, although I admit extremely difficult, to attempt some discussion of the way in which a mixture of output planning from the centre and greater freedom at the periphery might work.

It is in his discussion of French planning that Professor Wilson really first attempts to give reasons why overall and specific output targets may help growth, and why even with specific growth policies the economy may not achieve its maximum potential without such targets. But at each stage an argument that such targets may help is balanced by a potential countervailing disadvantage.

It is believed that management and labour are stirred to great efforts by being made to realise both the desirability of a high rate of growth and the possibility of achieving it. Firms that might otherwise have been content to jog along may change their ways; other firms that thought themselves reasonably progressive may be induced by the plan to set themselves still higher targets. Industrial development may be more rapid if it is in fact more orderly, with expansion less likely to be held up by shortages here and surpluses there. [p. 38]

If the management of a firm believes that most other firms and the Government itself will try hard to achieve the target, then it may be the more inclined to aim at rapid expansion, if only because the general rise in output should provide a wider outlet for its own products. [p. 58]

But in opposition to these arguments:

It is important to insure that the managers of unusual vision are given a chance to set the pace; they must not be held back and forced to accept a rate of change that satisfies the dullards who comprise the majority [p. 39]

rapid technological progress may require *unbalanced* growth [p. 39]
there is a real danger that if the national target on which many plans have been based is not in fact achieved, disillusion may follow and the last state may be worse than the first [p. 56]

Clearly Professor Wilson remains sceptical, but in his final summing up concludes that

there is a case for preparing forecasts and targets for national output and for its main industrial constituents. It is much more debatable whether for each industry syndicates should be established which should be required to produce 'plans' for future output. If there is to be 'indicative planning' it should be voluntary.

The trouble with the sceptical and reserved approach adopted by Professor Wilson is that, as he himself puts it, the basis for successful planning of this kind seems to be a 'confidence trick'. Each industry will become expansion-minded because it is convinced by the plan that the rest of the economy is going to expand more rapidly. Will the confidence trick work, unless all those who partake in it are enthusiastically sure that it is going to? Certainly there are some more familiar with the French scene than I who take the view that the rise of a new generation of enthusiastic managers in French business and government, convinced that more rapid growth was possible, was as important, if not more important, than the compilation of the statistical tables for the plan. If higher growth is a 'confidence trick' or a 'psychological conjuring trick'[4] or 'a matter of faith', it will need much more than statistics and discussion to make the trick succeed and to get a change of faith. The experience of the last twelve months hardly demonstrates, assuming this diagnosis of our ills to be correct, that the conversion was achieved by NEDC. Perhaps the new Department of Economic Affairs will be more successful.

The 'confidence trick' is in any case a difficult one to play in the United Kingdom. For it is not enough to convince each industry

[4] See J. C. R. Dow, *The management of the British economy, 1945–60*, Cambridge University Press, p. 398. Chapter XVI, 'Economic growth and economic stability', argues the case for the adoption of French-type planning in the United Kingdom with less reservation than Professor Wilson.

that if it expands its output the market will be there, since its customers will be expanding more rapidly too. The balance-of-payments situation requires that a substantial part of the expanded output be exported, and for this more than a 'trick' is needed. The 'trick' will work only if export prices are competitive and the economic environment encourages much greater attention to exports. This implies that continuous very high pressure of aggregate demand, with consequent dangers of demand and cost inflation, should not be used as the instrument for bringing about the conversion. Professor Wilson argues along these lines in his two essays on 'Inflation and growth' and a 'Policy for incomes'. It is, of course, hoped that, if only the long-run rate of increase in productivity and output can be raised, this in itself will make it easier to maintain stable prices and to secure agreement on an incomes policy, with average incomes rising no more than productivity. But if, as Professor Wilson argues, it is a condition of success for an incomes policy 'that there should not be a strong sellers' market for labour' (p. 52) and that we should operate at 'a level of unemployment slightly higher than has prevailed in Britain since the war' (p. 149), a move towards operating not quite so near the ceiling might, as Professor Wilson admits, mask for the time being any upward movement in the long-term growth rate. And if the upward movement does not show itself quickly, what happens to the 'conjuring trick'? To keep in play faith in a higher long-term growth rate, agreement on an incomes policy while operating with a greater margin of unemployment and capacity, and an environment which encourages greater attention to exports, will require juggling of a most sophisticated and intricate kind.

[9]

Managing an organisation[1]

I feel something of a fraud in agreeing to talk to you about this subject. I have no clear prescription to give about how an organisation should be managed. What I have to say is largely by way of random thoughts and reflections, arising in part out of my own experience and in part out of reading, not in a systematic way, some of the literature on the subject of management.

The first thing that has always struck me about any organisation with which I have had contact is the contrast between the formal structure and constitution of the organisation and the way in which it works in practice. Practically every organisation beyond a very small size has a constitution or formal organisation chart, and at the same time there is a strongly held view that in practice the organisation works in ways which are not, and cannot, be adequately portrayed in such a constitution. Indeed, one of the main problems in understanding how the organisation works and in managing it is to appreciate the interrelation between these two systems, which do not merely work in parallel, but in some mysterious way, which I must admit I have never been able to fathom completely, work closely together. For it is clear that both systems are indispensable. To attempt to work everything strictly according to the constitution and though formal channels of responsibility would undoubtedly lead to stalemate; but exclusive reliance on the development of spontaneous organic interrelations, arising from day-to-day working rather than predetermined procedure, would, equally, result in chaos.

Perhaps I could explain the contrast I have in mind in more personal terms by asking how one approaches the problem of getting things done in any organisation. The formal constitution or administration provides for clear channels of argument and

[1] This paper formed the basis of a talk in February 1962.

decision, and these seem to provide a definite framework within which to argue about issues and get action taken. But anyone who has worked in an organisation knows how frequently such channels prove maddeningly frustrating. Either because of the time taken, or the distortion of the issues as they get further and further away from their original source, there develops a feeling that the sense of understanding of what is going on is faint and unreal. Hence the reaction—both from 'above' and 'below'—that the 'official channels' or 'organisation' must in some way be by-passed. It is rare in books on organisation to find advice on how to engage in this gentle art of by-passing or manœuvre; on the contrary, there is usually the suggestion that once the ideal machinery of delegation, etc., has been set up everyone should abide by it, although there is usually a plea for 'flexibility'. It is only in the satirical literature, e.g. *Microcosmographia academica* or *How to run a bassoon factory*, that one gets hints on how to manœuvre.

Manœuvring usually depends on getting to understand where the focal points of decision really are, in terms not merely of individuals but also of groups and committees, which are a standard feature of all modern organisations. This one can learn only through 'feel' and experience, and it is certainly not true that in any two organisations committees with apparently the same functions exercise the same degree of influence in terms of the crucial role which they play. From the point of view of those managing from above, once they are clear what the nodal points are, they can use them either to make sure decisions are taken quickly and sensibly or to secure agreement in advance of formal decision through the 'ordinary channels'. Similarly, from the point of view of those 'below', some contact, direct or indirect, with such nodal points enables them to discover quickly what the chances are of getting some particular line agreed, rather than wait for a decision in the ordinary way. There may be situations in which the various individuals at these crucial points of decision form themselves, without consciously knowing it, into a caucus, who consult each other regularly and implicitly agree on the kind of line to take when the issues come up for discussion in the normal way. It is difficult to imagine an organisation working successfully without some feature of this kind. Imagine an organisation in which at all inter-divisional meetings those concerned turn up without prior knowledge or manœuvring with any of their colleagues, and there is really an attempt to arrive at some kind of agreement as a result of completely open discussion. Even with the strongest and wisest of chairmen, the task of concentrating discussion on two or three possible alternatives is likely to be extremely difficult, and unless matters are considered beforehand in a 'caucus-like' fashion, the decisions taken may be completely at cross purposes with what is being decided elsewhere in the organisation.

It follows that, for this web of interrelations or caucus-like system to be efficient, it must embrace all important aspects of the work of the organisation which are interrelated in important ways. It must make sure that 'X' is brought in and consulted if he is vitally affected.

If a 'caucus' can perform this kind of function, why not formally create one as a policy committee or standing committee? This is a difficult question to answer. The answer is partly that the caucus feature I have talked about, although powerful in practice, is by its nature vague both in its functions and in the group who belong to it. Also, one of the important features of the successful working of such a system is that its powers and influence should be exercised discreetly and even surreptitiously.

What are some of the main reasons for and elements in the manœuvring process? First, there is the contrast between the myth that an organisation—be it a business, a university or government department—has a single purpose and objective on which all those who work for it are agreed, or should be agreed, and the phenomenon in practice: serious conflicts between persons, division and sections, not merely about how to do things but about what should be aimed at, and about their own role and importance in the organisation. One of the most important features in management is, therefore, the creation of alliances and even conspiracies to achieve one's objectives. Looked at from the top, the manager needs to know where the main conflicts are and how to reconcile those in conflict in order to get things done.

One of the danger points is when repeatedly, on issue after issue, two divisions—or indeed two people—are always put into a position of conflicting with or opposing each other, so that the situation develops into one of almost open battle, and this becomes a standard feature of relations between the divisions, with the battle going on even when the issues do not seem to warrant it. If one can manœuvre administrative divisions and issues so that there is a shifting pattern of alliances and conflicts, this situation may be avoided. But it is still important to recognise their significance and to use them sensibly on particular occasions. It is tempting to assume that by suitable organisation and exhortation, conflict can be eliminated altogether, but I have yet to see a situation in which this happens.

In a university, departments are in conflict over allocations of money and staff, but the patterns of conflict can to some extent be manœuvred by the way these are dealt with. If the allocation is between, say, faculties, then the faculties will be driven into conflict with each other, and into presenting a united front in facing each other. If, in thinking of the wider purposes of the university, it seems that cohesion within faculties but separation between them is desirable, then such a system obviously has advantages. But if one thinks that connections between departments in different faculties are important, then the kind of management structure which induces faculties to oppose each other has clear disadvantages. One has to recognise, too, that there will be conflicts within each faculty, and to assess how strong they are in relation to inter-faculty rivalries. But the point I wish to make is that the recognition of these conflicts and alliances is important in managing the organisation. Certainly it is a mistake to assume that if you want people to work harmoniously and in a co-ordinated way the best thing to do is to separate them in a single institution or division.

Another feature of manœuvring and management in practice is to know the key figures who matter in the organisation, not always in terms of forming alliances to get things done, but to obtain—and to give—reliable information about what is going on, changes in the air, new policies being discussed and so on. In theory, everybody concerned ought to be kept informed, and in many organisations an attempt is made to achieve this through a mass of paper work, committees, news bulletins, etc. But unfortunately one of the features of this method is that it rapidly becomes self-defeating. For if it gets beyond a certain critical level—I am not at all sure how one measures this—the whole lot is ignored, and the communication of information in reality sinks almost to zero.

An alternative is for those who feel they must know to have their own network to use, which they can vary with time and with the personalities involved. But since the essence of the network is to pick out in practice speedy channels and the persons with the really vital information, it can scarcely follow the formal system of communication. Sometimes it can become almost a spy system, with someone given particular responsibility for keeping in touch with things on the ground. This has to be handled with great care and delicacy, otherwise there is the danger of revolt from those officially responsible and a tendency to treat the 'spy' as a 'favourite at court' and consequently to conceal rather than reveal information to him.

ECONOMIC MANAGEMENT

THE GOVERNMENT, THE PUBLIC AND THE EXPERTS

[10]

Changing economic ideologies in the United Kingdom[1]

In the last few years there has been a remarkable change in the passion and emotion with which economic issues are discussed in the United Kingdom. In the 1930's and in the immediate post-war period there seemed to be a deep cleavage of opinion between two groups taking radically opposed views of the way in which our economic system should be run. The rallying cries of these two opposing ideologies were 'planning' and 'free enterprise'. The supporters of each ideology argued that their view of the way in which the economic system should be run was fundamentally opposed to that of the other school. This controversy excited widespread interest in intellectual circles and among the general public. There was a flood of books, articles, pamphlets and talks on economic issues. Argument about the reform of our economic system always commanded an audience.

But in the last few years the sharpness of the ideological conflict has gone. There are, no doubt, differences of view on economic policy between the major parties in the United Kingdom, but as the last general election campaign demonstrated, these differences are largely of emphasis and on marginal matters. If the exaggerations of political propaganda are discounted, it is difficult to discern any deep, radical difference of principle about the way in which our economic affairs should be managed. Even the professional politicians find it difficult to draw a clear distinction between their own proposed economic policy and that of their opponents.

Not unnaturally, as controversy and political passions have died

[1] A paper delivered at the Congress for Cultural Freedom in Milan, September 1955, and amended in 1956 for delivery in Birmingham to the Ashley Society.

down public interest in economic issues has declined. Argument about the fundamental basis of running our economic society no longer excites much interest: the public seems to think that this problem has been solved, that it is irrelevant to the important problems of the day; or is frankly just bored and uninterested.

This change can be seen most significantly in the universities. I remember that in my student days in the 1930's economic policy and proposals for the drastic reform of our economic system were subjects which commanded great interest and caused great excitement and controversy among students—not only among students of economics and politics but among the student body in general. Only foreign policy, especially after the Spanish civil war, rivalled it as an issue which would arouse argument and keep discussion going into the early hours of the morning. The generation of ex-Servicemen returning to the universities in 1946 and 1947 were also deeply interested in these issues, although with a more mature outlook resulting from deeper experience.

Apart from Suez, it is not easy to discover what excites student attention in England today, but one can say with confidence that it is no longer issues of economics. The questions which agitated us in the 1930's and the ex-Servicemen in the late 1940's no longer seem important or interesting to the student body.

There were two great themes which provided the fuel for the fervent planning ideology of the 1930's and 1940's. The first was the crude and blatant inefficiency of the 'free' or 'capitalist' economic system. The great economic disasters and unemployment of the 1930's, following as they did in the United Kingdom a period of milder but chronic economic trouble in the 1920's, convinced the mass of intellectual opinion as well as the general public that a free economic system inevitably led to chaos. This view gained strength throughout the 1930's, and was reinforced by the experience of the disappearance of unemployment during the war, when the government took over control and, so it was thought, ran economic affairs by planning instead of leaving things to the operation of market forces. The contrast between the successful working of the economic system during the war at full employment level and the pitiful inefficiency and chaos of the 1930's had, not surprisingly, a remarkable effect on public opinion. Never again would we return to the 1930's.

The experience of the 1930's and 1940's seemed to reinforce the argument that an economic system could not operate successfully without conscious direction by a central guiding authority. The jigsaw puzzle of economic activity could not be expected to fit neatly together if decisions were left to the atomistic behaviour of individual firms and institutions, each proceeding without regard to the actions of the others. Only a central authority could see how all the pieces would fit together and could therefore plan the activity of each so that they fitted into a coherent whole.

The second great theme was the immorality and inequity of the 'capitalist' system. Criticism of modern capitalist society on the grounds that it depends essentially on the pursuit of private gain, that it puts private interest before the common good, that it treats individual misfortune harshly, and that it leads to great inequality of income, has long been a theme of those who demand a radical change in our economic system.

The great force and appeal of the arguments for a drastic change in our economic arrangements in the 1930's and 1940's arose from the way in which these two themes, inefficiency and immorality, met and reinforced one another. Both were to be remedied by the same prescription—the radical transformation of the economic system to give the government the central and predominant role in running it. Central economic planning would not only give us control over our economic destinies and enable us to run the economic system efficiently, but it would also put the public interest in place of private gain. Two major proposals for reform which were coupled with central planning—the nationalisation of industry, and more progressive taxation—also fitted into the same picture, for they would not merely be conducive to greater economic efficiency but would also result in a 'fairer' economic system, in which production for community consumption would be the predominant driving force.

Those who were opposed to these views likewise relied on two different themes. First, that central economic planning, nationalisation and high taxation would have the very reverse consequences of the claim of those who argued for them. An economy run by civil servants would be strangled in red tape. Second, that interference by the State in economic affairs on this scale would have disastrous political consequences. For a whole host of reasons which I hardly need to detail, the running of the economic system in this way, it was argued, would inevitably lead to a restriction of political freedom and liberty, and in the end to political dictatorship. And the experience of Russia and Nazi Germany was frequently cited in support of this view. Political liberty was compatible only with a free enterprise economic system.

The war transformed the whole context in which this clash of ideologies took place. For, with the exception of nationalisation, the major revolution which the radical reformers wanted actually took place during the war. The government assumed the central role in running the economic system, taxation revolutionised the distribution of incomes, and the 'common good'—winning the war—took first place as the prime consideration in running our economic affairs. So that in 1945, to a substantial degree, the issue was no longer what radical changes should be reintroduced, but how far we should try to go back to the system of 1938.

The argument that the government should accept the responsibility for preventing mass unemployment was already settled by the time the war was over. Economic opinion in Whitehall and general civil service opinion alike agreed that this was a major economic responsibility which the central government had to assume. There may have been differences of view—as there still are—on the degree of success possible in such a policy, on the relative importance of securing full employment at home and stability in overseas payments, and the instruments to be used in securing the objective. But that this was a sphere for the government and could not be left to the 'free working of economic forces' was no longer disputed.

It is now widely, almost universally, agreed that government fiscal policy is a most powerful tool for keeping the economy on an even keel. The view that a balanced budget should invariably be the objective of government policy is rarely heard in England today; we now argue about how big the budget deficit or surplus should be in order to keep the economy fully employed. This I regard as one of the great steps forward in economic policy.

But there was much more to the planning ideology than the maintenance of full employment. For great emphasis was always laid on the government drawing up a central plan or programme for the economic activity of the nation, showing the physical quantities of goods to be produced and the allocation of manpower to be employed. Such a plan would not only secure the co-ordination of production in an orderly way but would also have 'social priority' rather than 'the power of the purse' as its operating principle. The nationalisation of key industries would make the co-ordination of production—especially in investment—possible, as well as take us on the road to economic democracy by transferring the centres of economic power from private to public hands.

In the first five years after the war, we learnt in the United Kingdom how attempts to operate such a system work out in practice, and there is little doubt in my mind that the result of this experience was great disillusion and disappointment. Only rarely is central economic planning in physical terms now advocated as a policy, and such advocacy commands little attention or support. Those who had to operate the central allocation of materials, investment, imports and manpower soon learnt that in such a system arbitrary decisions, irrationality, chaos and haphazard rulings played a depressingly large role. The notion that central planning would lead to co-ordinated, rational economic activity, in contrast to the haphazard chaotic operation of the market system, soon proved an illusion. The notion that our economy could be run by a central plan into which all the parts are fitted by administrative direction is now put forward only by a lunatic fringe.

It is significant that very early in this period of experiment many of those who were politically committed to the government playing a central role in economic activity argued that planning should be operated through influencing prices, through taxation and subsidies, rather than through the control of resources. 'Planning through the price mechanism' soon became a fashionable slogan, and its popularity is itself an indication of how quickly the lesson was learned that rational, co-ordinated, detailed central planning of economic activity in physical terms is quite impossible in a complex modern industrial system. The shift away from physical planning and control began to take place during the Labour government's period of office. Indeed, it was a Labour Minister who claimed proudly that he was responsible for a 'bonfire of controls'. The idea that a price system is a great integrating instrument, that the pursuit of its own purposes by each economic unit will lead to co-ordinated economic activity, is once again acknowledged as an important and powerful truth.

The experience of the years after 1945 has also demonstrated that the argument about physical planning is largely irrelevant for the problem of maintaining full employment. Monetary and fiscal policy, it has been demonstrated, are the important instruments for keeping the economy on an even keel. Talk of manpower planning as a way to secure full employment, for example, soon disappeared. And even investment planning by central administrative control proved a difficult instrument to operate.

In this experience, nationalisation has been a red herring. The opposing ideological schools, it is true, talked about nationalisation and denationalisation in the language of 'planning' *v.* 'free enterprise', but this just served to obscure what was going on. There is no evidence that the nationalisation of coal, gas and electricity, for example, made possible a planned or co-ordinated fuel policy; indeed, the separate nationalised bodies appear to pursue their own policies very much as privately competing companies would. And practically every report on a nationalised industry argues more and more that the industry should be run on commercial principles. All talk of production for the 'common good' has disappeared. The Herbert committee on electricity is a remarkable example of this. Nor did denationalisation mean that a system of free enterprise or competition was introduced. The denationalised steel industry, for example, is subject to just as rigorous, if not more rigorous, official control, in respect of both prices and investment, now that it has been denationalised than it was when the Iron and Steel Board ran the nationalised industry. And this system of co-operative control, under the general scrutiny of a government board, is looked on quite favourably in the industry.

But whatever the issue of nationalisation is really about, it is clear that there has been much disappointment even among its most ardent supporters. The nationalisation of the means of production is no longer thought of as making possible a radical change in the operation of the economic system.

Has the lesson about central physical planning been learnt once and for all? I am not sure. I myself do not think that there is likely to be any renewal of widespread support for central physical planning as long as we succeed in maintaining full employment. I feel it is too early yet to be able to say how far our success in this direction in the post-war years represents good luck—the particular economic forces in operation at the time—and how far our better understanding and management of the economic system. As far as internal forces are concerned, there seems to me to be no reason why we should again suffer from mass unemployment, although I do not think we can altogether avoid fluctuations in economic activity. But if there is a drastic and sudden change in overseas demand, then the problem would be more difficult. If substantial unemployment resulted from such difficulties, I would not be surprised if the demand for central physical planning were raised once again. I do not myself think that planning of this kind would be a cure for the difficulties raised by such a situation, although I recognise that government control on a substantial scale may be necessary, especially in our foreign economic relations. *Ad hoc* administrative interference will, I think, continue and may vary in its importance. But I doubt whether we shall hear much more of arguments for a radical transformation of the basis on which the economy is operated. I repeat that this is subject to the condition that there is no substantial unemployment. If there is such unemployment, then I would not be surprised if the demand for consciously planned centrally guided administrative action were again to attract widespread support.

The anti-planning ideologists have also learnt a great deal from the post-war experience. One hears much less frequently than formerly the argument that economic control by the State necessarily leads to the restriction of political liberty, and that once we start on this slippery slope there is no turning back. It may be because of the long and deep-seated traditions of political liberty in the United Kingdom (and therefore it may be unwise to generalise from the United Kingdom's experience), but there is startlingly little, if any, evidence that during the five years after 1945 there was any attempt by the government to restrict the freest public discussion. And as long as discussion is free and unhampered, and the government provides all the material, as the Labour government did, on which its own actions and policy can be criticised, I find it difficult to take seriously the cry that economic control will inevitably lead to political slavery. Nor has the argument that in a controlled economy the bureaucracy will inevitably seek to extend its control further and further in order to correct its errors and conceal its mistakes been borne out by British experience. Indeed, I think there is evidence to the contrary: that the civil servants were the first to learn the lessons of the difficulty of running a centrally controlled economy, and that far from wanting to extend their control in the hope of making the system run more effectively they were only too glad to be relieved of this major responsibility.

And even the Labour government itself, committed though it was to economic planning, was zealous and desirous to maintain political freedom. It always shied away from the control of labour, wages or the trade unions. This may be explained in part by the trade unions' power in the Labour party and their unwillingness to concede to the State control over their functions and prerogatives. But I think there was more to it than this. Even those committed to planning demonstrated an impressive anxiety to be vigilant about public liberty.

Nor did the business community, traditionally ideologically opposed to planning, show any increased desire during this period to return to a 'free enterprise' system. Government interference, forms, allocations, etc, were always resented, and the business community was glad to see them go. But there is still the widespread view that it is the government's job to protect industry from any trouble that blows up, or that the government should encourage group arrangements by industry itself to meet such trouble. Business no more wishes to return to the fierce competition of the 1930's than the general public wants to return to the mass unemployment of the period. And whether controlled or not, business has enjoyed, with all its grumbles about taxation, ten years of continuous prosperity since 1945.

We are in a position now, therefore, where there is a widespread, almost unanimous, view that the government has the major responsibility for the general prosperity of the country and its external relations, and that any group suffering economic misfortune has a right to help from the government. To this, in my view, all other issues are subsidiary. As long as full employment is maintained, the old ideological conflicts are unlikely to be revived. I do not want to suggest that there is any great enthusiasm or deep faith in the justice of our present economic system. It is tolerated without any deeply held desire to change it in any fundamental respect; the erstwhile reformers, largely disillusioned by post-war experience, have no longer any fervently held plan for radically transforming our economic system. The one issue which still excites attention and some passion is the extent to which the government should go, forward or backward, in redistributing income and property through taxation. This acquiescence in our present economic arrangements may merely reflect the prosperity of the last ten years. For, notwithstanding the recurrence of 'economic crises', it is important to remember that for the mass of the population economic conditions have been improving perceptibly year by year.

Does this mean that there are no longer major problems of

economic policy which lead to deeply held differences of view? So it would seem for the present. Yet there are now problems emerging; but these problems do not fit easily into the old political and ideological divisions, and they are largely avoided by the political parties. How opinion on them will divide is not easy to tell.

One of the major results of economic and social change in the last generation has been to strengthen the power of the organised group in relation to the individual. The increase and incidence of taxation has strengthened the power of existing economic institutions. It is through the organised group that interests can be protected and pressure brought to bear on the government in exercising its major economic role in society. The government itself encourages the organised group, for it is only in this way that it can negotiate with conflicting interests and hope that, once agreement has been reached with representatives of the group, the agreement will be accepted by the interests affected. In wage policy and industrial relations all governments, whatever their political and ideological complexion, have virtually agreed to power being exercised, with the minimum of political interference, by the trade unions. But in return it is implicitly assumed that the unions will exercise this power responsibly, and discipline or educate their members to restrain them from 'abusing' this power. The individual worker must now belong to a trade union if he is to keep his job; the union will protect his interests, but in return he is expected to abide by the decisions and agreements made by his leaders. The 'unofficial' strike and inter-union strife threaten this implicit agreement between government and organised trade unions, and here also the weight of opinion seems to be in favour of giving more power to the organised group to discipline the individual, and to deal with inter-union conflict.

If there can be said at all to be an ideological basis for the new economic society, it is that the individual plays his role in society through his membership of the group; that the organised group will protect his interests in return for his loyalty; and that the group leaders will enforce discipline and responsibility in return for the power they wield. Government then becomes largely an exercise in the adjustment of group conflicts, and arbitration between them. I see the threat to liberty in the United Kingdom not in the limitation of political freedom in the traditional sense, but in the ever-increasing power of the institutionalised, organised group in relation to the individual.

[11]

The role of the myth in politics[1]

Is political behaviour to be explained and understood exclusively in terms of the interaction between interest groups? Is the whole machinery of government merely a device for securing a reasonably amicable reconciliation of these interests where they conflict? Is the notion of government as the pursuit of a wider public interest just a sham, a myth? If it is just a myth, one cannot help wondering why it has such a hold on so many of those who write and talk about politics; and indeed why the interest groups themselves press their case in terms of this very myth. For interest groups usually argue that the policy they are advocating is in the wider public interest, at least in the long run. Is this just hypocrisy, or is it significant that they feel it necessary to plead their case in terms of a higher principle of political behaviour?

I think that the principle of public interest as a criterion of action, impossible though it is to define, still plays a powerful role in politics. Indeed, it is largely through the reiteration of this principle, the theory that in the ideal political system action would be guided by this criterion, that we succeed in restraining the operation of interest groups. The ideal of the public interest and the practice of interest groups are both part of political life, and any satisfactory view of politics must comprehend both, contradictory though they are. We get a misleading view if we attempt to explain the reality of political behaviour exclusively in terms of one or the other. The reality is a complex interaction, admittedly not easy to disentangle or explain.

The tendency to construct theoretical explanations exclusively in terms of either principles or practice is common in writing and discussion of the working not only of politics but also of business,

[1] From *The Listener*, 21 June 1956.

and of other organisations such as a university or a private society. Our political system, for instance, is explained by some in terms of constitutional and political principles: the relative functions and role of the electorate, the House of Commons, the Cabinet, the civil service, and the parties. In these explanations there are principles which explain both how the system works and how it ought to work. Ministers are responsible for policy decisions, civil servants for advice and administration. The Cabinet represents the collective wisdom of Ministers operating at the highest level of statesmanship. The alternative approach emphasises what are thought of as the important features of political behaviour in practice—the influence of pressure groups; pandering to mob opinion; the force of personal ambition and the pursuit of power; party intrigue; ministerial decision and intervention as a confused, haphazard affair, guided more by the last by-election and the results of opinion polls than by any sense of public interest.

You have a parallel dichotomy in the analysis of business behaviour and organisation. On the one hand, the formal organisation outlined in a chart setting out the structure of the business; the functions and interrelations between departments; the channels of communication; the hierarchy of decision making, with the operating unit at the bottom and the board of directors in supreme control at the top. By contrast, there is the view, now very fashionable, purporting to be based on watching business behaviour in practice, and this emphasises what are called the informal organisations: the formation of cliques; the co-ordinating function of luncheon arrangements; business discussion in the golf club; the social relations between the wives of managers and wives of important customers. On this view of a business, one may discover that the authorities at the top of the hierarchy on the organisation chart never discuss anything but the most trivial matters, such as what colour to paint the factory, and merely rubber-stamp decisions which have been worked out and agreed before they are put to the board.

In the same way the working of a university can be described in terms of the formal powers and functions of the council, senate, faculties and departments, as laid down in the university's charter and statutes. Or one can draw a picture in terms of coteries of professors, how these are formed and exert their influence, the working of committees, and the influence of bureaucratic staff. The classic description of university life along these lines is still Cornford's delightful *Microcosmographia academica*. Similarly, in explaining the working of a small voluntary society: the written constitution usually gives supreme power to the annual general meeting; but in practice most successful societies are run by a small group of enthusiasts, who become a self-perpetuating clique. And the general membership is only too glad, grumble though it may occasionally, to see the clique assume the burden of running the affairs of the society.

How can these two views, in many ways contradictory, be reconciled? For I cannot myself believe that it is fruitful to elevate one view into the real explanation and treat the other as a mere sham. It would be more sensible to assume that the contradiction between theories which lay emphasis on principles and those which pay more attention to practice itself reflects the essentially contradictory elements in our complex political and social life.

Politics is full of such contradictions. Take the contrast between politics in practice as a rather dirty game, with politicians engaged in party intrigue and the pursuit of power, and politics as one of the highest forms of human activity, with the ideal of statesmanship seeking to safeguard the public interest in a dispassionate and disinterested way. Is this not a reflection of the dichotomy in our own behaviour? We are all, to a greater or lesser degree, mean, selfish, dishonest, lazy, inefficient and grasping; yet we have ideals of generosity, unselfishness, honesty, industry, efficiency and charity. Although we seldom live up to these ideals, our behaviour is affected by reaffirming them. In public life the ideal standard of political behaviour is in a sense a myth. As Mr Truman has said, 'a statesman is only a dead politician.' And yet when the behaviour of politicians is raised as a public issue through the exposure of some unsavoury incident, it is against this ideal standard that the erring politician is judged. The actions of Mr Belcher, as revealed before the Lynskey tribunal in the Stanley case, were probably no worse than those of many other politicians; yet Mr Belcher had to resign.[2] He was sacrificed in order to reaffirm the ideal of upright political behaviour.

[2] Mr John Belcher was Parliamentary Secretary to the Board of Trade in 1948 and resigned after the report of the (Lynskey) tribunal (*Proceedings of the tribunal appointed to inquire into allegations reflecting on the official conduct of Ministers of the Crown and other public servants*).—*Ed.*

Does this kind of public demonstration, amounting almost to a ritual sacrifice, in fact serve to raise and safeguard the general standard of political behaviour? One could argue that all this is just a form of social hypocrisy, and that incidents such as the Stanley affair merely serve to demonstrate to the astute politician how important it is to keep within the rules of the game, to be discreet in one's choice of friends and contacts and, above all, never to be found out. But I expect that most people would take a less cynical view, and feel that public demonstrations of this kind do serve to reaffirm the principle that Ministers should not receive favours from outside interests. Obviously it would be ridiculous to suppose that by such means we secure that politicians always live up to the ideal standards, or that our political system would work if they were sacked every time they fell at all below them. But even if we tolerate weakness and imperfection, we condemn them by the standards of the myth of upright conduct when they are blatantly exposed to public gaze.

Another principle central to our notions of responsible democratic government is that of ministerial responsibility for everything that is done by the officials in his department. But the work of a modern government department is far too extensive and complex for any Minister to be aware of more than a small fraction of the day-to-day decisions taken in his name. Sometimes this difficulty is met by drawing a distinction between decisions on general policy, which are for Ministers, and advice and administration, which are for civil servants. But this distinction is itself a fiction, and many of those who have studied the operation of government in practice would argue that policy is often little more than the cumulative result of day-to-day administrative decisions.

And yet there is no mistaking the force of appeals to the principle whenever anything done in a department, however trivial, becomes a matter of public political dispute and debate. The Minister cannot then escape responsibility by pleading that he did not know what was going on or that he was badly advised. From the moment the issue becomes public, argument proceeds in terms of the formal theory of the constitution that the action was his and that he approved it. And this theory, myth though it is, has real power. It means that if glaring error or inefficiency is revealed the Minister may be called to defend himself in parliament and may be forced to resign.

Crichel Down[3] was a classic case of this kind. The exposure of that affair, in all its complex and tortuous detail, did not lead people to argue that the work of a modern government department is so extensive that the Minister cannot be expected to know all that is going on; that we must contrive some way of distinguishing between ministerial and civil service responsibility. For such a distinction would offend against one of the fundamental myths of democratic government. On the contrary, by forcing the Minister's resignation we used the occasion to reaffirm the principle that officials must be obedient servants and that Ministers can and should control all matters of importance in their departments. There were, it is true, some expressions of uneasiness that the theory had too much fiction about it nowadays, and that it could not be entertained much longer. But in the end there was an almost unanimous view that the problem was best dealt with by reasserting the principle of ministerial responsibility.

It is the pretence that the Minister is always responsible, contrary though it is to the day-to-day practice of Ministers and officials, which makes possible the kind of action taken on such crucial occasions as Crichel Down. And incidents like Crichel Down and the Crabb affair,[4] provided they do not happen too often, serve to reaffirm the principle rather than to expose the pretence. The debatable point is whether the arrogance and power of officials is curbed by maintaining the pretence of their subservience, or whether it merely enables them to exercise powerful influence protected from public gaze and criticism.

The frequent contradiction between the formal organisation of business and its actual operation brings out a rather different aspect of the interplay between principle and practice. In any large busi-

[3] 725 acres of land at Crichel Down in Dorset were bought in 1937 by the Air Ministry as a bombing range and handed over in 1949 to the Ministry of Agriculture. Repeated applications by the original owners (or their successors-in-title) to buy back the land or rent it and farm it were refused. The Ministry of Agriculture equipped the land at considerable expense as a separate farm and sold it to the Commissioners of Crown Lands, who let it to a tenant. The appearance of a report on the affair led to the resignation of Sir T. Dugdale in July 1954 from his Cabinet post as Minister of Agriculture.—*Ed.*

[4] Commander Crabb disappeared in Portsmouth harbour in May 1956 in a frogman's outfit while engaged in underwater reconnaissance near the Russian cruiser *Ordzhonikidze*. It was not clear on whose instructions Commander Crabb was acting.—*Ed.*

ness, efficiency requires that provision be made for clear delimitation of spheres of responsibility, channels of communication and command, co-ordination of activity; and this is done in formal rules and organisation charts. But efficiency also requires that initiative and independence be encouraged at every level, and that everyone should use his own discretion in meeting the ever-varying situation facing the business. To achieve this the organisation must be flexible, which is merely another way of saying that there must be rules but that on appropriate occasions the rules can and should be disregarded. It is not only in the navy that there are two contradictory traditions of 'obedience to orders' and 'turning the blind eye'. But one cannot provide rules in advance for the occasions when the rules can and should be ignored. If management decisions on crucial issues of policy are to be effective, the fiction must be maintained that the rules are always obeyed. Only where there is such a fiction can one safely allow full play in practice to individual initiative and discretion.

The problem of combining effective control by the central authority with initiative and responsibility at lower levels is most acute when a large group of previously independent businesses are amalgamated into one organisation. The acknowledgement of the supremacy of the new central authority may be secured only by insisting for a time on a degree of centralisation and rigid obedience to rule which later might well be considered excessive. It seems to me that the Fleck committee's analysis of the operations of the National Coal Board illustrates a situation of this kind. The report draws special attention to the disregard at area, divisional and operating level of many of the important directives issued by the National Coal Board; and recommends that 'the Board should insist on their policies being properly carried out by the subordinate formations and should ensure that discipline obtains'. If through such discipline the Board succeeds in establishing the notion throughout the industry that it knows its business and is determined to see its orders enforced, it may later be able to relax the severity of its control. (Here I am expressing a view of my own, not that of the Fleck committee.) Once the supremacy of the Board has been established in practice and is fully recognised throughout the industry, strict obedience to rule can be allowed to operate to some extent as a fiction. When there is danger of mutiny the strictest adherence to discipline has to be enforced; where there is no such danger, discipline can be relaxed.

In some organisations the principles of the formal constitution exist as a safeguard, as a kind of safety valve, to be called into operation only in unusual situations. The normal day-to-day running of the organisation may be different from what one might suppose by reading the constitution alone. Yet here also, if the constitution is to be brought into play in unusual situations, the fiction must somehow be maintained that it is always in operation. This seems to me to be demonstrated, for example, in the way in which a university or a private society is run. In most universities—or perhaps I should say in most red-brick universities—constitutional authority over all academic matters rests with a senate or academic council. But there would be chaos if the senate attempted to consider and debate seriously all the issues brought before it. As a result, decisions in practice are taken by committees, by the vice-chancellor or by the administrative staff, and the senate usually acts as a mere rubber stamp. But the important fiction is maintained that these are recommendations which the senate can approve or reject, and there is a formal vote in each case. And this formality is not just a sham. For on some occasions a recommendation is questioned and debated and then the voting on it becomes, so to speak, a real vote. Such occasions have, of course, to be relatively rare. In practice, therefore, both the constitutional principle of senate supremacy and decisions by committee or other means operate in parallel. One cannot provide by rule in advance for the occasions when a senate should exercise its powers, and going through the formality—the pretence, if you like—that the rule is always in operation enables it to exercise its powers whenever it wishes—provided always that it does not do so too often.

There is a parallel situation in the way in which a private society is run. As long as the affairs of the society are going well, the annual meeting does nothing more than formally agree to the recommendations of the committee. There may be proposers and seconders for next year's officers, but in any well run society all this has been arranged beforehand and everyone knows it. But the formality is observed, and as each recommendation is put to the meeting, the chairman takes faint whispers of 'Aye, aye' to indicate unanimous approval of the proposals. Again this is not just a sham pretence that the society is run democratically. For if there is a body of members, outside the ruling clique, who feel strongly that things are going wrong in the society's affairs, they can stage a revolution at the annual meeting, and since the principle of the supremacy of the annual meeting is always there, no one can question their right to do so. But if they succeed in turning the existing clique out and get themselves elected instead, they in turn will operate by committee rule, notwithstanding their criticisms of cliques when staging their revolution.

It seems to me that all social organisation is full of contradictions of this kind. Myths, principles and ideals, as well as human weakness and fallibility and the demands made by the complexity and ever-changing variety of real life, all influence actual behaviour. If indeed there is a logic in social reality, it is a logic of inconsistency.

[12]
Government on the inner circle[1]

Every now and again in public affairs, as a result of some unusual incident, dispute or error, an inquiry is held, a tribunal is set up, a Minister resigns, and the veil which normally conceals from public gaze what goes on behind the scenes is for the moment torn aside. We then get, as an incidental by-product, a fascinating and revealing insight into the private conduct of public business. Then when the affair is over the veil is drawn back, and everything is once again wrapped in mystery.

In the last year or two there seem to have been an unusually large number of occasions of this kind. The Bank Rate Tribunal, Mr Thorneycroft's resignation and his unusually frank exchange of letters with the Prime Minister, the public competition between two groups in the aircraft industry for the BEA contract, the report on Mr Gethin's allegations about purchasing procedure in the British Transport Commission, and the court of inquiry into the dispute at Briggs Motor Bodies, were all important, not only because of the specific issues with which they were ostensibly concerned but also for revealing to the public a fleeting glimpse of the conduct of affairs, usually concealed behind closed doors. Indeed it could be argued that it is this picture given to the outsider which is the important part of these incidents and disputes rather than the particular way in which the issues immediately in question are for the time being settled.

To me, as an economist, it is this aspect of the Bank Rate Tribunal which was most striking. By sheer accident, as a by-product of dealing with the main issue—whether there was a leak of information—we learnt more in three weeks about what makes the City and the Bank of England tick than from years of laborious academic analysis. The minutes of evidence of the proceedings before the tribunal pro-

[1] From *The Listener*, 27 March 1958.

vide us with much more valuable source material than innumerable academic researches.[2] And it is not just the general public and the academics who learnt a great deal. I suspect that the City learnt quite a lot about itself too. One of the more ironical aspects of the debate in the House of Commons on the Bank Rate Tribunal report was the implied admission by members of the Opposition, including those who have held high office in departments concerned with economic affairs, that all this was new to them.

If I am right in thinking that the information which we obtain in this way is of great value in giving us an insight into the way things really work and in revealing to us the arguments and forces influencing those on the inside, why must we depend on the erratic chance of these incidents for such enlightenment? If there is to be fruitful and intelligent public debate we ought to be given more information of this kind in the normal course of events instead of having to rely on these abnormal crisis occasions. For, at best, they give us a partial and fleeting picture.

There are, of course, plenty of arguments against more regular open disclosure of the issues usually debated secretly and confidentially behind closed doors. These arguments are usually put forward with great force in the sphere of government. The case seems to be overwhelming on issues of foreign policy and defence. Here, it is said, there is the danger of revealing vital information to countries which are, actually or potentially, Her Majesty's enemies. This argument for secrecy finds its formal expression in the Official Secrets Acts. There is the subsidiary argument that disclosure to the public of the arguments that go on in the Foreign Office and the Defence departments would reveal differences of view, even disputes, with our allies, and that this information would enable our enemies, by playing on these differences, to drive a wedge between us and our friends. There is obviously a great deal in all this, but is it not usually driven much beyond the point at which concealment from unfriendly foreign powers is really important? For there is plenty of historical evidence that foreign powers have their own ways—frequently very effective ways—of discovering what is going on. It is the British, rather than the foreigners, who are kept in the dark. One can, for example, usually learn a great deal more about

[2] *Proceedings of the tribunal appointed to inquire into allegations that information about the raising of Bank Rate was improperly disclosed, December 1957*, HMSO, 1958.

the arguments going on inside British government circles from the American, French or Swiss press than from the British press.

This kind of concealment is most dangerous when the government engages in propaganda in foreign affairs. Then the British public is not merely kept in ignorance but is actually misled. I often suspect that some government statements on the hydrogen bomb have something of this character, designed more as part of the poker game with America and Russia than to inform the British public about the issues which are in fact exercising the minds of those in the know in Whitehall. Cornford, as usual, put the point beautifully: 'Propaganda . . . consists in very nearly deceiving your friends without quite deceiving your enemies.'[3]

The argument for secrecy is extended well beyond the realm of defence and foreign affairs, because the government in power usually treats the Opposition as its enemy, at least in public debate. The provision of inside information and the exposure of the debates and arguments that go on in the departments, in committee and in the Cabinet would give the Opposition and back-benchers ammunition with which to attack the government and to bait Ministers about their disagreements. This, it is argued, would weaken the standing of the executive with the public, and make strong and effective government difficult. Hence the rule—a rule, incidentally, enforced with increased vigour over the last fifty years—that Ministers should never disagree in public, and that government spokesmen should always speak with resolution about government policy. If, in fact, the government has no policy on some issue, or is still disputing what action to take, the spokesman escapes into vague, general, innocuous platitudes; but rarely explains to the public the issues in question, or why there is difficulty over the formulation of a policy. Unlimited dispute on the inside, but a united front to the public, is the general principle of most political organisations, albeit one that is enforced with different degrees of rigour. For the government this is made respectable, even hallowed, by the doctrine of collective responsibility.

The resignation of a Minister disrupts the system, especially if he refuses to give ill health or the pressure of private or business affairs as the reason for resigning. To insist on explaining in a published letter the nature of the dispute that led to the resignation is hardly

[3] F. M. Cornford, *Microcosmographia academica*, Bowes & Bowes, Cambridge, 1949, Foreword.

playing the game. The Opposition will rub their hands in glee, but government supporters will talk of 'rocking the boat' or 'letting the side down', and accuse the resigning Minister of arrogance in pitting his own narrow view against the collective wisdom of his colleagues. And the resignation will itself be used as an argument for 'closing ranks'.

All this would be less serious from the point of view of public debate were it not for another important doctrine of British government, that the government in power has the exclusive right of access to civil service advice and knowledge. This, coupled with the doctrine of civil service anonymity and ministerial responsibility, reinforces the tendency towards confidentiality and secrecy. The Opposition may be called Her Majesty's Opposition, and we may all be Her Majesty's subjects, but civil servants, although servants of the Crown, confine their advice and information to the government of the day. The rest of us have access to it only in so far as the government agrees to publication. Since anonymity, confidentiality and a monopoly of the facts are among the most potent instruments of bureaucratic power and influence, the civil service itself is not inclined to resist this particular doctrine. On this the Ministry and the civil service are natural allies, as one can see from the evidence which civil servants gave before the Franks Committee on Administrative Tribunals. Sir Harold Kent, the Treasury solicitor, stated explicitly in evidence before the Committee that 'one ought not to have a situation in which the conflict of departmental policies is thrashed out in public'.[4]

It is true that every now and again civil servants are called to give evidence before royal commissions or parliamentary committees, and this evidence is often published. In principle civil servants do not discuss so-called matters of policy on these occasions, but one can often learn a great deal from the evidence about what does go on inside the departments and about arguments on policy put to Ministers. For example, the evidence before the Select Committee on the Supply of Military Aircraft in 1956–7 is full of fascinating questions and answers on a whole range of controversial issues, such as the V bombers, the Swift, and the pricing of government contracts. And a great deal of it is very lively. One can imagine the twinkle in Lord Hives' eyes when he said, 'I have met some

[4] Committee on Administrative Tribunals and Enquiries, *Minutes of Evidence*, eighth day, HMSO, 1956, Q. 1961.

firms and I have said the only thing they produce is a good balance sheet every year. I have not seen them produce anything else.'[5]

But this usually involves reading between the lines, which is possible only if one already has a certain familiarity with the personalities and issues in the department concerned. I could use this particular report because of my inside knowledge from war-time experience in the Ministry of Aircraft Production. In any case, the argument is often about past policies—as in the committees on estimates or public accounts—rather than about those which are currently in the centre of the political stage.

Suggestions that civil servants should come out more into the public arena and explain issues of policy to the public meet with powerful resistance. For, it is argued, this would strike at the root of the doctrine of ministerial responsibility and would turn civil servants into politicians. This may be done in other countries, but the English arrogantly and complacently claim that the results in other countries show just how disastrous the whole idea is. For it goes without saying that the British way of doing things—in government at least—is superior in all respects to what is done elsewhere. There seems indeed to be little interest in how things are done in other countries. Sir Harold Kent said to the Franks committee, apparently unashamedly, 'I do not know very much about the Conseil d'État.'[6]

Another force making for concealment is the conduct of business by negotiation. One sees this everywhere—not just in government but also in industry, in trade unions and in the academic world. Business, it is claimed, in all these spheres is a delicate affair of negotiating compromises. This can be done successfully only if the participants can negotiate in secret conclave, or better still, as Cornford called it, by squaring.[7] If they are forced to negotiate openly in public they find it difficult to move from fixed, predetermined positions and are more concerned with prestige, face-saving and the clamour of their supporters than with the practical possibilities of agreement. On this view, public debate while the negotiations are

[5] *Second report from the Select Committee on Estimates, session 1956–57*, HMSO, 1956, Q. 1466. [Lord Hives was Chairman of Rolls-Royce and largely responsible for building up the company into a successful aero-engine producer. Devons saw much of him in war-time.]

[6] Committee on Administrative Tribunals and Enquiries, *Minutes of evidence*, eighth day, Q. 1982.

[7] *Op. cit.*, p. 22.

going on jeopardises the possibility of reaching agreement. And afterwards, you know the usual appeal: 'Give the agreement a chance; let's see how it works before criticising it.'

There is little harm in all this if politics is just the art of negotiating compromises between vested interests. But if not, if principle and a wider public interest should count, then secrecy on these grounds may be cause for alarm. For the greater the possibility of secrecy, the greater the temptation to the politician and administrator to be content with the negotiated settlement, regardless of principle and the wider public interest. More limelight is indeed one of the most effective ways of preventing politics from degenerating into a mere subtle balancing of the interests of conflicting pressure groups.

Then there is the argument based on the essential delicacy, intricacy and informality of the web of connections vital to getting things done sensibly. The whole procedure may indeed seem highly illogical to the outsider, yet it works. If it is subjected to too much scrutiny, the public will insist on rationality, principles and unworkable formal rules. The more irrational and muddled the procedure, the greater the pride the British seem to take in it. If it can be shown that present procedures are the accidental results of fortuitous events in our past history, so much the better. For this then demonstrates the great native genius of the British. They evolve workable systems without knowing it, whereas others worry about principles and formal organisations, and look what a mess they get into!

The system of relations that has developed in the last few years between the universities and the government, as a consequence of increasing university dependence on government finance, shows some of these characteristics. It is all rather obscure and informal; those who work it say that it works extraordinarily well, but are reluctant to reveal or discuss its working overmuch. If anyone suggests that the present system be altered in any way, or asks if this be necessary, the bogey that the universities will be examined by the Public Accounts Committee is usually enough to silence him.

To me, as an outsider, the very subtlety and informality of the system may itself be one of its weaknesses. For it makes possible influence over the universities, by suggestion, hint and innuendo—an influence which is so vague that it may be difficult to criticise but may yet add up in the end to a more powerful and extensive control than would be tolerated if this were attempted by formal rule and instruction. But perhaps I had better not go on with this illustration. For although I do not really understand how it all works, I am sufficiently involved myself to be accused perhaps by my colleagues of 'rocking the boat'.

The arguments for private and confidential debate which I have so far discussed are only a selection of those that are frequently used in defence of the practice. But I wonder whether there is not in all these arguments a deeper, although unacknowledged, reason for reluctance to admit the public to a full view of events: a mistrust of the general public; a fear that they will not understand or will be unwilling to face the truth; a feeling that the public must be cajoled, wheedled, seduced and exhorted, rather than convinced by logical argument and debate; a dread that if the whole complexity of the situation is revealed it will be misinterpreted and misjudged. These, plus the temptation to keep information secret because exclusive knowledge means power, seem to me to be the main motive forces behind the passion for cliques, confidentiality, and secrecy. There is so often the arrogant assumption among the inner circle of experts that truth is a commodity which the millions cannot face.

For whatever the force of the other arguments for secrecy, it is remarkable how easy it is, if you move in the right circles and have the right contacts, to find out what is going on. As long as it is 'between ourselves' and 'of course you won't let this go any further', even the civil servant will discuss policy and the inner workings of his department—always provided that you are prepared to use your contacts and information to explain and support the established line in public. Should you turn nasty and attack the hand that feeds you, however, your sources of information will soon dry up and you will find the barriers of secrecy erected against you even more strongly than before.

How can this attitude be reconciled with the notion that ours is, politically at least, a democratic society? I know that 'democratic' is a much overworked word and can now be stretched to mean anything. I have even heard it argued that the inner-circle system is democratic because it is essential for the proper functioning of a modern democracy. But to me—and I may just be a naive innocent in this—political democracy implies a full participation by the general public in the argument and debate about issues of policy which affect them. How can this discussion be sensible and intelligent if crucial information is confined to the inner circle, and the public is merely served with clichés and platitudes through public relations officers and information departments?

If it is given a chance the public has often a role to play in educating the experts and the politicians. Remember how the public had to demand of the government during the war that it should be told what sacrifices to make and what needed to be done. Even Churchill was surprised by the British working man's willingness to have his red meat rationed. Would we have plunged so ignorantly into the Suez affair if there had been a little more public knowledge and debate in advance about the arguments going on in the Foreign Office? The need to 'educate our masters' in a democracy can be read both ways. I was encouraged to find a similar view expressed by Sir William Haley in his Haldane memorial lecture. I had not dared to hope when I prepared this talk that I would get such formidable support for my argument.

To my mind, therefore, although one can think up many arguments and excuses in defence of government on the inner circle, there is an overwhelming argument for more frank and open discussion of public policy. To quote Cornford once again: 'There is only one argument for doing something; the rest are arguments for doing nothing. The argument for doing something is that it is the right thing to do.'[8]

[8] *Op. cit.*, p. 14.

[13]

An economist's view of the Bank Rate Tribunal evidence[1]

The Bank Rate Tribunal of December 1957 was set up to investigate particular allegations about improper disclosure of information about the raising of Bank rate. But in the course of the very extensive evidence given to the tribunal, interesting and important information was given about the working of the Bank of England, the City, and the Treasury—information which it would be extremely difficult to obtain by the ordinary process of research. In this article an attempt is made to distil and comment on some of the information likely to be of interest to the economist. Some of the topics of interest have already been discussed in two articles in *The Banker*,[2] and these will not be referred to in detail here.

Although we are not here concerned with the particular allegations which the tribunal was investigating, these have to be kept in mind in trying to use the evidence for other purposes. Witnesses were being asked to reveal and justify in detail their behaviour and actions during the crucial period, and in doing this they were led to make revealing statements. But, of course, they knew all the time what the tribunal was after, and this knowledge may have had an important influence on the slant they gave to their answers. This is particularly important in relation to one topic which will be discussed later in this article—the view held by the City on the

[1] From *The Manchester School*, January 1959, pp. 1–16.

[2] 'The Bank of England from within' and 'New light on the City', *The Banker*, vol. CVIII, March 1958. The first of these discussed the responsibility for fixing the Bank rate, Bank rate as a weapon, and the problem of dual loyalties of directors; the second discussed the impact of the September drain on four City houses, Lazard's liquidity crisis, the factors influencing foreign deposits in London, the underwriting of new issues, and the limitations on the Union Discount Company's freedom of market operations.

significance of Bank rate as an instrument of economic policy. In using the evidence given to the tribunal to form a view on this, one must remember that there might to a feeling, at least in the minds of some of the witnesses, that the answer 'yes' to the question 'Did you expect the Bank rate to go up?' would merely lead to further questions about why they held this view and whether in fact they had had access to inside information. Much simpler, therefore, to answer 'No' to the original question and to avoid further questioning. It is not suggested that witnesses were consciously telling lies, but that there might easily have been a bias in their answers, particularly when one bears in mind that they were being asked questions about opinions they held three or four months earlier.[3]

There is some support for this view in the proceedings of the tribunal. When one witness who sold a substantial volume of gilt-edged on the afternoon of Wednesday 18 September appeared to be unwilling to commit himself when pressed by Mr Milner Holland, a member of the tribunal, to state specifically whether the knowledge that a decision on Bank rate might be made the next morning played some part in his thoughts, Mr Holland said, 'I am not quite sure, but speaking for myself, I do not think it is yet a crime to have thought the Bank rate might go up. You did, in fact, ring[4] for that very reason'[5] [9794].[6] The witness then replied, 'Yes, that was so.'

The second general point to keep in mind in using the evidence is that the widest publicity was given to the proceedings of the tribunal in the press. The veil which normally conceals the working of the City from public gaze was quite suddenly torn aside. Every member of the public was being allowed to watch the detailed scrutiny of affairs of which he normally knows little or nothing. In these circumstances, important witnesses might have felt that the City was on trial before the public in a general sense. It would be only natural in these circumstances for there to be a 'closing of the ranks'.

[3] Bank rate was increased from 5 per cent to 7 per cent on 19 September, 1957. The tribunal was appointed on 14 November and heard evidence from 2 December to 20 December, 1957.

[4] To give instructions to sell.

[5] i.e., that 'you thought there might be a rise in the Bank rate' [9793].

[6] The references throughout are to question numbers in *Proceedings of the tribunal appointed to inquire into allegations that information about the raising of Bank rate was improperly disclosed*, HMSO, December 1957.

The role of the Bank, the Treasury, and the Cabinet in the Bank rate decision

The discussion about economic policy which finally led up to the Bank rate change and the other measures of economic policy[7] announced on 19 September 1957 revolved round three separate centres of the government machine—the Bank of England, the Treasury and the Cabinet.

In July the Chancellor 'gave instructions to the Treasury to consider possibilities of checking inflation by taking firmer control of the money supply' [10635] and on 7 August 'that during his absence abroad a study should be made in the Treasury of the possibility of bringing about a measure of deflation in the economy' [10570]. Sir Roger Makins, Joint Permanent Secretary of the Treasury, had two talks with the Governor of the Bank on 8 and 12 August and 'told the Governor the way the Chancellor's mind was working' [10572]. There was a further meeting with the Governor, and this time with the Deputy Governor as well, on 22 August, at which there was a discussion of 'the studies which the Treasury had made in accordance with the Chancellor's instructions' [10574] and at which the Governor gave 'his views on the desirability of a rise in the Bank rate' [10575].

The Governor was on holiday from 24 August to 14 September, and during this period Mr Mynors, the Deputy Governor, acted as Governor. Sir Roger Makins was also on leave of absence from 29 August to 5 September. During the period from 28 August onwards, Mr Mynors kept the Committee of the Treasury and the Court of the Bank of England informed about the measures to deal with the financial situation that were under discussion and told members of the committee that these might eventually include action on Bank rate.[8] Mr Mynors discussed the situation further with Sir Roger Makins on his return from leave on 6 September. During the week beginning 9 September there were discussions with the clearing banks on the proposal to limit bank advances. On 12 and 13 September Mr Mynors had further discussions with the Chancellor and Sir Roger Makins about Bank rate, and it seems that it was at this stage that the timing of the Bank rate increase,

[7] To hold down the total of investment in the public sector and the average level of bank advances.

[8] He also wrote to absent directors of the Bank on 3 September.

although not its extent, was considered in relation to the timing of the announcement of the other financial measures to be taken by the government.

On 14 September the Governor returned from holiday, and from that stage onwards the pace quickened and the network of consultation became even more intricate. The Governor and Deputy Governor spent Saturday together, returning to London on Sunday (15 September), where they saw Mr Parsons, the Executive Director of the Bank, and at six o'clock in the evening the Chancellor and Sir Roger Makins. At this meeting the figure of 7 per cent was first mentioned, with the statement by the Governor that his provisional view was in favour of an increase to this figure [7605]. The Chancellor asked the Governor to give the Bank's firm view by the following evening.

During the morning of Monday, 16 September, the Governor consulted some of the members of the Court[9] and told them that he proposed, subject to the Chancellor's approval, to recommend a 2 per cent increase in Bank rate on 19 September. The same evening (Monday, 16 September) he saw the Chancellor, who had Sir Roger Makins and Sir Leslie Rowan with him, and told him that although he had not yet consulted all his colleagues, he could give the firm view that the Bank considered an increase in Bank rate to 7 per cent on 19 September desirable [7631 and 7632]. The Chancellor asked the Governor to present the arguments for that view, 'which he did on the morning of 17 September'. The Governor, having in the meantime consulted further members of the Court, confirmed this view at another short meeting with the Chancellor the same afternoon (at about 2.15). Sometime on the 17th there was a meeting in the Treasury, with the Chancellor, the Economic Secretary and 'other Treasury officials', at which discussion took place about the raising of Bank rate to 7 per cent [10604].

At this stage the Cabinet comes into the picture. At a meeting at about three o'clock on Tuesday, 17 September, the Cabinet considered the terms on which the Chancellor would announce the other economic measures which the government were intending to take, and for the first time the question of Bank rate was raised. It was agreed that this should be left for further discussion between

[9] Lord Bicester, Mr Eley, Sir Charles Hambro, Mr Sanderson, Mr Babington-Smith and Lord Kindersley.

the Prime Minister, the Chancellor and the Governor. At 9 p.m. that evening there was a meeting at 11 Downing Street attended by the Chancellor, the Governor, Sir Roger Makins, Sir Edmund Compton and Mr Maude; followed at 10 p.m. by a discussion at 10 Downing Street with the Prime Minister, at which the Chancellor, the Governor, Sir Roger Makins, Sir Edmund Compton and Mr Bishop[10] were present. After some discussion 'the Prime Minister said he would not make up his mind whether the government should agree to the Bank rate being raised and, if so, to what figure, until the following morning' [10612]. The next morning, Wednesday, 18 September, the Chancellor saw the Prime Minister again and it was then agreed that an increase to 7 per cent 'would be justified'.[11] The Governor was informed of this at about noon on Wednesday, 18 September.

At 12.30 on Wednesday, 18 September, the Committee of the Treasury of the Bank of England met, the Governor and Deputy Governor proposed the increase in Bank rate to 7 per cent, and this was approved for recommendation to the Court the following day. On Thursday morning, at a Cabinet meeting starting at 10.30, the Prime Minister informed the Cabinet that he had reached the conclusion that the government should accept the view of the Bank of England that Bank rate should be increased to 7 per cent [10697]. Finally, the Court of Directors of the Bank met on Thursday, 19 September, at 11.45 a.m. and approved the proposal of the Committee of the Treasury that Bank rate should be raised from 5 to 7 per cent.

This outline of the events leading up to the final decision to increase Bank rate raises three interesting issues:

1. The relative roles of the Treasury and the Bank.
2. The position of the Cabinet in relation to the decision.
3. The contribution made by the directors of the Bank in advising the Governor.

On the first issue the evidence before the Tribunal does not in itself point to any firm conclusion. There is not sufficient informa-

[10] The Prime Minister's private secretary.

[11] There is no clue in the evidence to indicate whether the Prime Minister consulted anyone else about the proposed change, in the interval between the two discussions with the Chancellor on Tuesday evening and Wednesday morning.

tion revealed in the evidence to assess the relative importance of the roles played by the Bank and the Treasury in the final decision, or indeed where the main initiative came from. There is no disclosure of the kind of discussion or analysis that went on inside the Treasury or among the Bank's staff which led to the final recommendations, or what alternative policies, if any, were looked at and rejected. Certainly there is no evidence here to suggest that there was a distinct Treasury or Bank of England view or, if there was, how the difference was resolved in the final decision. The evidence merely gives us the formal moves, telling us who was consulted and informed, and when.

It may be significant that Sir Robert Hall, Economic Advisor to the Government, is not mentioned by name in the evidence as taking part in any of the high-level discussions between the Bank, the Treasury and the Prime Minister.[12] But in the evidence there is a reference to at least one meeting in the Treasury[13] at which discussion took place about the raising of Bank rate to 7 per cent when 'other Treasury officials' were present, and Sir Robert Hall may have been among these. The tribunal was given written statements from civil servants in the Treasury who in the course of their duties necessarily had prior knowledge of the increase in Bank rate, but the names of these civil servants are not revealed. For although the minutes of evidence taken before the tribunal have been published in full, written statements and other documents presented to the tribunal are unfortunately not included in the publication.

The evidence is more revealing on the role played by the Cabinet, and we have in the Chancellor's evidence for the first time a statement of the constitutional position. It is worth quoting some of the questions and answers in full.[14]

10675 Of course, responsibility for varying the Bank rate rests with the Court of the Bank of England?—It rests formally with the Court of the Bank of England and the Governor, but of course it is normally—it is always done in consultation with and with the approval of the Chancellor of the Exchequer.

10678 At about 3 o'clock on Tuesday, September 17, did the Cabinet

[12] The three Senior Treasury officials mentioned by name are Sir Roger Makins, Sir Edmund Compton, and Sir Leslie Rowan.

[13] On 17 September.

[14] The answers are by the Chancellor of the Exchequer to questions put by the Attorney-General.

consider the terms on which you would announce the other economic measures which the Government were intending to take, that is to say the measures other than the Bank rate?—They did.

10679 In the course of the Cabinet's discussion was the question raised whether those measures would be sufficient by themselves to meet the economic situation?—It was.

10680 Or whether they should be reinforced by any increase in Bank rate to either 6 per cent or 7 per cent?—Yes.

10681 *Was it pointed out that, by tradition, variation of Bank rate is not a matter for decision by the Cabinet?—That was, yes* [my italics].

10682 Was it agreed that the point should be left for further discussion by the Prime Minister with you?—That was the arrangement.

10683 And with the Governor of the Bank of England?—Yes.

There follow a few questions and answers about these discussions, and then:

10697 Were the Cabinet then[15] informed that the Prime Minister had reached the conclusion that the Government should accept the view of the Bank of England that the Bank rate should be increased to 7 per cent?—That information was given to the Cabinet.

10698 Did the Cabinet express approval of that conclusion?—*They took note of it* [my italics].

This gives a very minor role to the Cabinet and other ministers particularly concerned with economic affairs, such as the Minister of Labour and the President of the Board of Trade, in discussion and decision about one of the most important instruments of economic policy.

The Governor stated that he attached considerable importance to the advice that he received from the directors of the Court whom he consulted. His major argument was that

the problem that we were facing at that moment was a major exchange crisis, and the directors whom I wished to consult in addition to the members of the Committee of the Treasury were those directors who were particularly qualified to give me an opinion about the likely effect of a 7 per cent Bank rate on sterling [7733]

and

The specific point here, of course, was this: was a rather sensational rise in the Bank rate from 5 per cent to 7 per cent likely to be a really effective measure along with the other measures under consideration—which in

[15] At the meeting on Thursday, 19 September.

my judgement it was—or was there a risk that such a sensational measure as a 2 per cent rise from 5 per cent to 7 per cent might be regarded on the exchanges as some sort of panic action? [8115].

Unfortunately the evidence does not reveal what advice and answers the colleagues that he saw gave the Governor, nor how they assessed whether the foreign exchange market would be reassured or driven into a panic by the proposed 'sensational' increase. Of course, an indication of how they themselves would react might be important information, since the Governor might take this as a fair sample of the likely general reaction in the City. On this view the role of the part-time directors is important, not because they are experts in interpreting the economic and financial situation, but because they represent a cross section of the City, and give the Governor a valuable insight into the City's changing opinions, hopes and expectations.

It is perhaps interesting to note that the Governor did not state that he needed information and advice on how this dramatic raising of Bank rate might affect the internal economic situation. Indeed, he did not consult those directors, such as Mr Cadbury, Sir Alfred Roberts and Sir Harry Pilkington, who would be more concerned with this aspect of the policy, until the afternoon of Wednesday, 19 September. By this time he had already committed the Bank to 'the firm view' that an increase in Bank rate to 7 per cent on 19 September was desirable. And judging from the timing of the interviews[16] with these three directors, the 'consultation' can have amounted to little more than informing them of the decision.

The City's view of the economic situation in the summer of 1957

As has already been stated, there is little information in the evidence about the kind of diagnosis of the economic situation which was made in the Treasury or in the Bank in the summer of 1957, but there are many revealing statements by witnesses from the City about their view of the economic situation at the time, and their opinion of the government's handling of it.

One can give only a selection of the views expressed, but the following seem representative:

Mr W. J. Keswick, in a letter in September to Mr Hugh Barton, Managing Director of Jardine Matheson & Co., Hong Kong: 'I

[16] He saw Mr Cadbury at 2.10 and Sir Alfred Roberts at 2.20 p.m.

believe the trade figures are dreadful, and one hears on all sides ugly rumours about devaluation' [3850].

Mr H. J. Young, recalling a statement about the financial position of Britain by Mr W. J. Keswick at a meeting on September 16: 'As far as I can remember, he mentioned the adverse balance of trade, the loss of dollars . . .' [3339].

Lord Kindersley, recalling his attitude at a meeting on 28 August: 'I only wanted to say that I had just arrived back from Canada. I had left it three days earlier because I was really worried by the attitude of Canadian bankers towards the pound sterling in general, towards our inability to stop the wage spiral, and our ineffective (if I may say so) government at the time' [7343].

Mr H. R. Roberts, senior assistant general manager of the Royal Exchange Assurance Company, replied 'That, I am afraid, is what I thought' in answer to the following question: 'Were your own thoughts on the matter on more general lines, and did you rather come—so you say—to the conclusion that the situation was getting out of hand and that the government either did not know what to do to put it right, or if they did know they thought it would be politically inexpedient to do it?' [7030].

Mr C. A. S. Cooper, investment secretary to the Royal Exchange Assurance Company: 'While on holiday[17] did you do your best to keep yourself well informed on financial matters?' 'I did.' 'While on holiday did you study the press and especially the financial columns of the press?' 'I did.' 'Did you form a view while you were on holiday about the situation?' 'I did.' 'I think you have said that you formed the view that Her Majesty's Government's handling of the situation was inadequate?' 'I certainly did' [6578–6581].

The impression created by these statements and similar ones by other witnesses from the City is that City opinion was very much influenced in its view by superficial evidence about the economic situation, and by general opinion here and overseas of the economic state of the country. For the purposes of their own affairs, this may have been sufficient. No deep analysis of the longer-run economic situation is needed to support the conclusion that if others seem to be worried about the economic situation and do not have confidence in the government's handling of it, there may be a crisis, and it is as well to be prepared for it by being liquid.

[17] From 28 August to 16 September.

Nonetheless it is somewhat surprising that not a single witness who gave evidence before the tribunal appeared to be aware that the underlying trading position of this country was, for the time being anyway, surprisingly good, and that the balance of payments on current account was expected to be substantially favourable in the second half of the year 1957.[18] There had, it is true, been discussion throughout the summer about the menace of continuing inflation, and fears had been expressed in many quarters about what would happen to the balance of payments if inflation continued at the same pace into 1958. It looks as if when speculation against sterling started in the summer and the foreign exchange reserves began to drain away, many people in the City immediately jumped to the conclusion that this was because our wage costs were getting out of hand, that the government had not the courage to do anything about it, and so our trade position was deteriorating; and speculation against the pound was merely making the position worse. One wonders, for example, whether Lord Kindersley in his discussions with Canadian and United States bankers, which he frequently referred to in his evidence, explained, when they expressed such concern about the future of sterling, that the trading position of this country was really very strong, and that the pressure against sterling was almost wholly speculative?

Yet one must be careful in suggesting that the City as a whole was by its own sense of disquiet contributing to the speculation against sterling for which wicked Continental bankers are usually blamed! The witnesses who appeared before the tribunal were from this point of view a biased sample. They were in fact called to give evidence because they had been concerned with sales of gilt-edged during the crucial period. To give the right balance, it is perhaps appropriate to quote the following statement made by the Governor of the Bank: 'The surprising thing to me was that there was not very much heavier selling and more disquiet in the City at the time.'[19]

The City's view of the importance and effectiveness of Bank rate as an instrument of policy

It has often been argued that although changes in Bank rate and other interest rates may have negligible direct effect on economic

[18] In the event there was a favourable balance on current account of £154 million in the second half of 1957, and of £272 million for the year 1957.

[19] 16 and 17 September.

activity, yet they do exercise a substantial indirect effect by operating as a danger signal, a warning light, to the business community. On this view a dramatic increase in Bank rate might be important, not only to impress overseas speculators that the government means to defend sterling but also to convince the business community at home that the government really means to take charge of the economic situation. It is interesting, therefore, to examine what importance witnesses attached to a change in Bank rate. The following represent some important expressions of opinion on this point.

Lord Kindersley: 'No. I thought the other side of the argument, what the government were going to do, what the government would say, and what they would say about spending and how they would face up to wages in the nationalised industries, was more important than Bank rate, and I would not have liked to have seen the Bank rate raised without something like that going with it' [7397].

Mr J. V. O. Macartney-Filgate (a managing director of Lazard's): 'The opinion I formed was that, if any steps were taken, it was more likely to be a restriction of hire-purchase, further credit restriction, a general tightening up. I did not expect Bank rate to go up, although I thought it might be added to the general programme. I could not see that it was going to do any good' [5924].

Mr D. Meinertzhagen (a managing director of Lazard's): 'Because I did not believe that Bank rate by itself was a solution to our problems, and I did not know what other measures the government might take to deal with the situation. I recognised that some of them might involve a rise in Bank rate, but I looked upon Bank rate as a subsidiary matter to other measures which government might take' [6088].

Sir George Bolton (director of the Bank of England, member of the Committee of Treasury, and executive director from 1948 to February 1957): 'If the only information reaching foreign markets had been the possibility of a sharp rise in the Bank rate, in my opinion it might have had even an adverse effect on sterling, certainly not a good one' [8443].

Dr Hans Hock (a managing director of Singer & Friedlander, merchant bankers): 'How can the Chancellor,' I said, 'face his fellow bankers in Washington unless he does the maximum he can do at home? In fact I never thought of Bank rate. I thought of general financial measures' [8165]. Attorney-General: 'But the maximum he could do at home would comprise raising the Bank rate, would it not?' Dr Hock: 'It would be one of the possible measures. In fact it is well known in the City that the Governor does not trust Bank rate as a weapon in fighting inflation. He has said so at the last Bankers' dinner and he gave reasons why he did think it was not effective. I therefore thought much more in terms of some monetary measures with the intention of mopping up surplus liquidity of the banks' [8166].

If the statements of these gentlemen reflected a wider City opinion, then, at the time at least, confidence in Bank rate as an instrument of policy did not seem to be running very high.

The basis of decision taking

Many witnesses were asked by the tribunal to give an account of their sales of gilt-edged during the crucial days before the Bank rate increase, and were pressed to give an explanation of the reasons for their decision to sell. We have here, therefore, one of the rare occasions when business men were asked to explain in public the basis on which they took their decisions.

The cases before the tribunal fall roughly into two categories. First, those cases, mostly on a small scale, where someone, acting on behalf of his firm or on his own account, took a particular short-run view of the market and decided to sell. Second, the cases where a major decision was taken in a substantial business to sell gilt-edged on an appreciable scale in order to secure more liquid funds. It is the second set of cases that is more interesting, for here we see an attempt by witnesses to explain how they came to decide that they needed to be more liquid and the scale of selling that they thought necessary to meet the situation.

The important transactions were by Matheson & Co., Lazard Frères & Co., and the Royal Exchange Assurance. In each of these cases the Attorney-General, in trying to discover the basis of the decision to sell, cross-examined the witnesses in great detail about the operations of the firm, quoting detailed figures of transactions, deposits, etc. In nearly all cases, witnesses found it difficult to justify decisions in terms of this kind of detailed analysis of figures, and were inclined to fall back on statements about a general feeling or sense that it was the appropriate thing to do. The following are some examples of this.

Mr A. D. Marris (a managing director of Lazard's): 'What I think I would say in answer to your questions is that it is not just the relationship between call money and deposits that one has to take into account; one has to take into account acceptances as well. One plays this tune according to ear, and if you think the waves are running high you tend to want to get liquid, and I thought our deposits were low and we ought to get more liquid. It was not a considered judgment about percentages, I am afraid' [6916].

Mr J. V. O. Macartney-Filgate (a managing director of Lazard's): 'Yes, I think that reasoning is correct, but of course all this money which was going out and which, on the whole, was what I would call commercial money or quick-turnover money, was probably being accompanied by money coming up again for purely commercial purposes. If I wanted to sort of analyse the impact of the whole of that I would have to do quite a lot of research.' Q: 'And you did not do it in this case?' 'I did not do it because, as I say, one felt what was going on' [5920 and 5921].

Mr T. H. Brand (a managing director of Lazard's): 'You see, it is really—I do not want to overstate it, but it is an intolerable nuisance to have to look at these deposits and liquidity figures in my mind. They should not crop up, particularly at a time when you are busy on other things. I hate the position where we begin to, shall I say, sell gilt-edged once a week, and that kind of thing. It may be more personal than otherwise, but I am sure that is not the way banking business should be conducted if you are free to sell. You may be pushed into it' [5541].

Mr W. J. Keswick: 'I do not think there was anything provisional about it.[20] I think that we came to, or, if I may put it this way, we drifted to the decision that it was inevitable that we should recommend the sale of gilts' [4342].

Some minor points

Apart from the major issues of economic interest discussed so far, there are a large number of small points of information in the

[20] The decision to sell.

evidence about the working of the City, some of which are summarised below:

1. After-hours dealing in gilt-edged seems to be fairly widespread. One of the reasons given for this is that boards frequently meet in the afternoon and take decisions about their investments. Jobbers quote more cautiously after 3.30 because they are less closely in touch with movements on the floor, and in the ordinary run of gilt-edged the difference in price quoted might be as much as one-sixteenth [1904–8].
2. The gilt-edged market is not as 'perfect' as is usually represented in textbooks. Jobbers' quotations are for a 'normal quantity', ideas about what is 'normal' varying with circumstances, but usually for between £50,000–£100,000 of stock. For larger quantities the jobber quotes a special price and would usually know *before* quoting a price whether the enquiry was for a sale or purchase. In one example given by Mr Hunter (a partner in the stockbroking firm of L. Messel & Co.), he was able to get a price of 96⅝ for £50,000 of 3 per cent Exchequer stock, but only 96¼ for £500,000 [2065–9 and 4869–71].
3. The government broker never deals on behalf of the Bank of England on a Thursday morning before the Bank rate announcement.
4. The Capital Issues Committee grants approval for an issue upon the condition that the date of the issue has to be fixed with the consent of the Bank of England [7762].
5. The membership of the Committee of Treasury of the Bank of England, which meets each Wednesday to decide on what recommendation about Bank rate to make to the Court on the following day, was as follows in 1957: the Governor, the Deputy Governor, Lord Bicester, Sir John Hanbury-Williams, Basil Sanderson and Sir George Bolton. Lord Kindersley was not a member and explained why in the following statement: 'Because I am governor of the Royal Exchange and we hold our courts at the same time as they hold their Treasury Committee, and I would have to retire from the Royal Exchange if I was to go on to the Treasury Committee, and I would prefer not to' [7557].
6. The declaration made by every member of the staff of the Bank on appointment, the rule with regard to secrecy which all staff

have to sign, and the declaration signed by the agent of a branch, are given in full [8390, 8394 and 8397]. It is hardly surprising in view of these that one hears so little, except on such an occasion as the Bank Rate Tribunal, about how things are managed in the Bank of England.

[14]

Economic theory and economic policy[1]

The relation between economic theory and economic policy—how far economics can usefully help and guide issues of economic policy —is a difficult and complex question. What I have to say will not be a coherent and fully rounded treatment of the subject but merely a few disconnected comments on some aspects of this problem, which have exercised my mind lately. And I must apologise in advance for the roughness and inadequacy of these comments.

I want first of all to deal with an attitude which I shall call naive perfectionism—an attitude which you can gather from the name I have given it to be both misleading and dangerous. The naive perfectionism which I have in mind proceeds by constructing a theoretical model of an economic system without at any stage worrying too much about how far the model corresponds with or explains the real economic world. Having constructed such a model, the author or authors look at the real world and discover with horror that it does not correspond with the model. The conclusion then is —and here is the yawning gap in the argument—that the world must be made to correspond with the model. This method of relating economic theory to policy may lead either to advocacy of *laisser-faire* policy or to planning according to the nature of the model and political predilections of the authors. The *laisser-faire* modelists concoct a system which in theory seems to work wonderfully well and then proceed to argue that if only the government will make the correct institutional arrangements—e.g. by anti-monopoly legislation or 'neutral money'—the real economic world can be made to behave like the model. The planner's model is of a rather different

[1] This paper, in an earlier form, was given to the Nottingham Students' Society in March 1952. I have not been able to trace the occasion for which the version printed here was drafted, but it was probably later in 1952.

variety. He shows how in theoretical terms there may be impediments in the way of relating the 'optimum' situation—social costs, indivisibilities, the tendency away from equilibrium, etc—to a theoretical model of maladjustment in the system. But he also proceeds to argue that the government can be brought in to deal with theoretical maladjustments and to bring reality into conformity with a more perfect model: government location policy can take account of social costs, government nationalisation policy can deal with those industries where, because of indivisibilities, monopoly is inevitable and so on—in other words, that the government can bring about a reality which conforms to the model of planning theory.

Both these procedures, although they arrive at opposite conclusions, seem to me to be very much akin in that they both proceed by constructing a model of a perfect economic system which they wish to bring into being by forcing reality to behave in accordance with their model. They both wish to bring heaven on earth, and both regard this as a fairly easy proposition: the obstacles are evil, stupid, ignorant government, or evil, grasping businessmen, according to whichever view you take. On either view the main problem is to get rid of evil.

You may well say that you know of no economist who takes either of these naive views of the relation between theory and policy. And no doubt I have exaggerated—and purposely so—to make my point. But I still feel that the method, and indeed the language of economic theory, trap innocent students of economics into this snare very early in their study of economics. The notion of the 'optimum distribution of resources' which appears so often in general equilibrium theory easily leads the unwary student to jump to the conclusion that this is how the economic world ought to be made to behave. The notion of the optimum size of firms and the theory of marginal cost and price lead the unwary student easily to the conclusion that this is how a sensible businessman ought to behave. Indeed, the theory seems to the student at first sight to be so logical and rational that he often finds it difficult to understand how a businessman can behave otherwise than in accordance with the theory—unless, of course, he is stupid, ignorant and inefficient. And so if it can be shown that he does not behave in accordance with the precepts of the theory, the obvious conclusion is that one must get rid of him. Even the businessman is now caught in this snare, for if you invite him to explain how he runs his business he will first of all read a book on economics and then serve you up a garbled version of economic theory.

I consider this approach to the relation between theory and policy to be highly misleading and dangerous. I prefer to approach the whole subject from an entirely different point of view, which seems to me to be much more logical and also less likely to lead to the same wild axioms for economic policy that arise from the naive perfectionist approach. To me, economic theory is an attempt not to construct a model of what the perfect economic system would look like, but to explain the actual workings of an economic system. Any divergence between the model and reality would lead therefore not to the immediate conclusion that the model is in some sense right and that the reality is wrong and must be forced or induced to fit the model, but on the contrary to our asking cautiously how far our model gives us understanding of reality. This is the old-fashioned attitude to economic theory—what was known in my days as a student as positive economics. I shall leave unanswered for the time being how one proceeds from understanding to action, a gap which many people assume can be easily bridged. I will merely assert at this stage that there is no warranty for assuming that understanding, of itself, gives you power to act and control: in some circumstances, understanding may do the contrary (think of astronomy, here no one would claim that understanding gives power to control). If one understands, for example, the reasons for the imperfections in the economic system, the understanding may lead one to be able to act to remove or minimise the imperfections; or on the contrary may lead one to believe that the imperfections are of the essence of the system and that nothing can be done about removing them. *A priori* there is no reason for believing one rather than the other conclusion to emerge from understanding.

Leaving on one side for the moment the nature of the link between understanding and action, let me try and explain my view of the sort of understanding of the real world which economic theory gives us—or to a substantial extent can ever hope to give us. I find it easiest to approach this problem in rather negative terms, by looking at some of the things that economic theory does not do. First of all, economic theory deals with the general and not with the particular—this is what distinguishes it from economic history —so that whether it be the theory of price, or the firm, foreign trade or money it is characterised by its generality: this is indeed what makes it a theory. In addition it is, and must continue to remain, largely a qualitative generality. And this generality largely consists in showing how any part of what we call 'the economic system' is related to every other part. In other words, it shows us the interconnectedness of all the different parts of economic life. And it does this most successfully by constructing a price system in theory in which we can see how every part is related to every other part. This enables us to envisage how the whole thing 'hangs together' when we think of the system as a whole, or the function that each individual part plays and how a change in it will affect the rest of the system when we are looking at a small part.

Now there are many things about such a system which need to be kept in mind when we are trying to see how far it gives us understanding of the real world. There is nothing in the system itself which can tell us whether the world works like this. All that the system tells us is that 'this is how an economic system would work if an economic system worked like this'. We must therefore beware of forcing the world conceptually into this system and then thinking that we understand it. It is easy for economists to slip into the position of thinking they understand, whereas all they are doing is to pick out and distort reality until it fits into their picture. How, then, can we tell whether the system which we construct does in fact explain real events? It can be done in either of two ways. First, by seeing if, when we use this system to understand the real world, we feel it helps us; here it must be admitted that large parts of economic theory are at present not very helpful. Second, by asking whether the assumptions that the theory makes correspond with reality; this is not a very fruitful exercise, for since economics is concerned only with aspects of behaviour it would be surprising indeed if we found our assumptions corroborated. What we have to ask is whether the assumptions we make are an important element in reality, and this is much more difficult to test.

By its very nature, this kind of theory can deal only with consistent behaviour, since it would clearly be impossible to draw up a general system which portrays inconsistency. This means that theory can give us an understanding only of the general and consistent and not of the particular, individual, peculiar and inconsistent. This leads to two further qualifications to the understanding that economic theory gives us. First, it can be of little help in understanding those parts of economic behaviour where the peculiar and individual is more significant than the general: contrast the unsatisfactory nature of the theory of location or the firm with the theory of money or foreign trade. Also, even where it explains the general, it can give us an understanding only of general interconnectedness, and not of the particular interconnectedness at any point of time. This means that many branches of economic theory either consist of platitudes—e.g., in location theory, that firms will go where, from the point of view of markets, labour supply, etc, it seems best for them to go—or have to yield to economic history, as is often done in the so-called theory of location.

Even where the explanations are not platitudes, they are not very helpful in explaining any particular situation. Take, for example, the explanation contained in economic theory of the foreign exchange rate in the United Kingdom in 1949. All that the economic theory will do for us is explain the functional position of the foreign exchange rate as one price among a whole series of prices that are interconnected with each other. It will 'explain' the foreign exchange rate by tracing the network of this interconnectedness, distinguishing between those factors which are closely and those which are remotely connected in this way. Having drawn this pattern, we say we understand the foreign exchange rate in terms either of the function it performs—how changes in it will affect the balance of payments—or in terms of the other factors in the economic system—the level of prices at home and overseas, the extent of capital movements, etc, which determine it. But the moment we attempt to explain why the foreign exchange rate is what it is, either in terms of the quantitative significance of the web of interconnectedness—by how much a change of 10 per cent in overseas prices or a change of 5 per cent in wage rates at home will affect the foreign exchange rate—or why the foreign exchange rate in 1949 was 4·02 compared with 4·86 in 1939, we are lost. The understanding which theory gives us is, then, very much restricted. How much more restricted must our theory be in helping economic policy, in deciding what to change the exchange rate to, when we not only need to understand the factors determining it in quantitative terms but also need to forecast what will happen in the future to the various factors—e.g. the level of prices in the US—which will influence it.

Another aspect of the generality of economic theory is that, as at present taught, it is timeless and spaceless. By this I do not mean that we have no theory of economic development (although I for one don't think we can have one: it is the same will and the same wisp as is chased by some historians in trying to find laws of history); I mean that it is not related to any particular period of history or to any group of countries. The same elements of economics are taught in Egypt as in England, in Australia as in the United States, in Canada as in India. And although we may learn and teach a different economic theory from that taught fifty years ago, many economists approach this change not as a change due to the need to explain an economic society different from that existing fifty years ago, but merely as an intellectual advance such as has occurred in the natural sciences, where one can assume that the data being studied remain unchanged.

One can justify this universality in both time and space of the understanding which economic theory gives us by asserting that the fundamentals of economic life which economic theory seeks to explain or understand don't change and are little influenced by changing political and social organisation. I for one would be prepared to argue that this view is mistaken, but I shall have to resist chasing that particular hare. Or one can say that although social and political organisation have their importance they cannot easily be taken into account in economic theory, and that for this reason economic theory is limited to what is timeless and spaceless.

But if this is so the understanding which economic theory gives us must vary according to the importance of the role that political and social organisation in fact play in influencing economic phenomena. So the quantity theory of money will explain the phenomenon of inflation, whether it occurs in medieval England, modern Germany or a Central African tribe, because in relation to this particular phenomenon the particular form of social and political organisation seems to be of secondary importance. But the theory of wages in its most abstract terms (which merely tell you that, given mobility and knowledge, different occupations will have the same net advantages), although formally applicable to all societies, does not help you to understand the structure of wages in any particular society at any time. For the statement is so general as to become a platitude. To understand what determines the structure of money wages in any society at any time—and I take it that as economists that is what we wish to explain—we would need to appreciate the extent of the influence of non-monetary factors in making up the net advantages: that, for example, in certain societies at certain times white-collar occupations are preferred (if this be true). The extent of ignorance and immobility and their influence means that we can only explain the existing structure of wages, not in a general or universal theory, but in terms of what the structure has been in the past, i.e. in terms of economic history.

This contrast which I have drawn between the theory of inflation and the theory of wages has, of course, implications for the problem of the uses of these two points of economic theory in problems of policy. It will be seen that the quantity theory of money may have considerable importance in enabling a government to understand the implications of its monetary policy; on the other hand, it is difficult to see what use the theory of wages can be as long as it is expressed in general, universal terms and therefore has nothing to say about the significance or quantitative importance in the wage structure of immobility, ignorance or the social standing of occupations, let alone of the effect of a particular state of trade union organisation.

This point is often dismissed by saying that, although quite true, this is an unfair criticism of economics, since it cannot be expected and does not attempt to explain all aspects of social behaviour, that it must stop somewhere and should not attempt to explain political and social behaviour, that these must be left to other students who make these other aspects of social behaviour their special field of study. This, although true—and, of course, another and the normally obvious reason why economic theory cannot help directly in economic policy, for all economic policy is political and social at the same time—is not really relevant to the point I am making. My point is the rather more limited one that it is possible to explain only a limited group of economic phenomena in economic terms as normally understood, that others have to be explained in terms of political, social and religious behaviour; and since these aspects of behaviour cannot easily be explicable in terms of general laws, the economic explanation has to change continuously with the changing political and social context.

This leads me to another peculiar feature of economic theory which limits its usefulness when we come to try and apply it in policy. Although the theory deals with a social phenomenon (Robinson Crusoe economics can be used to explain some—but only the most elementary—principles of theory) and stresses the importance of such 'social' phenomena as division of labour, price, and organised markets, yet the structure concocted by theory does not portray a society at work; the economic aspect of life exists, so to speak, in a vacuum. It is true that a government is sometimes mentioned, but usually only in the theory of public finance. This means that the economic system is thought of as working atomistically or even automatically: so to speak, by nature and not within a particular social setting.

It follows almost automatically—although dangerously—from this that when we seek to use the theory to understand or explain reality we overlook the fact that the economic system works within a general social system, and that the working of the economic aspect of the system depends on how the system as a whole works. An economic system cannot, for example, be expected to work harmoniously in a general system which is full of conflict. That this is overlooked in economic theory can be seen from the fact that all the systems created by economic theory work harmoniously. It is true that theoretical systems sometimes portray disequilibrium, but none of them has room for, or takes account of, conflict. The moment we look at the real world we realise that this is not true: that, since economic phenomena are merely one aspect of social phenomena, to understand how the society 'ticks' will involve taking account of the overall social setting. So when we come to attempt to explain or understand the determinants of the general level of economic activity, or the forces making for inflation, we immediately begin to ask questions, for example about the attitude of trade unions. It is true that many economists would regard an inquiry into what determines trade union policy as outside the field of economics, but is it not just as important a determinant of the general price level as, say, banking policy? Certainly, if economic theory ignores it, the government, and economists themselves when they come to write on current issues, have to take it into account in diagnosing a particular economic situation; and it is obviously one of the most important elements in the government's economic policy.

I cannot resist mentioning one other important aspect of the peculiar nature of the understanding which we get from economic theory. This arises from the fact that what we are trying to understand in economics are not objective, unchanging phenomena which we can regard in some way as having an independent existence, as the natural scientist does. We are studying something which is a result of the interplay between ourselves and our natural surroundings. Our understanding of the economic system inevitably leads to our changing or attempting to change it, and unless you take the view that economic phenomena, even in their social aspects, are so determined that we can do nothing to alter them, that however much we alter institutions and politics the fundamentals are unchanged, our economic system is bound to reflect in some measure our understanding of it. This must mean that it is an ever-changing thing which we must seek to understand.

There is a tendency to confine economic theory to an attempt to understand a particular type of economic system as if this, although no longer closely resembling in outward appearance the economic reality we see around us, still in some fundamental sense continues to underlie the economic world in which we live. The phenomena that result from government action in all its multifarious forms continue to be regarded as excrescences merely obstructing, impeding or correcting the workings of more fundamental forces. Although we pay considerable attention to the implications of the actions of individuals and firms in such matters as the theory of price, we pay little attention to the implications of government actions. It may of course be true that the particular technique of economic theory cannot cope with the activities of government, since essentially that theory must assume an element of rationality and consistency in action. Whatever the reason, a theory that continues to be based virtually on the assumption that the government does not exist, or merely has the ring-holding function, cannot hope to give us much understanding of the real world in which government action plays such an important part. Curiously enough, even the government itself continues to rely on explanations given by this limited theory. For although it interferes with prices and the allocation of resources in all directions, it continues to assume that prices have the significance imputed to them in economic theory. It may be argued that this is a field for the student of politics and administration to study, but he certainly doesn't do so. We cannot, for example, rely on him to give us any sort of explanation of what determines government investment policy.

But I must at last explain how all this is related to economic policy, for you will realise that I continue to avoid building a bridge of argument between understanding and policy. Here I am afraid that what I have to say you will think weak and vague in the extreme. I proceed first of all to the conclusion which seems to me to emerge most clearly from my argument: that the understanding which theory—even where one can be assured of its correctness—gives us of reality is very limited, and that because of this limitation we can never proceed from the understanding which theory by itself gives us to make pronouncements about policy. The sort of argument, for example, which examines retail distribution in terms of theory, comes to the conclusion that this is a case of imperfect competition and therefore of misuse of resources, and immediately proceeds to argue that distribution should be rationalised or nationalised, seems to me to be jumping many stages of argument. Many of the so-called applications of theoretical understanding take this simplified form. Obviously, much more is needed for real understanding than is given by economic theory.

It is indeed curious that the economic theorist, who is supposedly trained to understand the interconnectedness of things, ignores the interconnectedness of the economic and non-economic aspects of social organisation. We are not likely, in my view, to be able to extend our understanding by developing economic theory along the path it has taken in the last fifty years. For we do not approach a theory which is more closely related to the real world merely by making the theory more complex. We must recognise that the approach of economic theory, however complex it becomes, will necessarily be limited, enabling us to gain insight merely into the general and universal aspects of economic life. To gain a wider and deeper understanding we have to join to theory a study of economic history (most empirical studies in economics are merely recent economic history), politics and administration, if not of sociology.

And let us beware of under-estimating the importance of the understanding which this historical approach gives us compared with the theory. The theory always fascinates the student because of its generality. It seems to be something firm, if not clear, to get hold of; when he has grasped it he feels he has really understood something which he didn't understand before. But ask yourself how important the theory is when you come to attempt to understand the affairs of the coal industry in this country today. How much more important it is to know something of the particular, peculiar facts about the coal-mining industry, for example its history, its present structure, the attitude of the miners and why it is what it is—whatever it really is, the policy of the Coal Board, and so on: everything that you get from steeping yourself in facts about the coal industry, using the economic theory in the background, not even as a technique of analysis but merely as a general framework within which to arrive at your understanding! Understanding is none the less understanding merely because it cannot be expressed in terms of universal laws or principles.

Given that theory helps policy only in that it gives understanding of what determines a particular economic situation, it has therefore a relatively minor role. And once we proceed to the next stage of attempting to elucidate the implications, that is, the effects of any particular line of policy, theory recedes even further into the background; for the understanding I have in mind in fact gives little capacity for forecasting. Since it attempts to understand mainly by the historical method in terms of the peculiar and individual situation—that is, what explains the economic situation in the United Kingdom here and now—it thinks of each situation as peculiar in itself, and the peculiar cannot be foretold. It can of course enumerate the various effects that a particular policy will have in terms of the general interconnectedness explanation, but little more. Or it can pretend to forecast the effects of a given set of policies in terms of a series of assumptions about the exact nature of the way the interconnections will affect each other in the future. But that is no more than saying that this is the way the policy will work out in practice if in fact the policy works out like this.

[15]
Economists and the public[1]

The public attitude to economists is schizophrenic and ambivalent: sometimes awesome and respectful, sometimes sneering and sceptical. Economists are alternately revered and reviled; praised and parodied; worshipped and cursed; ardently consulted as high priests of esoteric knowledge; derided as purveyors of witch-doctor astrology. The irritation and frustration of the public with economists are succinctly expressed in the jibe: 'where there are two economists there will be three opinions'.

What accounts for this situation? Is there hope of modifying it, either by changes in the way in which economists put their ideas before the public, or by educating the public to appreciate more clearly what the role of the economist is, or should be, in public debate on economic issues?

Theory and reality

The general public comes into contact with economics and economists when the latter write and speak in attempts to explain economic problems and, very frequently, out of this explanation, to recommend some particular action, or lack of action, in public policy.

Strictly speaking, economics as such, it is often said by the academics, is concerned not with recommending action but merely with understanding the working of the economic system and, where possible, explaining the consequences of alternative lines of action and policy. On this view, economics is scientifically and dispassionately neutral. Even the London School of Economics—which has a

[1] From *Lloyds Bank Review*, No. 77, July 1965. Based on one of the John Hinkley Memorial Lectures delivered at Johns Hopkins University, Baltimore, in November 1964.

reputation for producing social scientists, including economists, fired with missionary zeal to put the world right—has as its motto *rerum cognoscere causas*, 'to understand the causes of things', not 'reform the world' or 'get things done'. It must be admitted, however, that the founders of that institution—the Webbs and the Fabians—were innocently and naively confident that a truly scientific understanding of society would inevitably lead to only one conclusion for action.

Yet the very language of the analytical method in economics is hardly conducive to this neutrality. Consider some of the terms which are the basic language of economic analysis and the systems it creates: perfection and imperfection; rational and irrational; efficient and inefficient; mobile and immobile; optimum and sub-optimum; equilibrium and disequilibrium. This language and process of analysis itself implies—unless watched with painstaking care and humility—criteria for a 'better' compared with a 'worse' economic system. Of course, systems of analysis created in this way have extensive elements of abstraction and very often do not correspond at all closely with reality. But how easy it is, once an 'economic system' has been created in these terms, for the creators, Pygmalion-like, to fall in love with their creations. Should one be surprised if some economists, looking at the world with all its glaring imperfections, disequilibria, inefficiencies and irrationalities, should wish to transform it to correspond more closely to their beautiful creations?

The contrast between imperfect reality and the dream of perfection which impresses so many economists does not lead them all to the same conclusion about how to bring about this transformation. They are divided by a difference of view, held with almost theological fervour, about the cause of the imperfections, and therefore about the way in which perfection is to be achieved. There are those who see all vice in government intervention, all virtue in what is colourfully called 'the natural working' of the economic system. To these, the price system in the market is a thing of beauty, marred in its working only by the stupidities of politicians and administrators. Eliminate government intervention and 'the natural order' will be restored. Against those who believe in perfection through the restoration and preservation of what they call 'the natural order' are those who see vice, chaos, inefficiency and irrationality in such an unruly and unruled system, and propose by social control, through government, to bring about the change to perfection. It is ironical, but I think revealing, that the model of the perfect economic system which is the Utopia of the priests both of the market and of planning is remarkably similar: in one case given by nature, in the other imposed by man with the aid of government and the electronic computer. With the same model of the perfect economic system, the two schools hold completely opposed views as to how to bring perfection into being.

Both these systems of thought are, in my view, abuses of economic analysis, misleading the public into dangerous blind alleys. Fortunately, the lunatic fringe at either extreme has lost influence in the last few years, and the slogans implying that the perfect economic system can be brought into being either by a return to nature or through the sweeping and revolutionary operations of government no longer have the same mesmerising effect on the public which they had thirty years ago.

But the language and methods of economic analysis, still proceeding in terms of models of perfection or aberrations therefrom, continue to have an influence on economists and their relations with the public. The young student of economics, educated and trained in this technique, easily falls into the snare of thinking that he knows the answer to most of his country's economic problems. Only the avarice of business, the stupidity of trade unions, the conservatism of bankers, the vested interests of minority groups or the pusillanimity of politicians apparently prevent the correct remedies being adopted. How often have I read answers by students in examinations explaining quite briefly, but with unconscious certitude, what exactly the Chancellor of the Exchequer should do to cure Britain's balance-of-payments troubles, or the government and the Board of Trade should do to make industry more efficient and progressive! The suggestion that these may be difficult questions to which there are no easy, simple answers rarely appears. And the fault is not the students' but mainly the teachers'. For the student is encouraged, by the very formulation of the analysis and the questions he is asked, to believe that problems can be dealt with in a simple, straightforward manner if only economists—the right kind of economists, of course—were in charge. Is it any wonder that when such young men go out into business or Whitehall the arrogance which they display about their capacity to put the world right should frequently infuriate their employers?

Changing fashions

It may be protested, by the younger economists in particular, that all this is out of date: the economics of twenty or thirty years ago. Since then we have largely left general 'models', with their normative implications, and are more sensible and realistic in clothing and testing our theories with data from the real world. I admit this, but it is still true that there is a lack of humility, even in empirical analysis, in pressing claims for the relevance to policy of the latest academic exercises.

Economics is about human affairs, and there is a natural tendency for any economist searching for new truths to be excited by the possibility that his theories may have some relevance to the problems that worry his or some other society. That he may be rash in assuming relevance too quickly on inadequate evidence is an understandable failing. The new empirical economics has been much subject to this failing, at least in Britain. After the war, for example, exercises—apparently convincing exercises—were done showing that investment was the main determinant of economic progress, and that the pace of economic advance was slow in the UK because of inadequate investment. This became the fashionable explanation purveyed to the public. Soon, however, with little evidence that increased investment under government encouragement made much difference, research and development expenditure was seized on as the important variable. And this, in turn, has given way to the latest fashion, in which education is shown to be the prime mover. The speed at which fashion changes in current theory, as each bright researcher picks holes in the prevailing mythology, is quite staggering. Yet, at each stage, the 'new look' is put forward with the arrogant certainty that this time the theory is really right and capable of being taken as a guide-post to action.

Advanced countries are able to absorb this mercurial change in suggested remedies without too much difficulty or harm. But in under-developed countries the situation is pitiful. These countries receive ever-changing diagnosis and advice from the peripatetic group of economists tripping from one to the other giving them the benefit of the latest advances in the so-called theories of economic growth and economic development. In all this, there seems to be a recklessness in putting forward newly formulated but untried theories as guides to policy. Even before they have been fully worked out, they are handed over to or seized on by administrators or politicians as the basis of plans for action.

Contributions of economics

So far, the tenor of this article has implied that the puzzlement and frequent irritation of the public with economics and economists are the fault of the profession: that economists claim too much, prescribe rather than explain, propound answers rather than elucidate problems, and naively but arrogantly assume all too readily the applicability to the real world of the beautiful theoretical models which they use in their researches. If this were all, my answer would be simple. It would be to send the economist back to his study to do more work before inflicting his explanations on the public; and to advise the public to wait patiently until more reliable diagnosis and advice are available. But this is by no means all. There are many spheres of policy where economists have made, and are making, significant, even crucial, contributions to action. Indeed, it is mainly because of this that economists are listened to more and more. And in any case, the public is not prepared to wait patiently for the fruits of further research and study; answers are demanded, here and now, to some of the more difficult and searching problems of the day.

The contribution that economics has made, both to public understanding and policy, in the area of employment policy can hardly be overrated. It would not be an exaggeration to say that—the nuclear bomb apart—the greatest contrast between post-war and pre-war is the abolition of large-scale unemployment and of the violent swings of economic activity. This is among the major revolutions of our time. When one thinks of the atmosphere of strain, social conflict and incipient and actual revolution which was so characteristic of the 1930's, one must marvel at the miraculous change that has taken place. Certainly any economist in the 1930's, or even in 1945, would have regarded as a pipe dream a forecast, or hope, that in the twenty years after the war unemployment in the United Kingdom would not exceed 2½ per cent on average in any one year, and would normally be lower. To my mind, most of the credit for this revolution must go to economics and, *au fond*, to abstract economic analysis, and to the gentle and deliberate way in which economists have educated politicians, administrators and the general public.

It would be a mistake to believe that we now understand the workings of the economy so well that we can forever escape from having an unemployment rate higher than we have experienced since the war. In many ways, our capacity to contain heavy unemployment has not really been tested yet. But I do maintain that we have now a measure of understanding that should enable us to avoid the disasters of the 1930's. If we do experience them again, it will not be through lack of understanding. We ought no longer to expect the utter bewilderment, bafflement, perplexity and intellectual despair which was so characteristic of that period, To have brought about this change is no mean achievement. It is at least something to balance against the arrogant bearing of the economist and the confusion which, I have argued, he sometimes arouses on other matters.

Other lessons

Moreover, this major achievement of economics does not stand alone. There are other lessons the discipline of economics teaches which are of major importance to the public and which many economists continually and patiently try to explain to them. To take any one instance may make such contributions seem trivial, but this is worth risking to illustrate my point.

In England, for example, the potato crop usually starts with a few early potatoes in June, the main crop coming later in the summer from July onwards, supplies being stored for consumption throughout the winter and spring. In May and June there is often doubt whether supplies of 'old potatoes' in store will be enough until new supplies arrive. Sometimes the advent of summer and new potatoes is long delayed and stocks of old potatoes run out, whereupon the price of potatoes, both old and new, rises sharply. Then the housewives of Britain cry out at the inequities of life and the wickedness of greengrocers, and demand the intervention of the government to control supplies and prices. Along comes the economist to explain patiently how such regulation would not increase the supply of potatoes by one ounce; that at such a controlled price more would be in demand than could be supplied; that potato queueing would start, or supplies be diverted under the counter for favoured customers. So the public is introduced to an application of the so-called laws of supply and demand.

This is perhaps an example of no great moment, but it is through the accumulation of lessons of this kind that the economist makes his major contribution, not only in public debate but also in the interstices of Whitehall. Many people would be surprised at the extent to which, in discussion of a wide range of problems of government, it is the application of elementary, but none the less important, concepts of economics, rather than involved esoteric theory, that counts. It is this capacity—the capacity to use and explain simple concepts allied to a knowledge of the facts—that distinguishes the outstandingly useful and powerful contribution of the economic expert in business and government.

The political aspect

But, alas, this is not enough, either for the economists themselves or for the public. As one set of problems is solved, others, hydra-like spring up. Economists have always insisted that consumers have an infinity of wants, and that, even in the long run, over-production is merely an imaginary ogre. Whatever the truth of this, economic problems certainly seem to be capable of infinite propagation, and to their ever-renewed, even if changing, number the public demands answers, and demands them now. Many of these problems are, at present at least, unanswerable by economists. But that is hardly relevant. It merely means that they become political issues.

It has become the fashion in recent years for academics to take the hard-boiled view in their study of politics. Political philosophy, except as a catalogue of the theories of the great writers in the past, is neither taught nor much thought about. Academic political analysis sees political activity largely as the reconciliation, perhaps only occasionally successful, of the divergent vested interests in society. Legislative and administrative action must be explained, it is argued, by the pull and push of pressure groups—the farm interest, the trade union lobby, the City influence, the power of the big combines, and so on—all working through what is known as the 'old boy network'. I am not a political scientist and I hesitate to question the validity of this theory. In my—no doubt amateurish—observations of political behaviour, however, I find this theory misses a lot which has to be explained. There are occasions, maybe exceptional ones, when the politicians, executive, legislative and administrative, *are* trying to further the common interest. But in so doing they are frequently puzzled as to what that interest is and how it can be furthered. Politics is then 'the art of making decisions in relative ignorance', and our political system ensures that whatever decision a government may in its ignorance support there is an Opposition to put the opposite point of view. Indeed, I would claim that issues become political because of this ignorance, and that the political system is either a delicate or a coarse instrument, whichever way one cares to look at it, for arriving at decisions when we are in such a state of ignorance. It is, nevertheless, an essential feature of our society that we do not wish, indeed are not prepared, to acknowledge this ignorance. Rational scientific evidence is our touchstone. The arguments of both the government and the Opposition for the particular actions they propose are, therefore, couched in the language of certainty rather than of doubt.

It is here the economist appears once more. For when we are in a state of ignorance about how to deal with economic problems, they become issues of politics, and politicians are only too anxious to seize on the arguments of economists to put forward one solution rather than another. And they have no difficulty in finding such economists. It is one of the virtues, or perhaps vices, of economists that paucity of evidence is no impediment to their formulating theories and policy recommendations. Indeed, without the frustrating and irritating complexities of reality, propositions of a simple and elegant kind are much easier to formulate; and since the evidence to confirm or rebut them is often not available, they can be held and expressed with zeal akin to that of the medieval theologian. This is a godsend to the public and the politician, for it gives apparently rational and scientific support to proposals for political action.

We get, therefore, the curious and anomalous situation that where there is uncertainty in diagnosis, schools of opposing economists enter the political fray and propose remedies with dogmatic and arrogant certainty. It is rare in such situations for economists to declare that a problem is too difficult, that they do not know enough about it to make any worthwhile proposals, and so cannot help. True, there are a few who withdraw from the debate and retire into the cloistered calm of academic life. The public arena is then left to those who are prepared to support the opposing parties with pseudo-scientific argument. The danger that such argument may be recognised for what it is merely reinforces the tendency towards dogmatism. Ignorance merely increases certitude. There may be swings in fashion as to plausible scientific explanations, and deep rifts between opposing schools of thought, each maintaining its own position as correct beyond doubt. Disputes acquire the character of theological disputation, where, characteristically, opposing parties are 100 per cent certain that they have seen the light and that their opponents are in the outer darkness.

Two economic debates

Let me try to support this thesis by quoting two cases of public debate on economic problems in this country in which economists have taken great part. One is still a live issue, the other, for the time being at least, quiescent.

Growth and inflation. The first is growth and inflation. Practically every country in the world, from the richest to the poorest, is now concerned—one might say almost obsessed—with its rate of growth. That great invention of the economic statisticians, a system of social accounts (a very unusual invention, for one can, if necessary, build the social accounting bricks without straw, or even without clay), has made it possible for nearly every country to calculate its gross national product. GNP has almost become a part of everyday language. International 'league tables' of growth of GNP, or GNP per head, are compiled, and the placing of any country in the table is a matter of great concern, concern which has often—in Britain at least—been whipped up by economists. How to increase economic growth is one of the prime issues of public debate; and another 1 or 1½ per cent on the growth rate is seen as making all the difference between entering the promised land and remaining in the arid wilderness.

Let us now consider the problem that arises for policy: what effect does *employment* policy have on the growth rate? Will we achieve a higher growth rate if we operate at a level of capacity implying, say, a margin or 3 or 4 per cent unemployed, or if we operate close to the limit with, perhaps, a margin of only 1 or 1½ per cent? Here the schools divide. The first, supporting the 3–4 per cent thesis, argues that at that level the forces of competition between firms will keep them on their toes, anxious to introduce new methods, alive to innovation and technology; labour, too, to some extent fearful of unemployment, will be willing to co-operate in such ventures. Apart from this inducement to efficiency in particular firms, the economy as a whole will be more efficient: few hold-ups and bottlenecks because of shortage of stocks and particularly crucial supplies, and a reasonable distribution of investment funds between declining and contracting industries. So, the argument runs, although operating on a margin of 3–3½ per cent of spare capacity may seem a waste at any particular point of time, it enables the economy to achieve a higher long-run rate of increase in production than would otherwise be possible.

The opposing school will have none of this. With 3½ per cent unemployment and the state of the market which corresponds with this, it maintains, the businessman is so uncertain of sales that he is very cautious in his innovation and investment plans; and the worker, terrified of unemployment, will fight like a tiger, through his trade union, against any improved methods of production, including innovation, which are likely to reduce employment. This will mean, at worst, long-run stagnation, at best a very slow rate of growth. Operate at 1 or 1½ per cent unemployment, the advocates of this line of reasoning argue, and all will be changed. The employer, seeing a developing and prosperous market, will be anxious to expand and, finding labour short, will be only too ready to adopt new labour-saving devices. The worker, knowing the ease with which he could, if he wished, get another job, will be willing to see these new methods adopted. So, by operating nearer to the limit of capacity, the rate of growth of the economy will be raised.

Even if this were true, which it is not, say those in the first school, to operate at such a level of high pressure will lead to inflation and trouble with the balance of payments. The very reverse, say the others: for, with a high rate of growth and a large increase in productivity, it will be possible to promise the trade unions a bigger increase in real wages. Such a promise gives hope that the unions will agree to a wages policy which does not continuously drive up money wages beyond the rate of increase of productivity. As for the balance of payments, it is just the increase in production consequent on a higher rate of progress that will make increased exports possible. And so the ding-dong battle goes on, as between Tweedledum and Tweedledee, the policy implications of each being very different.

Now from the point of view of the argument developed in this paper, two points in all this are significant. First, the issue is a vital one for government: in its employment policy it has to decide what to aim at. Second, both schools are arguing about the issue largely in the light of ignorance. On the fundamental propositions essential to their argument, each side is speaking from a fixed position, which has very little, if any, evidence to support it. So the issue becomes a political one; and this, plus the ignorance itself, serves to sharpen the difference between the two so-called theories. In the political debate, the different parties can thus call forth support from reputable academic economists to give weighty, rational, and apparently scientific support to their conclusions.

The Common Market debate. Another example of a public debate on a topic of great economic importance, in which economists took a prominent part, is the question of Britain's entry into the European Common Market. Here again there were two schools of thought: one for, one against. Those economists who favoured Britain's entry argued that an expanded market would give our industries greater opportunities for mass production and large-scale operation, that increased competition in a free market would provide the spur to efficiency that British industry needed, and that association with the progressive, rapidly expanding economies of France, Italy and Germany would have a contagious effect on the British economy. In any case, they claimed, to stay out would have a very damaging effect on our trade with the Six, because of the discrimination there would be against us.

To these arguments the opponents of Britain's joining the Common Market had one reply: nonsense. The British market was already big enough for firms to reap all the advantages of economies of scale, they maintained, and if more competition from overseas was needed, why not lower British tariffs unilaterally? Moreover, the potential loss in trade with Europe was much exaggerated, and we should remember that if we joined the Six, Britain would have to buy her food from expensive sources on the Continent, rather than in the cheapest markets of the world.

Again, each side put forward apparently plausible arguments, but based on nothing so substantial as real evidence—the attempts made to analyse the possible effects on British trade were quite pathetic. Yet a decision had to be taken. The sheer impossibility of economics providing a conclusive answer made the issue political—it would, of course, have been a political issue anyway for non-economic reasons—and called forth a spate of apparently coherent economic arguments for and against.

Conclusion

Looked at from a detached, academic and strictly scientific point of view, in cases such as those considered above economists should say to the public, 'We are sorry, but the problem is very complicated, and we are not at all sure; indeed, anything might happen' (indeed, most economic analysis leads to this very important conclusion). There are a few economists who take this attitude, but they are usually ignored. In the Common Market debate there were a few who pointed out the difficulties of trying to assess the consequences, and phrased their analysis in what may be called 'on the one hand'–'on the other hand' terminology. But they were brushed on one side. The public has no patience with this kind of economist, who hedges his argument around with qualifications; he is suspected of evading his social responsibility. Thus the blame for this state of affairs is, in part at least, that of the public itself. It wants, it demands, clear-cut, black and white answers to problems that perplex it, and it expects the professionals to provide them.

It would be comforting to think that there was an easy remedy for this situation: that improvement could come through teaching more children economics at school, and in persuading economists to be less arrogant in their explanations to the public. This seems most unlikely to happen. We must, I think, recognise that, as long as there are difficult economic problems which economists do not altogether understand, puzzlement and frustration between the economist and the public will persist.

[16]

Decisions in ignorance[1]

In debate about public issues there are differences of view, not only because of differences in objectives and conflicts of interests, but also because when we all argue about what should be done and how it should be done we are arguing in a state of relative ignorance about how our society works and what determines its development. Yet, curiously, it is not this ignorance which is to the fore in the debate. Such is the overwhelming prestige of rational scientific analysis in our age that all remedies for action are propounded in terms of understanding and theories. Public action must be defended in rational terms, supported by evidence. We are thus in the apparently odd situation that, ignorant though we are, we demand that decisions should be taken in a rational, scientific way. Indeed, so overwhelming is this prevailing atmosphere that we will often grasp at any procedures as long as they can be dubbed scientific, in apparent unwillingness to face the harrowing alternative of recognising our ignorance. We will construct for ourselves pseudo-rational and apparently scientific systems as long as they give us a basis of confidence for action.

Let me take an example of a public issue where what I am arguing can, I think, be seen in almost pure form—the admission of students to universities. This has little to do with government, but that does not matter, since my argument applies to all decisions which have, if necessary, to be defended publicly. Indeed, the fact that it is not a political decision means that the element which I want to bring out can be seen in an uncomplicated form.

At present practically all universities get applications for admission, in many departments, from far more students than they have room for, and they have, therefore, to select among them. Few

[1] Announced as the first of four broadcast talks, this was in fact the last he was able to give (on 11 September 1965).

would now admit influence, family connections or prestige as admissible criteria for such selection. All must have the same chance, with the places going to the 'best'. And there must be a rational, defensible basis for picking the best. Examination results everywhere play an important part, but since these can be, and have been, attacked they are supplemented by reports from schools. These may be loaded in favour of the student, and not easy to discount. Then there is the interview. There a small group of university teachers will interview the candidates and assess, in the light of their own wisdom and experience of what makes for a promising university student, whom to select and whom to reject. So, with examination results, school reports and interview, a final list of the lucky ones is compiled. And this is seen by those taking part as an eminently rational system which 'takes account of all the evidence' and can thus be defended in public if necessary. And in these terms the public will in general accept it.

I think that the element of rationality is largely pretence, a pretence which we perhaps unknowingly indulge, in order to give both ourselves and the public the feeling that, as we so readily and frequently put it, justice has been done. The best of the applicants and the worst almost automatically select themselves on any criteria. The real problem is how to select from the middle lump. I doubt very much indeed whether we do any better by the procedures I have briefly described than we would by some random process such as picking names out of a hat. But think of the public outcry there would be if it were proposed to introduce selection by lottery! We may occasionally admit to ourselves that there is an element of luck in deciding which students get in, but we keep this dark and only whisper about it in private conversation. No university institution that I know of would include a statement to this effect in its published prospectus.

Perhaps no harm is done by this pretence of rational selection on the basis of evidence. For although we may do no better than we would by picking names out of a hat, perhaps we do no worse. Some time and energy may be wasted, but if the basis of selection is accepted and acceptable, decisions can at least be taken. And this is the essential point—select we must. This there is no avoiding, ignorant though we may in truth really be. And since admission to universities is now a public matter, this selection has to be done on a publicly defensible basis, which, I argue, militates against the confession of ignorance and encourages the belief that it can be and is done on a rational basis in the 'light of all the available information'.

For this system to be viable, it must not, of course, be subject to too much scrutiny and examination. Even those who operate it must not ask themselves too often what it is they are really doing. For if that happened, the whole method might be discredited, and would no longer be accepted as a basis for decisions. True, it would probably be replaced by some new, scientifically more fashionable basis —at present this would probably be a battery of psychological tests —with its own element of pretence. But the need not to enquire too closely if the public were to have confidence in it would apply to the new system in turn. It is a characteristic feature of such systems, therefore, that the full details of their operation cannot be open to public inspection and debate. For this would tend to damage that very element of confidence which the public demands.

Politics abounds with situations of this kind; difficult, contentious issues where our knowledge and understanding are limited, but where decisions have to be taken with confidence and determination. The temptation to grasp at apparently rational evidence is overwhelming if it appears to give a basis for decision. How do we distinguish between situations such as my university admission example, where the pretence of rationality may do no harm, since it probably gives us as good a basis for decisions as any other, and those where such self-deception may get us into yet greater difficulty and trouble?

It is this conundrum which I find quite baffling in issues of economic policy. For sceptical as I am about the depth of our economic understanding and of our ability to assess the consequences of one line of action rather than another, I recognise that, ignorant though we are, decisions have to be taken. And such decisions, we insist, should be defended in terms of knowledge rather than ignorance. Since the war, all governments in this country have proceeded on the basis that budgetary policy has an important role to play in influencing the general level of economic activity and unemployment, and economists have invented and elaborated a most complex system of statistical accounts for the economy as a whole designed to yield an answer for the Chancellor as to what his budgetary policy should be. But complex though his analysis is, it is of course a highly simplified picture of the real range and complexity of economic transactions, and is subject to much error and guesswork. Yet it yields an apparently logical and coherent picture of the economy and its potential development during the course of the coming year. It indicates not merely the direction of development, whether reflationary or deflationary, but also the magnitude of excess or deficiency of expenditure and, therefore, the magnitude of change required in the Budget. Of course, if the calculations are done on alternative estimates and guesses, they will yield different figures for the magnitude of change required, and it would be a bold economist who would argue that the rational element in his analysis would give him a single right figure. But when the Chancellor comes to present his budget he must have settled on one figure and be prepared to defend it. And it would not be acceptable to anyone in the House or outside if he defended it by saying that since we are rather ignorant about the forces in operation, he had put the three most likely estimates in a hat and selected one. Yet the process by which the final estimate was picked may amount to little more than this.

Obviously, it is difficult for anyone to accept this openly as a basis for action. Of course, if the Chancellor explains in his Budget speech—as he did until a few years ago—how he has arrived at his figure, there will always be critical economists outside arguing that it could equally well have been taken as higher or lower. I find it significant that in fact these explanations have been dropped. What the Chancellor does now is to review the economic situation, actual and prospective, and then declare, 'Having taken all these factors into account, I have decided that I shall need to raise £*x* million more in revenue.' The statistical link in the argument is no longer revealed, although of course all the calculations are still done in the Treasury.

The exaggerated pretence of rationality in the whole process was perhaps more harmful in the early years than it is now. For the formulation of the model of the economy in simple terms encouraged a belief that all the important elements in the situation were in fact embraced in it. We have learned slowly and painfully that much of the complexity of society was in fact overlooked, and that the problems of policy are not so easily dealt with. Yet there was the countervailing advantage that the exposition of the situation in rational, even pseudo-rational terms, gave, and still apparently gives, a basis for decision making, where decisions have to be taken. That the Budget has an important influence on the economic situation no one will now question, even if the effect is more complex than our present understanding can embrace. And one could argue, as I think I would, that on balance more good than harm is done by operating in this apparently rational and systematic way.

But it by no means follows that any and every attempt to portray the economy and its development in an apparently coherent and rational way will on balance be of advantage if it is used as a basis for action. It is at present generally taken for granted that many of our economic problems would be easier to deal with if we had a higher rate of economic growth. Does it then follow that an attempt to portray in statistical terms how this growth could be achieved will help us to achieve such a higher rate, or lead us to see what action needs to be taken? This issue will be once again hotly debated when the government's economic plan for the next five years is published.

A couple of years ago, when it became fashionable to argue the need for an overall economic plan and the National Economic Development Council was set up, the case for a plan was frequently put forward in terms of a kind of confidence trick. The only thing, it was argued, that really holds up a higher rate of growth is doubt by both management and workers as to whether the market will absorb the higher output. Each firm and industry hesitates to press ahead for fear that the rest of the economy will be laggard and will therefore not want the increased output. And with this hesitation fairly widespread, the doubt confirms its own validity. If only firms could be persuaded that there would be a continuing expanding demand for their products by other firms, then this hesitation would be replaced by confidence in continuous expansion. If it could be convincingly shown that a higher rate of growth is possible, then the battle would be won: the expansion would take place and would be self-supporting. Indeed, it was argued that continued production at this higher level would itself yield the goods for greater exports to help the balance of payments problem, and make a stop–go economic policy unnecessary. Whatever the influence of the plan produced by Neddy (*Growth of the United Kingdom economy to 1966*), it can hardly be argued that the experience of the last eighteen months supports the confidence trick case for having an economic plan.

The attractiveness of having a plan now is once again the apparent rationality of seeing how to rearrange the main elements of our economy so as to get it right. Yet our ignorance and uncertainty about the future are such that it is only by much assumption and simplification that we can draw up such a plan. No doubt when the plan appears it will include the necessary cautionary safeguarding words and clauses which will have meaning for the initiated, but its attractiveness as a public document will be its apparent reliability, certainty and comprehensiveness. The margins of error and guesses are not entirely to be revealed in their true nakedness. Indeed there is unlikely to be an explanation that the particular plan produced is only one among many that could have been produced, given slightly different estimates and assumptions.

From what has been revealed so far, it is very difficult to say what operational role the plan is likely to play in economic decision making. It may be that it will turn out to be little more than a pretty statistical exercise on what the United Kingdom economy might look like in four or five years' time, on certain crude assumptions about the future. In other words, it would merely show us that 'this is what the United Kingdom economy would look like in 1970, if it looked like this'. This is a harmless activity, if one ignores the scarce economic and statistical manpower that has gone into its compilation.

But I assume that its authors expect it to play a more significant role. Is it, for example, to indicate the level of output to be achieved for products and industries in 1970, and even perhaps specify which exports are to increase and which imports to be reduced? If so, in what sense are these to be operational for the industries concerned? Clearly, where an industry is government-controlled already, as are gas, electricity and coal, the plan may merely be giving figures that would perhaps have to be decided on anyway. But let us be aware that even here the inclusion of such figures in an overall plan does not itself give them any great sense or reliability. Since the government has taken over large sections of the fuel industry, it is inevitably involved in decisions about the future of those industries, but there is no particular virtue in being tied to a lot of figures for output in 1970 unless decisions have to be taken now implying firm output consequences for that year. For private industry the figures may be regarded as one more attempt, of a market research kind, to peer into the future likely level of demand for its products. But they may no more warrant firm and confident decisions now than other such market research exercises do.

It may, of course, be argued that it is not really the output figures that matter, but the implications of the plan in the need for greater efficiency, skilled labour, better management, reduction of restrictive practices, increased innovation and the many other things that are regularly said to be necessary in the British economy. But do we need an elaborate set of statistics, dressed up as a plan, to lead to this kind of conclusion? Is this yet another example of the impressive power of pseudo-scientific argument, but in this case without the excuse that the pretence is needed because it gives a basis for decisions which must be taken? But then I am anticipating. I can assure you that I have had no private sight of the plan. We shall be able to tell better when it comes out.

[17]

Intelligent laymen in Whitehall[1]

The high command of the administrative class of the home civil service is now firmly in the Treasury. One of the architects of the system which has led to this concentration of power was Sir Edward Bridges (now Lord Bridges), who was Secretary of the Cabinet from 1938 to 1946 and Permanent Secretary to the Treasury from 1945 to 1956. The book he has written in the Whitehall series[2] is, therefore, of great importance in giving a view, by one of its most eminent heads, of how the modern Treasury works. True, there has been a major reorganisation of the Treasury since he retired in 1956, following especially on the Select Committee report of 1957–8 and the Plowden report of 1961, but Bridges' book is post this reorganisation and purports to take account of it. Bridges modestly refers to his book as a 'rather prosaic account' and to his description of the work of the Treasury as 'a pretty dry factual catalogue'. To me at least this view of his book is completely misleading. I have never worked in the Treasury, but having been a temporary civil servant in the Cabinet offices and the Ministry of Aircraft Production during the war, and having continuing links from time to time with Whitehall since then, I find every page exciting and fascinating, just as much for what is not said as for what is. As an amateur academic observer of administration, both public and private, I find this one of the most revealing documents I have ever read. Never has the 'intelligent layman' philosophy of public administration been so nakedly exposed.

The Treasury is now in charge of financial and monetary policy, controls public expenditure, co-ordinates economic policy, and manages the whole civil service. Under the reorganisation of 1962 the

[1] A fuller version of the talk broadcast on 9 May 1964 and published in *The Listener*, May 1964.

[2] *The Treasury* (Allen & Unwin, 1964).

department is organised on a functional basis, with two sides, each headed by a Permanent Secretary, one in charge of finance and economic policy, the other of pay and management. This whole exercise is run by about 150 officials in the administrative class. The general theme throughout Bridges' discussion of how this work is done and organised is that this is a job for 'intelligent laymen'. 'In practically all walks of life,' he writes, 'the expert or enthusiast in a particular field does not have the final word, but has to get the approval of some layman or lay body. This is especially necessary in government affairs, where it is taxpayers' money which is being spent.' Or again:

the Treasury official dealing, say, with education or defence is thus not an expert in either of these fields, and will have no prior commitment about the matters with which he is dealing, derived from a long period of service in that field or a professional connection with it. But given his general background and his experience of Government service, he will start with at least the educated layman's knowledge of what happens in the field with which he is working.

Am I wrong in thinking that Bridges takes the view, characteristic of the administrative class in Whitehall, that professional knowledge nearly always implies biased enthusiasm, and that it would be dangerous if those with such knowledge had the final say in policy advice to Ministers? But what kind of probing and searching questions can these laymen ask, however intelligent—and there is of course no doubt of the brilliant intelligence of some at least of the laymen involved? It is one of the fascinating features of Bridges' book that he gives every now and again a brief picture of the day-to-day work of each division. On this particular point, I find his description of what the divisions controlling Treasury expenditure do starkly revealing. Take, for example, the bit on the 'Defence Policy and Material' division:

Let us suppose [he writes] that the particular Air Ministry proposal is a request to place an order for aircraft of a new type, the cost amounting to many million pounds spread over several years. The Treasury will ask how this order fits into the general pattern of defence policy as set out in the annual Defence White Paper.

Then next, and here presumably are the searching questions:

Are the numbers of new aircraft which it is proposed to order consistent with that policy? Are the Air Ministry convinced that the aircraft is technically satisfactory and that there is not a better one at an only slightly earlier stage of development? Are there special technical or production difficulties which might lead to greater expense? Would this particular aircraft call for further expenditure on extending airfields?

Surely, unless the Air Ministry is singularly unintelligent and inefficient, the answers to all these questions must simply be of the 'of course/yes/no' variety. How does the Treasury official know what to ask to probe beyond this vague and vacuous level? And I suggest that if he is to exercise any kind of check beyond the simple one of saying 'you cannot have so much money', the Treasury official must be able to probe further.

It may be argued that all this is pre-Plowden; that now departments are not asked niggling questions of this kind, and that the Treasury confines itself to discussing broad issues, such as the correct allocation of national resources. Maybe; although it is by no means clear that Bridges thinks that all is well now. Indeed, in the final chapter, which he calls 'Reflections', Bridges, discussing the Plowden reforms, writes:

> I ought to be satisfied with this: but I confess that I am not. I am troubled, as I have been for twenty-five years or more, by two things. The first is the degree of frustration and wasted time which is inevitable when any really large organisation, such as the Government service, is subject to detailed rules and regulations administered centrally, without sufficient scope for local interpretation. Secondly, by the conviction, based on most of a working lifetime, that the Treasury does its best work when it has strength of mind to keep to the big issues and avoid being drawn into the byways, however intellectually satisfying they may be.

And later in the same paragraph:

> In my bones I am sure that a greater freedom to departments in the steps they take to give effect to agreed policies would result in an even greater sense of responsibility than they all of them feel today, possibly in the initial framing of policies, and certainly in the measures necessary to carry them out.

But suppose Bridges is wrong—I cannot say whether he is or not—and that in fact the Treasury has gone much further than he thinks. My major questions still remain. Even on the 'big issues', can the intelligent layman in the Treasury without professional knowledge ask the relevant probing questions, and know whether the answers he gets are revealing and significant? And if responsibility for detail is now really delegated to the departments, are the administrative class in the departments, as intelligent laymen, able to initiate and check and effectively control what is going on? For, if Bridges had his way, presumably the questions asked about the new aircraft proposal, instead of being put by Treasury officials, would be put inside the department, but again by administrative-class intelligent laymen. But the dialogue between the departments and the Treasury would continue, as in the past, to be a dialogue between intelligent laymen. No doubt in this process laymen acquire great expertise in the 'dialogue' technique and on how to run committees, to keep the paper moving and to get decisions taken. Indeed, one of the ways of acquiring a reputation in Whitehall is to become known as someone who will stand no nonsense from departments. But is this enough? Is it an effective way of initiating and discussing even the 'big issues', let alone controlling and checking efficiency?

I must make it clear that I know of no ideal solution to the problem of controlling and evaluating the worthwhileness of alternative projects of public expenditure, or of securing efficiency in spending. Even though I am an academic, I realise that talking about the right way of taking decisions is quite different from actually having to take them, and I am not arguing that if the scientists and technocrats were in charge all would be well. I am asking for something quite modest to be tried much more widely than is done now. Bridges himself argues that experimenting with new methods is essential:

> Thus in discussing the problem of economic co-ordination and the role of Neddy [he writes] the matters dealt with involve a much better understanding than ever before with the world of business, industry and commerce; more effective methods of communication, in both directions. I am sure that this will be a helpful development from the point of view of the well-being of the country. This closer relationship—or improved methods of communication—is indeed, I feel, essential if the Treasury is to discharge effectively its duties of economic co-ordination. It may lead to big changes in the way in which the Treasury does this part of its work.

I would merely like to see more interchange of staff between the administrative and professional, especially scientific, branches of the civil service, instead of the present almost completely rigid distinction between the two from the point of entry onwards. Why, for example, should not staff from the scientific side of the Ministry of Aviation with administrative gifts—and many of the jobs at the senior level of the scientific and professional divisions in Whitehall are mainly administrative—be transferred to administrative posts? A sprinkling of assistant secretaries, under-secretaries, second secretaries and even permanent secretaries with some scientific background would, in my view, be a great advantage both in the departments and in the Treasury. This is not a novel idea of my own. I claim no particular originality in suggesting it. The Barlow Committee on Scientific Staff suggested in 1945 that there should be more frequent transfers of scientific staff to the administrative class. The Priestley Commission on the Civil Service, reporting in November 1955, repeated this suggestion. If I may quote at length to show that their proposals were not revolutionary:

> Two aspects [the Priestley commission says] of the question of career prospects for scientific and professional staff seem to us to call for comment. First is that of the opportunities for such staff to transfer to administrative posts. We regard this as a matter of importance not only in the interest of providing careers but also as a means of ensuring that those who are responsible for policy in departments such as the Ministry of Supply or the Post Office are able, by educational background and previous civil service experience, fully to appreciate the technical issues involved in the formation of policy. . . . We were assured that there is no ban in principle on such transfers, which do take place from time to time. We recognise that there are practical difficulties in increasing the number of them. For example, it is in general desirable that transfers should take place not too late in life, but many good young specialists are reluctant to sacrifice their chosen professions and careers for the unfamiliar ground of the work of the administrative class. We are also aware that the most highly qualified specialists do not necessarily make the best administrators. We think, however, that despite the difficulties the positions should be carefully watched and argue that the service should not lag behind outside practice in this matter.

Whether 'the position has been carefully watched' I do not know, but nothing much seems to have happened, except in the use of economists who, although professional, are not included as scientists in this argument. The Zuckerman committee on 'The management and control of research and development', reporting in 1961, make a similar plea, adding the important point that there is an advantage too on the scientific side in having some scientific staff who served for a time on the administrative side. The Zuckerman committee referred to the Priestley commission's recommendation, and commented, 'In fact, the number of such transfers is negligible.' As far as I can discover, this comment would still be true in 1964.

The need to transfer scientific staff to the administrative side more frequently is made even more urgent because the number of entrants to the home civil service who have a scientific background is pitifully small. Between 1950 and 1962 about 600 entrants have been admitted to the administrative class of the home civil service through open competitive methods I and II; of these only twenty had degrees in the natural sciences. Here again, I am not including economics or other social studies as science. Indeed, it is particularly curious that Bridges does not even discuss this issue of the use of scientists in administration, since he clearly thinks that the great development in the use of economists—their working alongside administrators in one division, and their occasional transfer to administrative posts—is a great step forward in the working of the Treasury. Modestly he does not in fact mention the enormous contribution that he himself has made to this change. If there is a case for using professional economists in this way and not leaving economic and financial issues to intelligent laymen, why is there not a case for using staff with a technical and scientific background to work with administrators in mixed divisions or as administrators in charge of non-technical divisions?

Indeed, I am sometimes worried by the sweeping victory that economics is now winning in Whitehall. Everybody is now talking about cost—benefit analysis, and the rates of return on projects, just as they did about 'effective demand' towards the end of the war. As long as you can turn all your calculations into percentages of GNP you can apparently get away with quite a lot. I am not against the use of economists in the civil service, nor am I against having a substantial number of administrators who have a background in economics; on the contrary. But knowing as I do how arrogant some academic economists can be about their expert knowledge, and how much of this arrogance is passed on in their teaching, I can see some danger here that the new witchcraft will have too easy a victory, and will be used to decide issues where, in my view, it is not really useful. Again, part of the trouble arises because the intelligent layman is not in a position adequately to appreciate when economic expertise is useful and when he is being taken in. The lay civil servant is often schizophrenic in this situation, alternating between being impressed by economic argument, particularly if it is expressed in a statistical form, and being completely suspicious of the whole corpus of economic knowledge.

It may well be argued that the parallel to the employment of economists in the Treasury is the employment of scientists in the departments, and no doubt there is a good deal of interchange and argument between scientists and other technologists and the intelligent laymen in the departments. But it remains, I think, true that these two groups think of themselves as quite different because transfer from one group to the other is rare and because discussion between the departments and the Treasury is usually conducted not by the scientists but by two sets of intelligent laymen debating technical and scientific issues in their wisdom or ignorance, however you care to look at it. But even if the position in the departments is satisfactory, which I very much doubt, I still think there would be great benefit within the Treasury itself in having at least some administrators who have at some stage of their career worked on the scientific and technical side.

I know that among scientists, just as among economists, there is sometimes an arrogance, an unjustified implicit assumption that the methods of science can and should be used to answer most questions of policy. Here again the 'intelligent layman' is schizophrenic, thinking how brilliant the eminent scientist is, and how stupid and naive he is in dealing with matters of policy and politics. Surely this attitude on the part of the scientist arises in part at least because he has never had to bear the burden of taking decisions of the kind that face administrative staff, and has had little experience of dealing with policy matters in relation to politics. He frequently comes into the civil service already despising politics, despising the administrator, and his experience when he is kept in a separate group—even though he may have close contact with intelligent laymen on finance and policy—merely reinforces his view. Many of the administrative staff he knows are nice chaps with brilliant minds, but they have been ruined by becoming Treasury-minded and do not understand science. As for the political game, this completely baffles and infuriates him.

The fashionable view is that politics is nothing but the pursuit of power and the reconciliation of pressure groups. What is overlooked in modern theories of government is that politics and public administration (and private business and administration too) are also the art of taking decisions in a state of relative ignorance. If scientists understood this and had administrative experience, they might approach problems of policy and politics with more sympathy than they do at present.

You will, I hope, realise that my ideal model of a senior civil servant is a man who, whatever his subject when he entered the civil service, has had experience during his career in an administrative division, an economic division, a scientific or technical division, a statistics division and perhaps even a technical costs or contracts division. And I use the word division purposely because I think that, to secure my objective, he must work, so to speak, mixed up with others with a different background—not, as at present, in close or remote parallel with them. If this worked over a period—and I am arguing that it is worth trying—I would then contemplate the possibility at least that, with perhaps a few exceptions, everyone beyond a certain level—say Assistant Secretary—would be in a service with a single description and not 'administrative', 'technical', 'scientific' or 'economic'.

There is, of course, the still wider issue of interchange between the civil service and business and industry. Bridges recognises that, given the way in which government, not only at the Treasury, is now involved in economic affairs, it is necessary that Whitehall should know much more than it does at present about industry, and not at three or four stages' remove. I am always astonished in London at the remoteness from industry and business, apart from finance. I find this just as much among academic economists as among administrators in Whitehall. When I was in Manchester I used occasionally to meet factory managers and to go round factories and talk to people about the problems they faced. On the occasions when I came to London and happened, for example, to say that I felt that nonsense was being talked about the cotton industry or about the way in which manufacturers and trade unionists reacted to government policy, I was staggered to find that those with whom I talked treated me as a great expert on these problems and were avid for more information. I used hootingly to laugh at them and tell them that my knowledge was very fragmentary; but they would not accept this, and I suppose, compared with their metropolitan ignorance of anything north of Watford, they may have been right.

I know there are great difficulties in arranging for people from outside to be brought into the civil service. I do not have in mind the short-term appointments where experts are brought in by particular Ministers with each change in government. I don't think this is a particularly good idea. I would like to see an attempt made to attract promising men at the age of thirty or outstanding men at the age of forty from industry and business into the civil service. I know this is extremely difficult and that the flow is likely to be in the reverse direction, but why cannot something be done, at least to make transfer to and from departments and the *nationalised* industries possible?

I have dealt only with one major issue raised by Bridges' book; there are many other fascinating ones. Whether, for example, it is necessary or desirable to have the enormous concentration of power which is now in the Treasury; whether the Treasury staff at its senior level should be given the superior status symbol of an extra £600 a year compared with the departments. Whether, as Bridges argues, there is on balance an advantage in having establishment and management of the civil service in the same department as economic policy and economic co-ordination. The way in which Bridges writes about these and other important problems is certainly not a 'dull, factual catalogue'.

There will, I expect, be many in Whitehall who will say that in my argument about intelligent laymen I have got it all wrong, partly because things have changed since Bridges retired and partly because I don't understand what is going on anyway. They may be right; if they are, I would plead for more open discussion of these issues and not just by retired civil servants and ex-Ministers. At present, even when something is published about the civil service, as in the Plowden report, it is doctored before publication, and what is published is written in what Professor Mackenzie has called mandarin prose. In order to understand what this stuff means one has to translate. Professor Mackenzie, who is an expert philologist in the field of mandarin prose, attempted this in a brilliant article in *The Guardian* in May 1963. As he wrote in a note to that article, 'Much is of necessity conjectural, but this version has a certain internal coherence which gives it plausibility.' If we are to discuss these issues without recourse to the philologist's technique, which I know has many risks, the civil service must be willing to discuss these issues more openly. At present there is, I think, an unholy alliance between Ministers and civil servants which secures secrecy on the principle of civil service anonymity and Ministerial responsibility. This is a political fiction which has been pushed much too far in this country.

I am particularly terrified by it when the intelligent layman civil servant adopts a mock arrogant modesty, arguing that he merely advises and the Minister decides, but laughs cynically with his colleagues about politicians and Ministers when they are not there. Governments are more likely to be discredited or credited (if I may revive a neglected use of this positive) through the gossip of civil servants in the inner circle in London than in any other way I know.

[18]

Economic management in Whitehall[1]

State control and free enterprise, planning and the market system have become emotive words, politically and academically loaded terms of praise or abuse. They are no longer useful in furthering understanding of the way our economy works or in discussing issues of operation and policy. We need a new terminology which is less given to doping the race-horse before it leaves the stable.

In discussing the work of the civil service and the machinery and organisation of government, especially on the economic side, to me the central feature of our economy which distinguishes it from that of fifty years ago is that it is now a 'managed' economy. Whitehall is faced with the problem of how to staff and organise itself to manage the economy, and to manage itself. Under the post-Plowden reforms, the Treasury, which regards itself as *the* central government department, is split into the 'pay and management' side and the 'finance and economic' side. It is implicit in the present system that these two need to be separate but joined, and that general economic management, policy and co-ordination should be centred on the Treasury.[2]

Many features of the present system have come under heavy fire lately. The tendency, for example, to rely on the amateur rather than the professional—indeed 'amateur' is now a dirty and 'professional' a 'U' word. I have myself criticised the 'intelligent layman' philosophy which predominates in Whitehall. The setting up of a series of special bodies on particularly difficult economic issues—the Three Wise Men, Nic and Neddy; the need to have a Plowden enquiry for the Treasury to reorganise itself; and the ideas now

[1] Amended text of broadcast talk given on 26 June 1964 and published in *The Listener*, 2 July 1964.

[2] The 'pay and management' side of the Treasury was transferred to the newly created Civil Service Department in 1968 (i.e. some years after this talk was broadcast).—*Ed.*

floating about, especially from Opposition members including Harold Wilson himself, for a Ministry of Planning or Production—all suggest that there is still something to argue about, even after the recent reorganisation of the Treasury.

To me some of the central issues worth debating are: What is and should be the job of the pay and management side of the Treasury? Does it need to be so closely tied with the rest of the Treasury or would it be better in a separate department? Should the Treasury itself be confined to money, finance, taxation and control of expenditure? If so, is there a need for central initiative and co-ordination for non-monetary and non-fiscal aspects of the economy? Where should this central initiative and co-ordination lie? Should the Economic Adviser to Her Majesty's Government and the Economic Section remain in the Treasury? These and other aspects of managing the economy are highly controversial issues, economic, political and administrative—issues, in fact, of political economy, touched on in many ways in the Third Programme interviews by Norman Hunt of Enoch Powell, Harold Wilson and Jo Grimond, in Bridges' comments on these interviews, broadcast last Monday [22 June 1964], and in his recent book on the Treasury.

It is time we all recognised that the major task of the higher civil service is no longer administrative but managerial. I ought to explain how I view the distinction between these two approaches. The administrator—the 'pure administrator'—is primarily interested in keeping the machine going. His slogans are 'Keep the paper moving', 'Get through the agenda', 'Get the minutes out', 'Avoid awkward issues', 'Never get the Minister into trouble'. It does not really matter to him what is decided or whether the right things get done as long as the machine is kept moving smoothly. The managerial type, by contrast, has his eye on the trouble spots, is anxious to take action in anticipation, to see that crucial issues of policy are raised and dealt with and to ensure that the structure of the organisation for which he is responsible is appropriate to this kind of activity. Given the task that the civil service was undertaking fifty years ago, the administrative approach was perhaps appropriate at that time; now it seems to me quite inappropriate.

The management function of Whitehall is bedevilled by the mythical notion that Ministers decide policy and civil servants administer. I find what Enoch Powell had to say on the relations between the Minister and the civil servants rather puzzling. He recognised that civil servants should and do advise on policy, and that the department is 'an indispensable instrument for the preparation for decision, and of course it's an indispensable instrument for the execution of decision'. Then he argued that 'the advice tendered to the Minister is of course unitary, and you can't give a man two opposite pieces of advice at the same time. And therefore it is the function of the department, when the advice comes to the Minister, to come down on one side or the other or to present a course of action.' All very sensible, as long as the notion of 'unitary advice' is not pushed too far. And here comes my first puzzlement. 'This is one of the tests,' he said, 'of ministerial competence—to be able to detect, when a problem comes forward, whether hidden in it somewhere there is a contradiction, an unresolved discord.' But why should the Minister have to discover this for himself? Why should not the case put to him include the arguments for and against and 'the elements of unresolved discord' within the department?

Then again, Powell kept on stressing the notion, odd to me, that the department puts 'the facts' to the Minister, and he in the light of the facts and in discussion with those who know 'the facts' decides policy. I do not wish to argue that one should not *attempt* to distinguish between 'facts' and 'policy'. But on most issues of economic policy, both central and departmental, this dichotomy is ensnaring and misleading. It may enable us to maintain the important fiction of Ministerial responsibility, but it has the crucial disadvantage of leading us to mistaken notions about what the civil service, especially in its senior branches, is doing or ought to be doing. On any major issue—roads, traffic congestion, the distribution of industry, mergers and monopolies, full employment or growth—'facts' and 'policy' are inevitably interwoven, and the way in which the 'facts' are interpreted, indeed the decision even to get at the facts, itself implies what the policy issues are. What, for example, are the 'facts' about the effects of mergers, or the 'facts' about the relation between full employment and growth which can be separated from policy or alternative policy implications? Why bother to collect 'facts' about mergers if mergers are not a crucial issue of policy?[3]

There is already evidence that there is recognition in the Treasury that the managerial, as distinct from the administrative, function is important in Whitehall. There has been a major advance in

[3] These paragraphs were omitted from the broadcast text.

applying new managerial techniques, especially in O & M and the use of machines and computers, and there are the beginnings of major changes in long-term budgeting and the more sensible use of government accounts. And the Treasury is no doubt asking itself, as British business is, what makes good managers, and how can they be trained? And will the new management schools have any contribution to make? In criticising the 'intelligent layman' philosophy which permeates Bridges' book on the Treasury I was particularly concerned to rebut the implicit view that Whitehall managers should come primarily from the administrative class. I do *not* hold the view that professionalism and technical expertise by *themselves* make good managers. On the contrary. In public and private business, good managers may come from those with an academic background and actual experience in arts, science, technology, economics or any of the other social sciences. But the essential feature of a rising and successful manager is that he should have experience of more than one branch of the business, not be confined to the administrative, technical or accounting sides. And it follows from this that beyond a certain level—I suggested Assistant Secretary level in Whitehall—where most jobs become managerial, rather than mainly technical or administrative, there is a strong case for a single, rather than a many-headed service.

The management side of the Treasury is also the focal point for considering whether departments are appropriately organised to do their jobs properly. And this function increases in importance as the Treasury decides to exercise less control over detail and gives more responsibility to departments. No doubt a good deal of argument and discussion goes on in departments and between departments and the Treasury on structure. But there is little evidence as yet that the Treasury takes much time or trouble to find out how problems of structure are dealt with in business and whether anything useful is to be learnt from academic studies of management. As Bridges said in his talk, the civil service faithfully put into action Labour proposals for nationalisation in the immediate post-war period. But it had apparently no clue about the appropriate structure and organisation for them. Only after twenty years of painful experience and enquiry by outsiders are we gradually evolving a workable system for these enterprises. Mr Powell seemed to think that because businessmen are interested in profits their background and experience is inappropriate to Whitehall. I think he is quite wrong on this. It may be true that in peace-time there is no room, either at the senior civil servant or Ministerial level, for the buccaneering business tycoon, but there are plenty of outstanding managerial businessmen who could move over without difficulty, if they wished, to Whitehall problems, just as many outstanding Whitehall civil servants, especially of the managerial kind, have moved over to business in recent years. I am sure that the management side of Whitehall, especially the Treasury, has a lot to learn from much more dialogue with business on problems of organisation. Perhaps this will develop in time, but at present it is pitiful to find that on the management side of the Treasury there is hardly anyone, apart from the Permanent Secretary himself, who has a responsibility for being knowledgeable about the facts, and thinking how analysis of these and experience elsewhere might be used to raise, let alone answer, questions about organisation and structure in Whitehall. True, there is a division in the Treasury called Management Services (General) which on paper has this function. But it is quite a small division, and has many other functions, particularly in exploring the further use of management techniques.

This whole issue of management and structure is crucial to the successful development of government in this country, and in my view much more has to be done than is allowed for even in the Plowden report and recommendations, which, in the published version at least, places far too much emphasis on techniques. These functions of selecting and training managers, looking at the structure and organisation of departments, together with pay, promotion and conditions of service, are certainly enough to warrant, in size, seniority and quality, a staff equivalent to a department. But why in the Treasury?

Before attempting to answer this question, let us explore the work of the other side of the Treasury—the finance and economic side. Here the Treasury is operating at various levels, sometimes actually doing primary administration, as in some aspects of domestic and overseas finance and payments, sometimes controlling and supervising, as in (say) public expenditure on health and education, and sometimes at a different level still, as in general economic policy, co-ordinating and taking an overall view. It is in relation to this general activity that the economists in the Treasury, particularly the Economic Adviser to Her Majesty's Government and the Economic Section, play their main role.

Is it sensible to have all this activity and Pay and Management brought together in the Treasury, or should these responsibilities be rearranged? Bridges thinks that on this point all is well. Harold Wilson argues that this overloads the Chancellor and the Treasury and that the Treasury is obsessed in times of crisis with the balance of payments aspects of our problems. Under his government, he said, a Ministry of Production or Planning 'would be responsible for co-ordinating decisions about expansion in the physical field, deciding what industries we need to encourage, either by tax means or by other methods'. In Bridges' broadcast comment on this he said nothing about the overloading point, but was obviously worried about the suggestion that there should be a Ministry of Production as well as a Chancellor of the Exchequer. He argued that this would create tension and confusion and 'that some one Minister must be responsible for the oversight of the totality of our resources, and for deciding, under Cabinet authority, how that totality is to be assigned and allocated'.

I think, and of course I may be wrong or arrogant over this, that both Wilson and Bridges have missed a very important point in discussing this issue. All major departments concerned with economic affairs—the Board of Trade and the Ministries of Labour, Power, Transport, Housing and Local Government, Public Building and Works—are, or ought to be, managing and co-ordinating departments. I know that apparently there is always someone at the Treasury who has a responsibility for each of these departments where staff or expenditure is involved, and can therefore be said to be co-ordinating; but this is almost a complete farce in, say, distribution of industry policy, or manpower training policy (if indeed there is one). Of course there ought to be co-ordination between distribution of industry, housing and transport policy, in relation particularly to regional economic development, but is there any evidence whatsoever that the Treasury can or should and could do this kind of co-ordination? Or that a Ministry of Production, dealing in physical resources as Mr Wilson suggests, could do anything useful with actual operational matters still in these separate departments? Again, the Board of Trade has substantial divisions supposedly knowledgeable on British industries, overseas markets, trading conditions, productivity and even perhaps manpower problems, and clearly ought to be thinking of British industrial problems from a general, not a narrow departmental point of view. Here again, the notion that some Principal at the Treasury can take a more sensible general overall view is nonsense. Nor do I think that when Neddy does a review of British industries, as in its report on building—it adds much, if anything, to what is known in the departments.

In my view, therefore, the important question missed by both Wilson and Bridges is: what aspect of economic co-ordination is the Treasury competent to take care of? I think that the Treasury can and ought to look after the general level of economic activity and the balance of payments, since the Treasury *par excellence* can influence these through fiscal and monetary policy. But there are, as I have argued, other major aspects of general economic policy and economic co-ordination which are not adequately dealt with in the Treasury. If the Treasury is to be expanded to deal with them, it would mean demoting the departments even further and an even greater concentration of power at the Treasury. There are strong reasons against this.

But can the other departments—especially those on the economic side—be relied on to take the kind of initiative and co-ordinating activity which we have grown to expect from the Treasury on the general level of expenditure and the balance of payments? Perhaps not, at present, because they are not fully aware of what they ought to be doing. There are, however, signs of change. Appointing Heath as Secretary of State for Industry, Trade and Regional Development as well as President of the Board of Trade is one. The beginnings of 'research units' at the Ministry of Transport, the Ministry of Labour and other economic departments is another. This use of the term 'research', by the way, is rather misleading: what is needed, and what is in fact being started, is some ordered investigation of what is going on in the economy, as a necessary condition for initiating policy, instead of waiting until troubles become acutely obvious before dealing with them.

It is, in my view, pressing ahead with this development in all the main economic departments (and of course Aviation and Defence have many important economic aspects too) which is needed rather than setting up a new Ministry of Expansion or Production, *à la* Wilson. Wilson referred every now and again to his experience of Whitehall during the war. I do not know which particular bit he had in mind, but I wonder whether he remembers the attempts to run a Ministry of Production in war-time? On the whole I thought the venture a failure. Perhaps he disagrees. If he does, I would be very interested indeed to hear why.

The Economic Adviser to Her Majesty's Government and the Economic Section, at present in the Treasury, play a very important role in helping and advising the Treasury on action on the overall level of the economy. But they could also help enormously, and to some extent already do, in prodding departments on other aspects of economic policy and in helping to co-ordinate their activities and to raise major issues of policy at the centre. And I do not myself see that this second role is in the long run less important than the first. If I am right in my argument, should the Economic Section and the Economic Adviser remain in the Treasury? During the war and for a time after the war they were in the Cabinet Office, and I think they would now be more appropriately placed there. This would have the added advantage of giving the Adviser a measure of independence, which his title implies but which he can hardly have in his present position at the Treasury. The Economic Section could then act as the focal point for all central economic initiative and co-ordination, not merely that relating to overall expenditure and the balance of payments (the Treasury would, of course, still need a strong staff of economists). Being in the Cabinet Office, the Economic Adviser and the Economic Section would serve, as they should, the Cabinet as a whole rather than just the Chancellor. They could then be part of the Prime Minister's staff—or, if there is to be an overlord in charge of economic affairs—they would, while technically still available for the whole Cabinet, in practice, work for the overlord. But overlordship raises a whole host of political and managerial issues.

There would be a further advantage in having the Economic Section in the Cabinet Office—it would work even more closely than at present with the Central Statistical Office, and ensure that the central statisticians were used by departments and took more initiative in bringing forward emergent issues which they could see arising out of their examination of the figures. Indeed, I would go even further and re-amalgamate the CSO and the Economic Section, as they were originally before the break was made early in 1941. This may be sheer nostalgic sentimentalism on my part, since when I first went to the Cabinet Office in 1940 the two were together, and I felt that the whole show worked much more fruitfully then than after they were split. But I think there is more to it than sentimentalism. Statisticians, if left by themselves, get obsessed with statistics and facts as such, and do not realise that, in some aspects at least, the facts are needed to illustrate particular policy problems. A good economic statistician in Whitehall should be sufficiently close to problems to be able to take the initiative in bringing to light new problems emerging from the facts, and which are unknown, in their early stages at least, to those who do not see the facts from day to day.

How does all this relate to the question that I left over: whether there was a case for splitting off the pay and management side of the Treasury as a separate department? Bridges argues that the pay and management side and the finance and economic side should be together because to separate them would be a 'false step and would have greatly weakened the effectiveness of both management and financial functions'. If, as I have argued, the Treasury's main co-ordinating function should be related to the overall level of economic activity and the balance of payments, if the major economic departments should play a greater role in economic management and co-ordination, and the Economic Adviser and Economic Section should go to the Cabinet Office, I doubt whether Bridges' point still holds so strongly. Also, let us not forget the need, which Bridges ignores, for greater integration within the Treasury of the 'taxation' and 'finance and economic' sides. Perhaps the Treasury could then tackle the task of absorbing the Board of Inland Revenue and the Customs and Excise departments, if it were relieved, as I suggest, of some of these other burdens. Certainly there is need for more investigation into taxation policy and the effect of particular taxes. It might be easier to achieve this if the chairmen of these two boards, who are paid the same salary as second secretaries in the divisional Treasury, were made responsible to the Permanent Secretary instead of being directly responsible, as at present, to the Chancellor.

I know that there is no conclusive argument on managerial issues of the kind that I have been raising. Any solution has advantages and disadvantages; what I do claim is that there are clearly still problems worth discussing.

Every now and again in this talk I have referred to what Harold Wilson might do in his government. To avoid any misunderstanding, let me say quite clearly that I do not think that these are merely problems for a Labour government, if elected. The red herring of nationalisation apart, the issues of managing the economy which I have tried to raise affect any government that I can conceive of being elected in the next decade or two. For they will all be committed to managing the economy.

[19]

Inflated economists in Whitehall[1]

In the past few years the shortage of economists has become progressively more acute. Government has been persuaded of the usefulness of the latest economic techniques, such as cost–benefit analysis, and has come to realise the value of having economists participate (here I must declare my interest: I am employed by the Ministry of Defence as a part-time consultant) in discussion about policy in other departments as well as the Treasury.

Big business has come to realise that economists can be of value, not merely in intelligence services, general forecasting and dealing with Whitehall, but also in analysing internal business problems. The universities have expanded their economics departments rapidly, new universities have been set up, and many other higher education institutions have started social science departments with emphasis on economics.

But, as this demand has mounted, little has been done to increase supply. Some universities, recognising that you cannot train professional economists in three undergraduate years, have begun to make arrangements for postgraduate courses and teaching. The flow of good UK students for these courses has been disappointing because of the superiority, both academic and financial, of US graduate schools, because of the employment opportunities in this country immediately on graduation, and because of the low level of State and local authority graduate awards. The LSE last year managed to raise money, privately, to award more attractive graduate studentships, and has for the first time a substantial group of first-rate United Kingdom students in its graduate school.

Clearly, with such a divergence between demand and supply, the

[1] Published in *The Guardian* on 12 March 1965 under the title 'Economising on economists'. Devons took strong exception to this change of title, of which he was not informed.

situation was potentially inflationary even six months ago. In the past six months the new government, with its plans for increased employment of economists in Whitehall, has added yet further twists to the inflationary spiral, and, in my view, if they persist with these plans, we shall escalate into the worst kind of runaway inflation in the market for economists.

Six months ago there were twenty economists employed in government departments on policy work. Now there are fifty. True, about ten of these have come from Neddy's staff, some of whose work has been transferred to the new Department of Economic Affairs. The rest is a net expansion.

In addition there are plans for recruiting about forty more economists in the next twelve months! All this while universities are trying to expand, two new graduate business schools have to recruit staff. The colleges of advanced technology and technical colleges are setting up social science departments, with economics high on the list, and business, both nationalised and private, is crying out for more professional economists.

Beyond this, the operation of the Resale Prices Act, the National Board for Prices and Incomes, the proposed expansion of the Monopolies Commission, the regional planning boards and councils, the new Confederation of British Industry, as well as practically every committee set up by the government, will require more and more economists. Where are they to come from?

The main inflationary departments are the new Department of Economic Affairs and the Ministry of Overseas Development. It is difficult for an outsider to judge the sensible needs of the DEA: there is so little information about what its functions are in relation to those of the Treasury and the other economic departments. We know, of course, that the DEA is now preparing a general plan for Britain's economic development and that maximum use is being made of advanced economic techniques (DEA *Progress report* No. 1, January 1965). This sounds good, but tells us very little about what the Department, and the economists it employs, will actually do. For detailed information the only source at present is the godsibologists (for the uninitiated, 'godsibology' is that new branch of political economy and sociology which bases its analysis on a plausible mixture of fact, esoteric jargon, half-truth, rumour, gossip and anonymous Ministerial and ex-Ministerial statement), and I prefer not to rely on these.

In any case, one of the outstanding economic godsibologists—Mr Samuel Brittan—has now joined the DEA, and cannot be expected for the time being to make anything but official statements. We must wait until the plan is actually published to see what DEA is up to. But when the plan figures have been manufactured, what do the economists do then? Sit and think about how to get the plan achieved? I have never found that 'sitting and thinking' works very well outside academic cloisters. Very little thinking normally takes place, and those concerned find even sitting rather difficult.

I urge the DEA in using 'advanced economic techniques' to do some work on the 'political economy multiplier'—the number of economists demanded elsewhere for every one employed by the DEA. The main effect so far of appointing economists in the DEA is to raise the demand for economists elsewhere. Every government department, nationalised industry, trade association, trade union, big business, now wants economists to answer the questions that the DEA and the little Neddies are asking.

I suspect that the political economy multiplier is at least five, but this is only a hunch, and I hope that the DEA will make a scientific estimate. Indeed, if it takes account of the *most* advanced techniques such as dynamic feed-back analysis, it may well find the system explosive!

The employment of large numbers of economists by the Ministry of Overseas Development is even more puzzling. Surely they are not going just to 'sit and think' about economic aid and development? Perhaps they are going to decide who should get more aid? Is so much more to be spent that fifteen more economists are needed to advise on its allocation? Presumably they will not be silly enough to think that they can work out in Whitehall development plans for overseas countries.

It is particularly disheartening to find that a government with economics so well represented at the ministerial level should be taking such inflationary action. The Prime Minister himself was, in his youth, a promising economics don. No doubt he no longer thinks of himself as a professional economist, but he must remember the theory of what happens when 'too much money chases too few goods', and the same theory applies where 'too much money chases too few economists'. Does he want a 'free for all' with 'rationing by the purse'? Maybe not. But the alternative is a plan, with rationing by allocation and priorities. If there is such a plan, cannot he take us outsiders into his confidence and let us know what it is?

May I urge on him the need to put in hand a 'cost–benefit analysis' of the alternative uses of economists, an analysis which will take into account the wider public interest, not merely the private interest of the government or individual Ministers and departments? I do not know who should do such an analysis. Not the DEA, since it has a private vested interest in the result. The management side of the Treasury perhaps ought to do it; but the civil servants there must be in a difficult position. For I suspect that they do not want to give Ministers the slightest excuse for thinking that the Treasury is doing anything to frustrate their policies.

But whoever does the exercise will have to face the uncomfortable fact that in the short run, at least, 'supply' is limited. Even in the longer run the situation is not promising, given the limited facilities likely to be available at some universities and the apparently difficult position that the University Grants Committee faces when it has to find the money for the new universities and to take over responsibility for the CATs.

I expect my argument will be misinterpreted as reactionary opposition to the employment of more economists in Whitehall or to the particular individuals brought in from outside. This is not my argument. More economists are needed, and some of the appointments will add greatly to effective economic discussion in Whitehall. Sir Donald MacDougall and Mr Nicholas Kaldor, for example, are excellent appointments. Mr Kaldor is one of the outstanding economists of our generation, and combines in a rare way a brilliant originality in theory with a perceptive understanding of policy problems (of *this* country), even though I do not agree with many of his conclusions. He has his weaknesses and failings: who hasn't? We should count ourselves lucky that when he left Hungary he decided to make his home here.

My worry is about the scale of expansion that this government has embarked on in recruiting economists, apparently without thinking out carefully why they are needed and what they are to do; the apparent lack of attention to supply; and the complete disregard of the effects of their actions on the universities, business and others who desperately need more economists if they are even to approach achieving what the government is demanding of them.

[20]

Plan for economists

A brief for the Prime Minister[1]

1. Since I wrote my article in *The Guardian* on 12 March on the inflationary demand for economists in Whitehall evidence accumulates, and not godsibological[2] evidence, that we are approaching the point of escalation. The demand for economists mounts, the market is now like an Eastern bazaar completely out of control, and the need for determined action—even for planning—is desperately urgent.

2. News of the latest distorted twist of the spiral reached me on 17 March in a circular letter 'to a few Heads of Economics Departments' from the Civil Service Commission announcing that the government 'is setting up [*sic*] an Economic Service' with established posts. The grades in this service are: Economic Assistant £965–£1,606), Economic Advisor (£2,259–£3,087), Senior Economic Adviser (£3,135–£3,985) and a 'small number of higher appointments'. We are told that six posts of economic assistant 'are now to be filled', and that the Commission 'should be very glad if you could bring these posts to the notice of any suitable qualified young economists (aged 20–30) who might be interested'. 'Students graduating this year may also apply, but their appointment will be subject to their obtaining a first or second class honours degree.' This is sheer madness, for the following reasons:

(*a*) The LSE and perhaps one or two other universities are at last beginning to build up graduate teaching with UK students. Do you want to ruin these efforts by snatching graduates into

[1] Published in *The Guardian*, 26 March 1965.

[2] 'Godsibology': that new branch of political economy and sociology which bases its analysis on a plausible mixture of fact, esoteric jargon, half-truth, rumour, gossip and anonymous Ministerial and ex-Ministerial statement.

government service when they are still in their nappies, by offering them £1,000 a year? What would the UGC, the Ministry of Education and the Treasury say if *we* proposed that the State studentships in Economics and Statistics should be £1,000–£1,200 a year?

(*b*) A career service for economists in Whitehall is absurd. At the adviser level and above, to be of use to government, economists must move in and out of Whitehall to the universities (including the business schools when they are really going concerns), business, nationalised industries and, I hope, trade unions. A 'confusion of economists' with forty years confined to the 'inner circle' in Whitehall will dispense little but outlandish and fossilised economic advice. And the young man going in as an 'economic assistant', if he wants to have a permanent career in Whitehall, should be encouraged—I would make it a requirement—to spend some years in posts where he is not in a dreamland writing detached, but perhaps impractical and irrelevant, notes on economic policy. Maybe it is intended to ease transfer to the administrative, statistician and even the scientific class. But there is no mention of this in the letter.

(*c*) 'The successful candidates in the present competition,' we are told, 'will probably be appointed in the first instance to posts in the Treasury, the Department of Economic Affairs and the Ministry of Overseas Development'. No mention of the Board of Trade, the Ministries of Labour, Transport, Housing, Agriculture and Food, Power, Technology, Aviation or Defence! Are we to assume that these have all the economists they need, or have a lower priority for economists than the ODM?[3] Or are they in future to get all their economic advice from the DEA?

(*d*) The DEA must be given a chance. But from new evidence, again non-godsibological—the actual questionnaire the DEA has put out—the DEA is wildly extravagant in its use of economists. I cannot imagine what the DEA will do with all the replies—if it gets them—to the countless questions it asks. Donald MacDougall and Eric Roll,[4] at least, ought to know

[3] Ministry of Overseas Development.—*Ed.*

[4] Director-General and Permanent Secretary respectively of the Department of Economic Affairs in 1964–5.—*Ed.*

better. This is not planning, but sheer economic and statistical mesmeric extravaganza.

3. No doubt, Prime Minister, you and some of those who advise you will say, 'Take no notice of Devons; we know he is an anti-planner.' This is not true (I certainly do not walk with Enoch); but true or not true, it is irrelevant. 'All right,' you may say, 'but you are merely critically destructive.' On this occasion, at least, I have constructive proposals to make. They are:

(*a*) Get the DEA to look at *actual* planning experience before it launches out on wild, utopian pseudo-planning ventures.

(*b*) Estimate the marginal product of economists at the ODM, their potential marginal product in other economic departments, and redistribute the economists so that there is a rough equality of product at the margin.

(*c*) Extend the work of the Centre for Administrative Studies to cover more administrative staff, including those at senior level.

(*d*) On supply, support those universities which have started efficient graduate training in economics and statistics.. There must be direct grants for this; the UGC or the Ministry of Education cannot handle it.

(*e*) Get agreement with economics and statistics departments in some universities on a broad programme of relevant investigation and research that would be of interest and use to government; and provide direct finance to support it. Urgent action is needed.

(*f*) Points (*d*) and (*e*) imply government contracts with economics and statistics departments of a few universities for a programme of graduate training, investigation and research. I do not myself like ear-marked grants, but if the government increases demand as it has done, special action to increase supply must be taken. We can also learn from American experience in government contracts with universities and avoid some of their worst mistakes. Contracts must be with *departments* and not individuals; otherwise professors will spend much time in Whitehall negotiating for contract renewal.

(*g*) At the LSE we already have a successful graduate training scheme and have raised enough money from business to finance about fifteen UK studentships a year (£750 plus fees a year for the first year). We want to increase this to forty or fifty.

(*h*) How much would this cost? I do not know about other universities, but a contract with the economics and statistics departments of LSE for £20,000 next year, rising to £100,000 after five years, would have a dramatic effect on the flow of trained UK students and on relevant research.

I do not want to raise false expectations. We shall not be able to solve all the government's economic problems. But I am convinced that if you give us the tools we can at least start the jobs. Try it for five years, and if it fails it can easily be dropped.

4. I realise, Prime Minister, that you must be preoccupied with foreign affairs and have little time to deal with the issues I have raised here and on 12 March. But think of the political implications. I suppose you have set your heart on being an honest broker bringing peace to Vietnam. I realise the attraction of an election battle cry 'Vote for Wilson—the Saviour of the World'. But can you pull it off? I fear that our position as a world power is too weak, and the Americans do not trust you as they did Attlee. Your public image in the US is a slythy tove too clever by ninety-nine hundredths; and the Russians trust no one, not even themselves. In any case, ponder on your own comparative advantage; surely it is in getting the economic affairs of this country straight? At present the danger is a repetition of 1945–50: a government committed to planning without any idea of how to plan. Surely you learned something then which you can pass on to the Minister for Economic Affairs? Remember the disillusion with planning after two or three years of Labour mismanagement. Then you made a virtue out of necessity by claiming great credit for 'a bonfire of controls'. What will you have this time, 'a bonfire of economists'? Has the Labour Party, with so many economists, learnt nothing about economic management (a less emotive term than planning)? Has the Labour Party a deep-seated suicidal instinct?

5. Some may advise 'Wait for Heyworth'. Heed them not. Remember the consequences of 'Waiting for Robbins'.

6. This may make you angry, but the godsibologists tell me that at least you read what angers you.

UNIVERSITY AFFAIRS

[21]

Lotus grove of Academe[1]

Public debate about the future of the universities increases in intensity daily. It is now not merely the most important subject to write about, it is the most fashionable one. Happily, argument about higher education is still confined to top people and to lively minds. It is the quality dailies and weeklies, the monthlies and quarterlies that are full of articles on this important problem. Masters of Oxford and Cambridge colleges, vice-chancellors, headmasters of public schools, members of the House of Lords, and all those eminent public figures who bear the weight of responsibility for making sure that the Robbins committee makes the right recommendations—all these, and, perhaps most telling of all, the BBC Third Programme, are delivering themselves of homilies, weighty and trenchant, on this vital topic.

Yet I am beginning to wonder whether in all this debate the really significant point is not being overlooked. Everyone talks and writes about the need to increase the number of places at the universities, to improve methods of teaching, and to help those who have known only a miserable and uncultured working class background to attain the delights and wonders of middle class life. True, reference is sometimes made to the needs of research—after all, this is National Productivity Year—and if research can help economic growth and increase the gross national product, then clearly the volume of research ought to be increased. But is it right to think of teaching and research as the major function of a university? How many members of university staffs are burning with passionate zeal to teach—to raise the level of the ignorant from failure to pass or from a pass to a lower second? As for research, remember what Cornford wrote in *Microcosmographia academica*—the only really scientific analysis of academic life—'The

[1] From *The Listener*, 14 March 1963.

principle of Sound Learning is that the noise of vulgar fame should never trouble the cloistered calm of academic existence'.

What, then, are universities for if they are not for teaching or research? Clearly, to me, to make provision for an intellectual leisured class. Intellectual leisure gives freedom to think, to read, to write, to ruminate and to argue with colleagues. It implies that we are not tied down but use our time as we think fit; not according to a plan or programme laid down by someone else—the college, the university, or the University Grants Committee—but according to our own wishes and inspiration. Some teaching and research, especially if you like doing it, may be included in the way in which you use this freedom; but it is the possibility of intellectual leisure which really attracts people to academic life.

Think—and I suspect you will not need to think hard or long—how important and delightful intellectual leisure is. Let me make it clear that I am now not speaking from my own direct experience of university life at Manchester and the London School of Economics. I know so much about these that to base any argument on them would obviously be biased and prejudiced. It is much better to analyse the situation from material based on hearsay and gossip, and it is at Oxford and Cambridge that we can see and analyse intellectual leisure in its quintessence. There, as I understand it, the dons can think, argue and gossip to their hearts' content about the really important issues of life such as the nature of man and his language, the origins of the universe or the use of the semi-colon, and the eminent statesmen that they have met.

The significant thing about this inspired thinking is that no one knows the causes and sources of inspiration. It may come at any moment, quite unexpectedly: perhaps when lying late in bed in the morning, or at midnight in the senior common room when thought is stimulated by good food and drink, perhaps even as one closes one's eyes and leans back in an armchair to listen to a student's weekly essay. Brilliant ideas and thoughts cannot be forced. You may have to accept with philosophical calm and resignation long periods of idleness and triviality, in the hope (sometimes, I fear, a vain hope) that one day inspiration will come. We must accept this as long as we do not know what it is that causes inspiration. Surely we must realise that inspiration cannot be planned—not even on a quinquennial basis. If we recognise this, it may be that there is some point in listening to the essays of even stupid and ignorant students. For ignorance is a challenge; there is at least a worthwhile hypothesis that challenge calls forth a response, perhaps in this case a response of new and inspired thought.

I hope I have convinced you that intellectual leisure is worth while. But you may ask, or you should ask, why should the public pay to keep a privileged class like this just so that they can contemplate at leisure? To answer this question I shall have to introduce you to modern economic analysis, and you will, no doubt, find this is a bore. But I am not ashamed of being an economist. Everyone will agree that in the crown of the social sciences economics is the brightest jewel. I am, I hope, sufficiently humble to admit that the social science crown is a little tarnished, but the jewel of economics shines bright and clear.

Economic analysis has made great progress in the last thirty years. Through the development of mathematical and statistical theory, through econometrics and the techniques of empirical testing, we have come to realise how little earlier economists really understood. We need no longer rely on common sense; we have unerring scientific criteria. Instead of merely asking whether public expenditure is worthwhile, we now apply what is called 'cost–benefit analysis'. You must be an economist to understand the power as well as the sheer beauty and elegance of cost–benefit analysis. The essence of the theory is that if we wish to decide whether to spend public money on a project, we must compare the cost with the expected benefits. Does it not thrill you to be introduced to one of the major scientific discoveries of our age? But here comes the rub. How do we calculate and compare cost and benefit? For cost you might, in your innocence, think we can get what we want from the white paper compiled by the University Grants Committee. But unfortunately, for my purpose the figures are completely useless. The tables on staff at the universities exclude Oxford and Cambridge and the figures of expenditure are not complete anyway. But it is obvious that in principle they could be obtained, and that is all we are concerned with in *advanced* economic theory.

So much for the cost side. What about the benefits? Here quantification—the keystone of scientific method—is more difficult. But fortunately the qualitative arguments are so overwhelming that the difficulty of quantification need not worry us. First, there is the enormous benefit to the dons themselves—and do not forget the indirect benefits. Brilliant students are quick to recognise the value of wisdom acquired through leisure. And when they get into the Treasury they will carry on the tradition that it is through wisdom, unhampered by technical knowledge, that advice on important matters of public policy can best be formulated. Then think of the calls made on dons to serve on government committees, and to act as advisers and consultants. Could they do this if the university did not allow them plenty of leisure? And what would the BBC do, especially the Third Programme, if it could not call on the dons? How disastrous if the public were deprived, for example, of the benefit of those penetrating, coherent and valuable discussions between philosophers. Do I need to add more? Surely the benefits, even though not quantifiable, are well in excess of the cost?

But I must enter a reservation here. Will the public and those at the Treasury who now have such a large say in fixing university salaries really understand the issues? Would it not be wiser, at present at least, to confine any discussion of this kind to the inner circle in the universities? Let us carry on, I suspect they would say, and claim that the function of dons is to teach and do research —this the public will understand, and urge the government to support it; once we have the money we can use some of it to support academic leisure, and since we know this is clearly right, no harm will be done.

But I do not altogether agree with this view. Perhaps I am old-fashioned and naive, but I feel strongly that 'honesty is the best policy'. The duplicity in the present image presented to the public even leads me to wonder in depressed moments whether my colleagues at Oxford and Cambridge really believe in the pursuit of wisdom for its own sake or whether they too have become infected by the gnawing worm of social purpose. If they are not prepared courageously to defend the principles of academic leisure, how much more difficult it would be to claim just a little of it, and all the background luxury which is apparently necessary for it, in other universities. I urge my colleagues not to allow themselves to be prostituted by the lures of economic growth.

Perhaps after all some of the dons at Oxford and Cambridge might be willing to speak out in this way. For they could readily argue that in the future there should be some specialisation between the universities. Teaching is important, they recognise; but the comparative advantage of Oxford and Cambridge is in intellectual leisure. The application of the theory of comparative advantage—again, a most powerful tool of economic analysis—might clearly in their view lead to Oxford and Cambridge being the main centres for academic leisure and the other universities the main centres for teaching, and staff–student ratios could be adjusted to allow for this. I wonder, however, whether this takes account of the most recent advances in dynamic economic analysis. For remember what I have said. Who knows the causes and sources of inspiration and wisdom? Perhaps the contemplation of dark satanic mills may also inspire path-breaking ideas, and the challenge which comes from mixing with ordinary people in Manchester, Leeds or Birmingham may result in a response at least equally valuable as the parochial challenges at Oxford and Cambridge. Looked at in this way, every university has the right—nay, the duty—to provide for intellectual leisure for its staff.

Many may, I fear, maintain that I have been merely arguing in a circle. My answer to that is clear: 'The nature of God is a circle.' Or if you consider that blasphemous, I quote Rilke and Hofmansthal: 'Nothing is wiser than the circle,' and 'whoever knows the power of the circle does not fear death.'

To me my case is clearly overwhelming. But I am worried that the value of academic leisure is being overlooked in all the anxiety to move up higher in the international league table of the population–student ratio. In throwing out the baby of reaction and conservatism in our universities, let us not throw out the bath-water of a thousand years of British academic tradition.

[22]

Evidence presented to the Robbins committee[1]

Redbrick, Oxbridge and the new universities

The English university system is peculiar in having the older universities, 'Oxbridge', with enormous intellectual and social prestige compared with the remainder. This disparity between Oxbridge and the rest is reinforced by many aspects of the public student grant system, the selection of students, the ability to raise finance, etc.

It is a much disputed matter how far this disparity is mainly one of social prestige and amenity and to what extent it is important also in the intellectual quality of staff teaching and research. In comparing Redbrick and Oxbridge, it is important to draw a distinction between science and arts, and not to make propositions relating to the universities as a whole. One of the main administrative differences between Oxbridge and Redbrick is the college compared with the departmental organisation. The departmental structure puts the professor or professors in charge of the department and, therefore, of teaching and research in his subject in a way which is quite unknown in Oxbridge. This departmental structure has substantial advantages in subjects such as the natural sciences, where successful teaching and, even more, successful research depend on there being an organised body of staff and research workers in the subject co-ordinated under single direction. Where successful work depends on being able to organise a group of colleagues and research workers as a team, there are great attractions and advantages in the departmental organisation, especially for the professor. The departmental system of Redbrick universities also implies the allocation of finance, buildings and equipment on a

[1] These five pieces were presented in evidence to the Robbins Committee on Higher Education in 1962.

departmental basis, again giving the professor a large measure of independence and autonomy in the use of resources within his allocation.

These features of Redbrick organisation and administration are of much greater significance in science than in arts subjects. For it is in science that research depends on there being a substantial team of staff and students working in the same field, and it is in science where modern research demands expensive and elaborate equipment. It is true that in recent years Oxbridge has developed departments in this sense in some of the natural sciences, but they are still complicated in their operation, particularly in the operation of teaching and supervision of research, by the main college structure. For a senior Fellow in one of the natural sciences at Oxbridge the opportunities afforded by a chair at the Redbrick university have many attractions, attractions which may be sufficient to offset some of the lack of amenities associated with Oxbridge and the drabness of the physical surroundings of many, but not all, Redbrick towns. Running a department has necessarily administrative burdens associated with it, but these again may be offset by the attractions of being a master of one's own show.

It is a feature of the departmental organisation of the sciences at Redbrick that the professor builds up around him a team of teachers and researchers whose main interest is in the same broad field as his own. If he goes to an appointment elsewhere, many of this staff will go with him. This means that his successor often has at his disposal vacant posts which he can fill with staff in fields in which he is interested. Thus an appointment to a chair at Redbrick is not merely academic promotion but gives the holder an opportunity of developing his subject in a way which may not have been open to him previously.

In arts subjects the position is usually quite different. Research, even where it is of outstanding importance to the staff, rarely proceeds on a team basis. It is not usually important in arts subjects to have a group of colleagues and research students working in the same field. Expensive equipment is also not usually required; the main requirement for research being a good and extensive library. From this point of view, the departmental organisation of Redbrick universities has few attractions for the staff compared with the college organisation of Oxbridge. Indeed, for the senior members of staff, and especially the professor, being in charge of a department may be a burden rather than an attraction. Having the responsibility for organising a large staff and body of students, even in his own subject, may interfere with rather than assist the development of his own research.

If this argument has any validity, it would mean that the Redbrick universities have considerable power in attracting eminent scientists to chairs in relation to other universities, but that such power does not exist in arts subjects. In particular, a senior Fellow in science at Oxbridge looking for opportunities to develop his own research interest might well be attracted by the offer of a chair at Redbrick; whereas for a Fellow in arts such an offer might imply a restriction rather than a development of his own writing and research opportunities. The relative isolation of a Fellow at Oxbridge from the administrative apparatus of a department in arts subjects may indeed be one of its important attractions.

This distinction between the attractiveness of science and arts departments at Redbrick universities, especially from the point of view of the professor, seems to be supported to a substantial degree by a brief analysis I have made of the careers of professors at Redbrick universities in the main sciences (physics, mathematics and chemistry) and arts (English, modern languages and history) subjects. This analysis covered the careers of 162 professors at English provincial universities; 86 in science and 76 in arts subjects. Of the 86 in science, 60 had done postgraduate work in Oxbridge and 26 had been Fellows. Of the 76 in arts subjects, 29 had done postgraduate work at Oxbridge and only nine had been Fellows. At London University the difference between science and arts is not so marked, although here too the relative attractiveness of a chair in science to an Oxbridge Fellow seems to stand out. Of 38 professors in the science subjects at London nineteen had done postgraduate work at Oxbridge, and of 39 in arts the number with postgraduate experience at Oxbridge was the same. But twelve of the science professors had been Fellows at Oxbridge, and only five of the arts professors.

The character of arts departments at Redbrick universities also seems to be substantially different from that at Oxbridge. At Oxbridge there seems to be a substantial—indeed a preponderant—body of students who read arts subjects as a general education without a career directly connected with the subject in mind. In the Redbrick universities there is a preponderant element who are reading a subject with the intention of teaching it as a career. This is particularly true of women students, who comprise a much higher proportion of total students at Redbrick than at Oxbridge. According to the analysis of first admissions done by Professor Glass and his colleagues, out of 269 women students first admitted to Redbrick universities to read English or foreign languages, 170 gave teaching as their intended career. For history and geography the comparable figures were 85 out of 147, and for combined or general arts courses 128 out of 172. For men, of 187 reading English or foreign languages, 68 said that they intended to teach; in history and geography, 89 out of 198; and in general arts, 122 out of 276. At Oxbridge, by contrast, of 590 men admitted to read English and foreign languages, only 76 gave teaching as their career, and of 601 men reading history or geography, only 85.

There is also an important distinction between arts and science in the age at which staff are first appointed to chairs. In this case the position seems to be similar at all universities, although it may have more significance at Redbrick, with its central feature of departmental organisation and the professor in charge. At provincial universities 64 per cent of Professors in Science (Physics, Chemistry and Mathematics) were under forty when first appointed, compared with 47 per cent in arts (English, foreign languages and history). In arts 30 per cent were over forty-five when first appointed; in science only nine per cent. This disparity in age of first appointment can be interpreted in many different ways—for example, that in science, academics develop and show their outstanding abilities at an earlier age than in arts subjects; or that the universities have been willing to take greater risks in appointing young men to chairs in science than arts. Whatever the reason, the higher age of first appointment, and in consequence the tendency for arts departments to be run by older professors, has an important effect on the outlook of arts compared with science departments.

The features of arts compared with science departments that have been dealt with here raise important issues for the future of arts departments at the Redbrick universities. In the sciences their position is relatively secure. Given the advantages of the departmental organisation, their substantial technical and research equipment, they can hope to continue to compete effectively with Oxbridge and the newer universities which have acquired independence since the war and those which are now being newly established. But in arts subjects the prospect seems very different. Compared with the newer universities their amenities are poor, and from the academic point of view they have no particular attractions for staff. There seems to be no reason, on the face of it, why students or staff should prefer to study at Manchester or Liverpool or Leeds, compared with Exeter, Nottingham, Brighton or York. Indeed the very reverse may be true. Once there is a tendency for the arts departments at Redbrick to decline relatively in this way, there will be forces in operation reinforcing this tendency which it will be difficult to reverse. For deterioration shows itself in ever greater difficulty in attracting good staff, which leads to a decline in reputation, discontent and frustration in the departments, especially among the junior members of staff, and desire among those with initiative and ideas to seek posts elsewhere.

In many ways the growth of the newer universities is bound to have serious consequences for arts departments at Redbrick which cannot be avoided. For their initial advantages, compared with their position in the sciences, are quite trifling. But there is a feeling that the scales are being weighted against them by the privileges in buildings and other amenities, apart from the natural ones of better sites, being granted to the newer universities. There is a lot that the Redbrick universities can do themselves to make their arts departments more lively and exciting, but if they are to have a chance of succeeding in doing this they will have also to be accorded some of the facilities which make for a civilised and attractive academic atmosphere. This is not likely to happen if they are regarded as places where expansion can take place relatively cheaply, with most of the new facilities, ideas and public regard devoted to the development of the new universities.

Government financing of the universities

The development of the present system of financing the universities mainly through the system of a central allocation by the Treasury to the University Grants Committee, and an allocation by the University Grants Committee to individual universities, has come about through a series of historical accidents. The main virtues claimed for it are that it manages to combine a high degree of independence in the universities notwithstanding their reliance on public finance for a major part of their budget.

I wish to argue that the degree of independence secured by the universities under this system is much exaggerated, and that the UGC system, whatever its merits in the past, is now inappropriate in its present form for running and financing the universities.

The independence of the universities which is maintained under this system is in many respects symbolic. On two major issues, the appointment of staff and what is taught, the universities have, it is true, been left quite free, but on other matters—for example, their general rate of expansion, the direction of expansion, the attention devoted to research compared with undergraduate work—freedom has been preserved only by the universities doing what the UGC wants them to do, and by their being prepared to have a general programme, subject to UGC supervision and criticism, co-ordinated for them through the Committee of Principals and Vice-Chancellors. This network of rule—the Committee of Vice-Chancellors, the UGC and the Treasury—operates in an atmosphere of secrecy far removed from day-to-day discussion in the universities themselves, and gives the impression within the universities, not of great freedom and independence, but of rule by remote authority over which they have no control and who debate and decide issues by criteria of which they have no knowledge. The general public, too, is kept almost completely in the dark about the issues which exercise the minds of the vice-chancellors' committee, the UGC and the Treasury. It has, significantly, taken a disagreement between the UGC and the Treasury to have a major issue of policy debated in public. This in itself has revealed the weakness of the UGC system, for the proposals of the UGC and justification for them have barely been revealed to the public. Even the universities are individually still in ignorance as to the effect on them of the latest policy decisions.

Any reform of the UGC system should take into account two major issues. First, the need for greater public participation in the debate about government policy in relation to the universities, and second, whether matters can be rearranged so that it is clearer than at present over which issues the government, *via* the UGC or some other system, should or should not exercise control.

As long as there is an assumption that students reaching a certain standard at school are entitled to be supported by the public in a university course, a substantial amount of university funds for current expenditure will have to come from public finances. But need it come, as at present, through a single five-yearly grant, centrally allocated in some way to individual universities? While such a system persists there will be an inevitable tendency towards uniformity of standards, central suggestion if not direction as to which subjects merit expansion, what should be the appropriate relationship between size of staff and student body, and (even more important) what privileges and exceptions should be allowed to individual institutions to depart from these standards. There is already a suspicion—whether the suspicion is warranted is another matter—that Oxford and Cambridge are treated as privileged, and that the new universities are being allowed, even encouraged, to do things which will soon put them also in a privileged position in relation to the older Redbrick universities. There is a view that expansion at Redbrick can be obtained relatively cheaply, and there is a suspicion that this view influences the Treasury, if not the UGC itself, in its attitude to some of the problems which expansion at those institutions raises.

As long as there is a central overall allocation of money for current expenditure, as under the present system, the suspicion that this allocation and the implied conditions attached to it are influenced by strange and peculiar views on the part of the inner circle of those who determine UGC and Treasury policy will remain. One of the ways of overcoming this difficulty would be to make a much smaller proportion of finance available centrally in this way. A simple way of going some way towards doing this would be for the universities to raise their fees to correspond more closely to the cost of dealing with students and, as a consequence, for a much larger proportion of their income to come through fee income in this way. All universities have fees at present, and they have gone through the farce of adjusting them once or twice since the war. The point of these trivial adjustments, which have still left the fees ludicrously low in relation to cost, is difficult to fathom. An adjustment which brought fees up to a figure roughly corresponding to cost, which on average must at present be £600 a year, would give a university with 5,000 students an income of £3 million. Under such a system, fees would be given to the student as part of his grant, as at present by the local education authority or other granting body. Such a level of fees would make the grant, including maintenance, for a fully supported student around £1,000 a year. Arranging for public support to be related in this way to the student grant would also make it clearer to the public how much publicly financed university students are really costing, although some might think this revelation to be unwise. It would also, incidentally, mean that overseas students paid fully the cost of their courses here, instead of being heavily subsidised as at present.

Under such a system, uniformity of fees between universities would not be necessary. Indeed, there might be some advantage in lack of uniformity, with each university deciding at what level and in what way it wished to provide courses. The attractions and disadvantages of expansion to individual institutions, and the different ways in which expansion might be financed, would also be clearer. It would then be for the government directly, or indirectly through local authorities, to decide how many students to finance, instead of, as at present, trying to get agreement on numbers first and then issuing an allocation of finance, agreed with the UGC or not, afterwards.

Such a system might also introduce an element of competition between the universities, and perhaps induce the universities to pay greater attention than they do at present to the wisdom of some of their main lines of expenditure. Central salary negotiation, with uniform salaries throughout the universities, would of course complicate the operation of such a system, although it should not make it impossible. It must, however, be admitted that with such a centralised salary system the incentive to continue with the present general central allocation of finance is increased.

If such a system of financing *via* fees were adopted it would still leave capital grants for expansion, or for new universities, to be dealt with centrally. And the central authorities would still have the major problem of deciding what number of university students to support. This would have the advantage of concentrating attention on these two issues, instead of having attention widely dispersed over the detailed current programmes of individual universities.

I recognise that the decentralisation of current finance in the way in which I have suggested is not likely to get wide support. And I put forward the following points which I would regard as important within the present general scheme of things.

1. A discrete five-year planning period is an unsatisfactory way of financing the universities. It leads to a position of standstill as the last year draws to a close and the figures for the next

five-yearly period have not yet been revealed. I suggest that the period of planning be a *running* five-year period—a system which is, I believe, now widely used in Whitehall. Under such a system the UGC would always be able to look ahead at least four years and at best five years.

2. Capital grants should be treated in the same way as (1), except that, for the time being at least, they should extend over a seven- or ten-year running planning period.
3. The differential in students' grants, according to whether they go to Oxbridge, Redbrick or the new universities, or live at home, should be drastically narrowed, if not abolished.
4. The present system by which the UGC is an advisory committee to the Treasury should be changed, first by removing it from the Treasury, and second by giving it some more full-time members and some staff.
5. More information about the work of the UGC should be made publicly available, so that there can be reasonable public debate about the important issues of policy.

Criteria for admission to the universities

All students wishing to enter a university have to satisfy the technical standard of 'university entrance requirements', but satisfying this standard does not give the student the right to admission. For most universities and departments within universities set standards higher than this minimum. Whether they set such standards because they think the technical requirement is too low is a matter of dispute. In practice it arises because most departments are faced with more technically qualified applicants than they have places for. On what basis is this selection made and how satisfactory is it?

For most universities and departments there are three criteria: the level of marks at GCE, the reports of headmasters and headmistresses, and the interview. In operating these criteria the admissions procedure of the universities has become increasingly complex, and with the growing pressure on university places more and more time is spent in dealing with applications for admission. The universities are all the time seeking a system which will give the 'best' applicants admission, but I doubt whether they can succeed in this achievement except in quite an arbitrary sense. The problem is not one of selecting the outstanding students and rejecting the poor ones, for on any criteria these tend to select themselves. The issue is how to select a proportion of those in between who fall within a relatively narrow band, whether on examination performance, reports or interview. It is my contention that, looked at from outside, any method of selection applied to this group is bound to be arbitrary, whatever lengths those responsible for admission go to. Indeed, because of the necessarily arbitrary element in selecting a part of those who so nearly resemble one another, those responsible for admissions may clutch at any procedure which appears to make the selection more defensible both to themselves and to the public. The interview is obviously a procedure of this kind. It makes it possible for the universities to feel that they have taken into account qualities in the candidates which do not show in examination marks or reports, and it persuades the public that some rational method has been used to select between applicants who are very close together on these other criteria. But it is very doubtful whether, apart from the best and worst, who can easily be selected on other criteria anyway, the interview is anything more than a useful device for picking, where some picking has to be done. Is there any justification for the view that the interview selects the best, or that it gives a better result in the event than tossing a coin to decide who should or should not be admitted among this middle group of applicants?

If, as I argue, there is inevitably this arbitrary element in selection for admission, is there not a case for recognising it, being more generous in the initial admissions standard, and making greater use of the first year's course at the university to select those who should go on to complete a degree? Instead of trying by more and more devices, in my view inevitably unsuccessfully, to perfect methods of selection so that the 'best' are admitted, let us recognise our inability to do this and give a greater proportion of those who knock at the doors of the universities a chance to enter.

Such a policy would, of course, inevitably mean a greater rejection rate at the end of the first year. For there is nothing in this proposal which would enable the universities to deal with larger numbers in total than they would be able to do otherwise. It may, of course, be argued that at the end of one year at the university there will also be an arbitrary element in the results of the test which will be applied to decide who should be rejected and who should be allowed to proceed. This is no doubt a valid argument to some extent, but the element of arbitrariness is quite different from that at the point of admission. For the test would be within the university system of teaching and examination, and the student would be demonstrating whether he was able to make profitable progress within that system. Such performance would provide a relatively good prognosis of how he would perform in later years, in a way in which prognosis on the basis of school performance does not.

A more generous policy of admission with a higher proportion of rejections at the end of the first year would have other incidental but not unimportant consequences. At present the competitive pressure for admission is such that the schools are inevitably under pressure to train for the competitive struggle. It is always possible to distort the educational process and to train pupils in the examination or interviewing technique to try to squeeze the extra 5–10 per cent of marks. If all schools do this, as they are tempted to, none will be better off in the struggle for university places, but in the process the standard of education among the students—about which the universities complain so much—will be damaged. Another feature of the competitive struggle is to induce pupils to stay on in the sixth forms at school for three or even four years in the hope that they will achieve that extra margin that will give them admission to a university. Would it not be better for all concerned if these extra years were spent at the universities rather than at school?

It can be plausibly argued that the benefit of attending a university for the student is not mainly the formal education he receives, but the opportunity he has of discovering how to educate himself and of developing a wider outlook on life through being a member of a community of students. Even one year of this as a break between the relative narrowness of school life and starting a job may be of some value. And at least a larger number would feel that they had been given the opportunity of enjoying a university course.

Postgraduate teaching at English universities

There is a tradition, perhaps just a myth, in English universities, that in an honours degree course a student is brought to the frontiers of his subject and that if he then stays on at the university to do graduate work he is ready to do independent research. As a research student he will have a supervisor who will guide him in this research. The extent of guidance that he gets varies a great deal, but it is in most cases confined to a particular, fairly narrow, research topic.

It is my contention that such a system confines graduate education in this country too narrowly and that there is scope for developing postgraduate training of a broader kind which students should receive before they proceed to concentrate on a specific and narrowly confined research project. The development of such postgraduate teaching might also have incidental favourable effects on the scope and content of undergraduate courses.

I have not sufficient knowledge to argue the case for this view over the whole field of university studies, although I think that it merits consideration. What I argue is related particularly to economics. Whatever may have been the position in the past, it is certainly not true today that a student can be brought up to the frontiers of the subject over a period of three years. Attempts may be made to do this, but they involve enormous cost and even then are rarely successful. In order to get ahead in economics, the study of other related subjects, such as politics and history, may be reduced to a point where the student is encouraged to take a narrow specialist view of his subject, and the significance of the narrowness largely escapes him. Even within the confines of economics, he must specialise still further if he is to be familiar with the niceties of the latest fashionable controversies in the professional journals. The outstandingly brilliant student may succeed in understanding these, but at the end of three years his knowledge is narrow and specialist, and there are many parts of the subject to which he is an almost complete stranger. The average student, however, is unlikely to have grasped the significance of even the specialist aspects of the subject he has studied. He will merely have acquired a limited technical competence in answering examination questions. Where the attempt is not made to design the three-year course up to the frontiers of knowledge, the need for further training for students to become professional experts is obvious.

If one starts with the background material of either narrowly trained specialists or more widely taught but less 'advanced' students, it is doubtful whether the appropriate immediate graduate work for those who stay on is research on a specific research project for a thesis. Very often the student is not yet sufficiently at home in the general principles of the subject to know what his specific interests are or where he can profitably do research. Even if he has a research topic that he wants to follow, this usually means a reinforcement of a tendency to narrow specialisation. What is needed for most students is a further year's general course of study of an organised kind, during which time they can acquire a better general grasp of the essentials of the subject, and can also discover for themselves in which particular field they wish to do research if they stay on longer. Such a fourth year of study would be mainly on the basis of lectures and classes as at the undergraduate level but at an advanced level.

If it were accepted that a fourth year of general study is necessary to turn out professionally qualified economists, various things follow. The continuing dispute about the degree of specialisation appropriate at the undergraduate level would be reduced. For both students and staff would then accept the undergraduate degree course as a general rather than a specialised training, since there would be opportunity for study and teaching of the more advanced and specialised aspects of the subject in the fourth year. It would, of course, have to be generally recognised that normally such a fourth year would be necessary for anyone who wanted to be professionally qualified, and the opportunity to stay on for a fourth year would have to be available for those students who had shown sufficient merit in their first degree.

It would not be possible nor economical to institute postgraduate courses of this kind at all universities. If, as is suggested, such courses were organised on the basis of lectures and classes, a given minimum number of students would be needed to make the system worth while instituting. A university making provision for such graduate courses would draw its students from a wide range of graduates from the country as a whole.

If the provision of postgraduate training of this kind is regarded as desirable—and it is generally recognised that training for a fourth year is necessary to acquire professional competence in the subject—finance would have to be provided to enable and to induce those of sufficient merit to stay on for the fourth year. It would not be sufficient, in my view, to extend the present scale of grants and scholarships for a fourth year. This is unlikely to provide sufficient inducement, or to attract to postgraduate courses here those English students who at present go to American universities. Something more substantial would be needed, say at the level of about £600 a year.

An organised postgraduate course would also make it possible to deal more satisfactorily than at present with the large number of overseas students who come for postgraduate training to British universities. Most of these students express a desire to do research, but it is clear when they come here that what they need, perhaps even more than their counterparts coming from English universities, is a thorough training in the basic principles of the subject and, when they have acquired this, some study at the more advanced level. Given the level at which they have studied the subject before they come, a two-year course, consisting of the final year of the British first degree plus the first postgraduate year as envisaged here, would be much more appropriate for them than attempting some research project. If they succeeded in this kind of course they would then be ready and equipped to do some specific piece of research if they wished to stay on to do so.

Those who are familiar with American as well as British graduate schools will recognise that what is proposed here is that we should go some way at least towards adopting the American pattern. There is little doubt that American universities in their graduate schools provide for the training of technically proficient economist students in a way which British universities do not. It is not without significance that some of the best of British graduates recognise that if they want a rigorous training in economics at an advanced level they are more likely to get it in the United States than in this country.

If we are to provide an adequate flow of professionally trained economists for industry, public service, and the universities, and at the same time resist the tendency towards a high degree of specialisation in the first degree course, a fourth year should become a standard feature of our arrangements for university teaching of economics in this country. The universities will, however, find it worth while introducing such a system only if funds are available to induce the best selected students who want this professional training to stay on for at least a year's postgraduate training.

The government of the universities

The rapid growth of the universities in recent years has thrown up a wholly new series of problems in their government and administration. These are due partly to rapid change and partly to larger size. One of the odd features of the situation is that each university has met and dealt with these problems with very little knowledge about how they are met elsewhere. It is not clear whether each thinks of its own problems as peculiar, but the universities have certainly acted as if they had little to learn from what goes on elsewhere.

Any explanation of the way in which a university is governed and administered raises the usual problem of attempts at explaining how institutions work. One can fairly readily explain the formal structure of the university and the powers which the various organs—court, senate, council, faculties, departments, etc—have according to the written charter or constitution. Or one can attempt to explain how the system works in parctice—a much more difficult task, since this may bear little relation to the formal constitutional position. But little attempt has been made to study university government and administration at either level. Yet there are many issues which exercise those within the universities where knowledge and understanding of what has been tried elsewhere would be of great help, at least in making those issues clearer if not actually directly helping to solve them. I outline below some of the issues which I have in mind, all of which have become increasingly important in recent years:

1. Every university is having to face at intervals the issue of how much further to expand, if at all, and what facilities it needs for such expansion. How are decisions on such major issues of policy taken within the university? How 'democratic' is the decision-making process? How far, in particular, do junior members of staff feel that they have participated in the crucial discussions which have led to the final decision?
2. What autonomy is given to the departments and faculties within the university system? Has this autonomy increased or lessened as the university has grown in size?
3. What is the system for promoting staff? Is this done on a departmental, faculty or university basis? How does the machinery for considering cases for promotion work? Is any attempt made to keep to a particular ratio of different grades of staff within departments, faculties or the university as a whole?
4. How are senior appointments, to chairs and readerships, made? Do lay members sit on the appointments committee. Is outside academic opinion sought? If so, how is it arranged?
5. What is the division of functions between the administrative and academic staff? Does the academic staff take part in

decisions about finance and buildings, or are these left entirely to the administrative staff?

These are merely a few of the questions where knowledge of how things are done elsewhere would be of benefit to a university. I draw from this the conclusion that it would be highly desirable to have more work done than at present on the administration of universities.

[23]

The size of universities and university departments and the need for new university institutions[1]

I start with the general proposition—which I am not going to attempt to defend—that there is little merit in our trying to arrive at any sort of agreement about the 'optimum' size of department, faculty or university. There are advantages and disadvantages of size and growth, and where the balance lies at any particular time will depend on a whole range of complex circumstances.

I am, however, prepared to argue that as a department, faculty or university grows beyond a certain point, there is a natural tendency, unless official measures are taken to counteract it, for size to lead to increased academic specialisation and separation and to growing complexity of administrative organisation. These two tendencies reinforce one another. As the machine of administration becomes more complex, each department finds it increasingly frustrating to have to go through the central apparatus to get what it wants. It tries, therefore, to get more and more control over its own affairs, whether in appointments, teaching or research. When control is decentralised in this way, there is inevitably a temptation to keep to one's own department and to specialise one's contacts with both staff and students.

The machine of university government becomes so complex that few, if any, of the staff, let alone the students, understand how it works. There arises a disturbing murmuring about a mysterious 'they' who control university affairs. It is, of course, characteristic of a situation of this kind that nobody is able to specify who 'they'

[1] A paper presented to the Conference of the Universities of the United Kingdom, December 1958.

are. The sense that the university is an academic community in large measure in control of its own destiny is very much weakened.

I speak from limited experience only at Manchester University. And even in relation to Manchester I do not wish to exaggerate the dangers I am talking about. But I think the symptoms are there. And I would be surprised if they do not exist in other universities of similar structure, size and rate of growth to Manchester. Manchester has now reached a size, both in staff and students, where most of the 'academic' advantages of size are exhausted and further expansion will, in my view, merely aggravate the dangers I have been referring to.

The dangers of a weakening in this sense of community in the university are reinforced by the growth and increasing complexity of the control apparatus—both government and university—for controlling the universities. I know that most of those who participate in the working of this delicate system say how splendidly it works. And their views are reinforced by visitors from overseas, who are always aghast with admiration at the British capacity for making a virtue out of irrationality. But whatever virtues it has, the way it works serves to heighten the feeling among those of us who are on the periphery that we are subject to the control of a mysterious and remote 'they'.

We all know, of course—indeed we are told this at frequent intervals—that the vice-chancellors' committee, the UGC and the Treasury do not control the universities. They merely suggest, advise, co-ordinate and offer us money, which we can always refuse if we don't want it! But the very informality and indirectness of the machine's operation is itself one of its most frustrating features. For how can one discuss and argue about the influence these bodies exercise when in theory they exercise no control at all? But I am getting away from the main theme of this session, although I think, myself, that it is related to it.

My main argument is that we are already meeting many acute problems of size and growth, and that we need to take more conscious action to attempt to counteract the more obvious evils. Since many universities are faced with similar problems, I think we could learn a lot from each other's attempts to deal with them. Most of us live in complete ignorance of how things are managed in other universities. It is interesting that academics, willing though they are to dissect and criticise other institutions in society, do not take readily to a dispassionate examination of the institutions in which they work themselves. They are also inclined to think that the problems of universities are peculiar, whereas I am convinced that many of them—especially those related to size—bear close affinities with those of large-scale business and government departments.

Indeed, if we ourselves were to set about studying in an organised and comparative way how our universities work, who knows, we might even be able to explain the system to new members of the staff, instead of leaving them to try to find out painfully for themselves, with the result that they usually give up the attempt in frustrated despair.

If problems of size are already with us, as I'm sure they are at Manchester, how much more acute are they going to become in the next few years with still further expansion. It is quite clear from its recent report that the UGC is conscious of these problems, and they are expounded at some length. But they are not in my view adequately dealt with. The UGC report faces each issue squarely in the face—and then passes on. In nearly every case, proposals for dealing with these problems clash with the demand for more numbers. At each stage, when it comes to an operational decision, the UGC explicitly or implicitly favours numbers, and usually with the minimum immediate expenditure.

Take for example the section on 'Educational problems in the universities'. Most of the suggestions imply a much higher quality of staff than we have at present and—more important for my immediate point—much more individual attention to students by supervision, discussion and social contact. The report emphasises that with the increasing proportion of 'first generation' university students this, rather than lecturing, is the crucial educational activity. Indeed, there is the suggestion that unless the university can teach the student 'how to think' there is little point in having him at the university at all.

All very laudable, no doubt, although some of the sentiments suggest that the members of the UGC live in a dream world of their own making. Be that as it may, all this implies more facilities per student, both of space and teaching, and more time for universities to think how to cope with these problems, instead of being overwhelmed with the tasks of further expansion. But the report makes no attempt to resolve this conflict, and the implication behind its backing for increased numbers is that it is prepared to see serious attempts to solve some of these problems postponed for a decade or more.

This is especially serious for a university like Manchester, because there seems to me to be evidence that the UGC is particularly pressing expansion on the older provincial universities, since this seems in the short run to be the easiest and cheapest way to meet the demand for more numbers. For most of the newer universities, particularly those which have reached university status in the last decade, have set great store on having a high proportion of their students in residence. Expansion at these institutions usually means comparable expansion of expensive residential accommodation. But at universities such as Manchester the proportion of students in residence is low, and on the present ratio one can apparently get more easily and cheaply—from the UGC point of view—an increase in numbers.

Student accommodation is one of the most pressing problems at Manchester. But in other aspects of building too we have, no doubt like others, been working under grave physical handicaps since the war. A couple of years ago it looked as if we might have an opportunity to get things on a more satisfactory basis in the next few years. But the scale and timing of grants for building is such that the new expansion will now be upon us long before the buildings are up to deal with the *last* bout of expansion.

Why then, you may ask, does Manchester agree to expand, if it is going to create such difficulties? Partly because the offer of money for expansion is too great a temptation to resist. Also I think because there is a suspicion—and who is to say that it is unwarranted?—that if we did not agree to expand we should be at a disadvantage in persuading the UGC to give us what we need for our present numbers. Further, most of my colleagues seem to accept without much question the view that the UGC is best able to say what in the national interest is the right contribution for Manchester to make to the overall increase in numbers. They assume, of course, that the facilities for this expansion will be available in the right quantities at the right time.

Indeed, within each university the temptation to jump on the expansion bandwagon is well nigh irresistible. How much easier for the department which can point to expansion to lay claim to a share of the limited facilities for new staff and buildings!

Naturally, if one merely takes a short-run view, and looks at the problem of expansion quinquennium by quinquennium, it appears obvious that any expansion in numbers must come from existing institutions, and within these a major contribution must come from the older provincial universities. But if I am justified, even to some extent, in arguing that many of these universities are encountering acute problems of size, then this is in itself an argument for taking a longer view of the adequacy of existing institutions. For it is only the long view that will be of use. If we want new institutions to make a substantial contribution in fifteen or twenty years' time, discussion about their character and location needs to take place now. Traditionally, as I understand it, the UGC has not regarded itself as responsible for taking the initiative in setting up new institutions. It has waited until institutions that have developed spontaneously have put forward a claim to be included on the UGC list once they were well established. Most of the new universities of the last decade—Nottingham, Leicester, Hull, Southampton, Exeter—developed in this way. The college at Keele in north Staffordshire and the new venture at Brighton[2] are, of course, departures from this tradition. There is, however, little indication in the UGC report to show whether it regards these two as the forerunner of a new system for setting up university institutions. I know little about what went on behind the scenes in the decision to sponsor these ventures. There is only one brief paragraph about Brighton in the UGC report, and it is perhaps significant again that the report takes a short-run view and emphasises that the 'initial capital cost' should be lower than elsewhere because it will not be essential to provide living accommodation in the first stages of development.

I end, then, with the question whether, given the need to develop further new university institutions, the present system for initially sponsoring them is at all adequate.

[2] Now (1970) the universities of Keele and Sussex respectively.—*Ed.*

MISCELLANEA

[24]

Serving as a juryman in Britain[1]

It is with considerable diffidence and hesitation that I give a public lecture on a legal subject. For I have no professional qualification in the study of law, either British or American, and I fear that I will say many things which will merely reveal my ignorance. But I am emboldened to take the risk because my subject, 'serving as a juryman', is not one of which professional lawyers have any experience. For in England, and I believe in the United States as well, lawyers are understandably precluded from serving on juries. Although a great deal has been written, mostly by lawyers, about the role of the jury in the legal system, none of it, in England at least, is based on information about what goes on in the jury room.

Let me make it clear at the outset that what I have to say is based entirely on two periods of jury service which I was called for in Manchester a few years ago; the first period for the quarter sessions and the second for the assizes, each period for about a week. On each of these two occasions, I served myself on juries for two cases, neither of which lasted more than a single day. The rest of the time I spent sitting around in court, listening to other cases, waiting to be called. But in some of these cases, which I merely listened to, I had nonetheless an opportunity of discussing, perhaps unlawfully, with the jurymen concerned after the case was over, what had gone on in the jury room, and what had influenced the jury in arriving at its conclusion.

It is this question which is the central theme of my lecture—what evidence influences a jury in its findings. But I must repeat, at the risk of boring you, that in answering this question I am

[1] This paper was originally given as one of the John Hinkley Memorial Lectures at the Johns Hopkins University in the autumn of 1964 and was subsequently published in *The Modern Law Review*, September 1965, pp. 561–70.

merely giving a view of my personal experience, which is confined to a small number of cases and for all I know may be quite unrepresentative.

First of all, let me give a little background information as to how a jury is selected. This is of some importance because, as I hope to show later, the class composition of a jury and their social experience and knowledge may have considerable importance in influencing their assessment of some of the evidence placed before them. In England each local government authority has to keep up to date a list of registered voters, and this list (often used by market researchers) specifies with a letter J which of the electors is eligible for jury service. There is a general property qualification; at the time when I was called, owners of property with a value of more than £10 a year freehold or £20 a year leasehold, and householders renting property of a net annual value of more than £30 a year in London and Middlesex and £20 a year elsewhere were included in the jury list. This effectively excluded the bulk of the working class wage-earning group; for although these annual value property figures seem very low, in fact they were not actual market values of property, but nominal valuations for tax purposes, which were at the time still based on 1939 valuations. Within this group a long list of occupations was exempt, a list which must have been compiled some years ago—members of Parliament, doctors, lawyers, ministers of religion, Post Office workers, Customs, Exise and Board of Inland Revenue officers, and Inspectors of Factories.

I tried to find out how people were picked to serve on a jury panel. But the law books that I consulted in England are silent on this. The process of selection seemed to have worked in a peculiar way in my own case; for my legal friends were certainly surprised that I should have been called twice within a period of two years. On the second occasion, too, those who were called were heavily concentrated in my local area of suburban Manchester, for most of the panel came from three or four adjoining streets.

I was also curious to discover how the jury was picked for a particular case in the courts from the assembled panel. The textbooks suggest that it is a random process, with the method of securing this randomness varying from court to court. It certainly was not random in my case. I was called to attend on Monday morning; all day Monday and Tuesday morning I sat at the back of the court hoping that I would be called for a case, but I was not.

To put it mildly, by mid-day on Tuesday I was bored, angry and frustrated. I approached the police sergeant who seemed to be in charge of affairs, engaged him in general conversation, flattered him not very subtly by saying 'how difficult his job must be,' and explained that I was getting bored just hanging around not being called. He commented in a strong Lancashire accent—which I will not try to reproduce—that sometimes some of those called for the panel did not serve at all. I hoped that that was not going to happen to me. 'Leave it to me,' he said. 'The next case should be quite interesting.' Sure enough, the clerk called my name for the next case. A lesson no doubt in the application of the theory of personal relations.

Before getting to the central theme of the lecture—what influenced the jury in arriving at their decisions in particular cases—I would like to say a little about the general atmosphere in which the jury operated.

First, what struck me was the great contrast between the way the officials—the clerks and the police—treated us, and the attitude of the judges. The clerks and the officials treated us, so to speak, as 'jury fodder', conscripted by legal process: therefore without rights or deserving of consideration. We were herded into rooms, kept waiting without any indication as to when we would be called, or how long our service was likely to run; roughly dismissed with a rude grunt, if we dared to ask: 'Is it safe to go off for an hour or two?' Indeed, we began to feel that we were the criminals awaiting trial.

But once in the court room, the atmosphere changed. We were no longer 'jury fodder' but part of the English legal system; twelve citizens good and true. The judge, particularly, treated us with great respect and almost ostentatious kindness, making us feel that we were his equals; that indeed we and he were the only sane, normal people in the whole place. We were the guardians of reason, common sense and everyday language—the fictional 'reasonable men' beloved of the law—in a tangle of doubtful evidence, police jargon and far-fetched legalistic arguments.

Indeed, on one occasion the Recorder of Manchester interrupted a case for about a quarter of an hour to address us on the iniquitous way in which his court was being used by the circuit judges, just because Manchester corporation had done nothing yet to rebuild the Manchester assize courts, which had been destroyed by bombing during the war. He appealed to us as good Manchester citizens and ratepayers to see to it that action was taken to restore his premises to its proper use—that was, of course, for his court. This Recorder was indeed a rather eccentric judge—I was going to add 'and perhaps not representative', but I do think that is necessary. His name was Mr Noel Goldie and his court was called, quite openly, by the police 'Goldie's Follies'.

When I sat in the jury box on my first case, I was impressed with the following. First, that Englishmen must have been of much smaller bulk when the jury box was first designed, for we were miserably cramped and had to sit bolt upright for long periods; perhaps it was an astute move to make us so uncomfortable that when we did retire to the jury room we would be so weary that we would make our decision quickly. Second, how difficult it was to keep track of the evidence without taking notes. But no paper and pencil were provided. Perhaps I ought to have spoken up and asked the judge if I could have some. The fact that I wanted to take notes may just be an occupational failing; but as I shall show later, this implicit reliance on the memory of the jury, especially when the case was a complicated mass of evidence depending on an intricate web of times and locations, had important consequences for the way in which the jury arrived at its conclusions.

Nobody really told the jury what it was supposed to do. True, the judge in his summing up talked to us at some length about the evidence and kept on emphasising 'matters of law are for me; matters of fact are for you'. But I do not think that most of the jurymen understood what this meant—or if they did, they took little notice of it. At no stage did any judge state clearly and boldly, 'This court is concerned with (*a*) whether the man is guilty, (*b*) what the punishment should be. (*b*) is not your concern *at all*, but is for me to decide within the limits of the law; (*a*) you and I have to decide together—for I have to make clear to you what the law is, and you must then decide in the light of the evidence whether you think this man did what he is accused of.' No doubt plain language of this kind is out of place in a court of law, because my phraseology would be ambiguous and uncertain in its meaning to lawyers. Legal language may be certain, but it is over the heads of the jury, and tends therefore to be very largely ignored. Similarly, I think that expressions such as 'reasonable doubt', 'reasonable man', 'reasonable case'—terminology beloved of the legal theorist—have little meaning for the juror when he meets them for the first time. Perhaps when one has done a week or two's jury service one begins to learn, but by then although one has learned from experience one can no longer benefit by it.

No one told us how we should proceed when we went into the jury room to consider our verdict. For example, that we should elect a foreman. On my first case when we went into the jury room, we stood around, looking at each other rather sheepishly, not knowing where to start. One amongst us then volunteered: 'I know all about this, I've been on a jury before. We have to elect a foreman. Since I know all about it, perhaps you would like me to be foreman.' We all murmured our assent.

You will gather from all this that we all felt in very strange circumstances, not knowing quite what was expected of us or how to proceed. All this could have been avoided if the panel that had been called had been addressed at the outset by, say, the clerk of the court for a quarter of an hour, explaining to us the procedure of the court, our role in it and the way in which we were required to fill that role. But a little instruction of this kind would no doubt be thought by the lawyers to be tampering with the open-mindedness of the jury.

All this is preliminary, for the substance of my lecture is concerned with how we arrived at our verdict in the cases we dealt with. My main conclusion, which I can state at the outset, is that you could never tell what bit of evidence would influence the jury, and that frequently they were influenced in arriving at their verdict not merely by whether they thought the accused was guilty but also by whether he should be punished. If they thought there were special circumstances, even if they thought the accused guilty, they were likely to find him not guilty to make sure he was not punished. As the police sergeant with whom, as I indicated earlier, I had struck up a talking relationship, said to me, 'I've been serving in this court for nigh on twenty-five years. I've listened to hundreds of cases. At first I used to try to assess in advance in each case whether the jury would bring in a verdict of guilty or not guilty. But having experienced some of the craziest decisions imaginable, I've given it up. It's a complete waste of time to try and guess what the jury will do. You might as well toss a coin.'

The first case I would like to deal with, which I call 'The Case of the Officious Bureaucrat', concerned a man who was being prosecuted for re-selling used national insurance stamps. The accusation was that the man had got hold of some national insurance cards, steamed off the stamps, rubbed off the cancelling dates, and had used them again, thus avoiding paying the national insurance contribution and defrauding the insurance fund. The main evidence came from a Ministry of National Insurance expert, who told us of tests he had done on the gum which had been used to stick on the stamps, and the small bits of fibre that were still attached to the stamps. The first demonstrated that two kinds of gum had been used, one of which was not the kind used on the reverse side of the stamps as issued; the second that there were some bits of fibre adhering to the stamps, different in texture from those of the current card, and clearly giving evidence of some previous adhesion.

Then came evidence from a Ministry of National Insurance official, about how the cards were handled in the Ministry of National Insurance. This was to get clear a small technical point on other evidence which was brought to show the stage at which the employee had the opportunity to purloin old cards. The official, who seemed to me to be quite a junior one, gave his evidence clearly, but somewhat disdainfully, cryptically and officiously—or so it seemed to me—in answer to questions by prosecuting counsel. He was almost the prototype of the petty bureaucrat. Defence counsel was apparently quick to realise this. He started his cross-examination in a slow, drooling manner, purposely I think, wanting the official to think that he, counsel, was a fool, and just did not have the least glimmering of understanding of how an efficient office organisation—like that of the Ministry of National Insurance—was run. As these admittedly rather stupid questions went on you could almost sense that the civil servant was losing his temper, and at one stage he replied to one of counsel's questions, 'That is irrelevant.' Counsel now changed his mien completely; from an apparently silly, rather sleepy, inefficient cross-examiner, he became alive and as sharp as a hawk. He riled the witness, who, getting angrier and angrier, got to the point of making the fatal reply, 'That is a silly question.' You can imagine what happened then; the judge intervened, admonished the witness and told him to answer and not to comment on the questions, which the witness did from then on, but in an obviously sulky and surly manner.

In his summing up the judge concentrated on the evidence of the technical expert, pointing out that it had not been seriously challenged, and that the defence had no explanation for it. He hardly mentioned the officious clerk's evidence, since this was on quite a minor point. And he pointed out to us that the onus was on the prosecution to prove guilt.

The point of all this is its influence on the jury. When we retired to the jury room the jurymen turned to each other saying, 'Did you hear that little pipsqueak of a civil servant?' 'These petty bureaucrats, they need to be taught a lesson.' 'I would not like to have to work for him.' When the self-appointed foreman asked for our views on the case, I said that the technical evidence seemed to me to show conclusively that the stamps had been re-used, that this was not rebutted by the defence, and that the accused had given no explanation whatsoever except just flatly to deny having used old stamps. This seemed to me conclusively to point towards his guilt. The others disregarded this altogether and just said one after another: 'But look at that tinpot dictator'; 'these officials'; 'it might happen to us any day'; 'I'm not going to find him guilty'; 'let's teach these civil servants a lesson'. So they all argued for 'not guilty'. I argued with them for about twenty minutes that they were not directing themselves to the evidence; I called attention to the judge's summing up and argued that the officiousness of the civil servant was really quite irrelevant. But it was no use; this was what impressed them, and they were determined to do the official world one in the eye. I gave way and we returned a verdict of 'Not guilty'.

The second case, which I call 'The Case of the Unidentified Intruder', was concerned with a man accused of 'breaking and entering' a domestic household. The evidence can be summarised briefly. First, a married woman, who explained that she went out to work daily during the week, coming home at around 5.30. She usually locked the doors, and thought she had done so on the particular day in question. When she came home she found the back door open, she heard a noise upstairs, and then a man rushed down the stairs past her out of the back door. She was so upset and the man dashed by so quickly that she did not see his face and could not identify him. The next witness was a fingerprint expert, who explained that he had examined various fingerprints in the house and that they were identical with those of the accused. He explained that to be sure of a fingerprint identity one had to be able to point (I think it was) to eight characteristics, and that in this case he could identify fourteen, so that he had no doubt whatsoever that the fingerprints were those of the accused.

The accused just flatly denied being in the house, and it was his counsel, in cross-examining the housewife, who had elicited the information that she had not really seen the intruder's face. In summing up the judge drew special attention to the evidence of the fingerprint expert, pointing out the significance of the certainty given by the number of identical characteristics he had found, and indicating that in view of this the fact that the woman was not able to identify the intruder did not really matter.

At this stage the jury withdrew. I ought to point out that this was not a case where I was a member of the jury, but I discussed it at some length with the foreman of the jury afterwards. After about half an hour the foreman of the jury reported that they were in disagreement and unable to reach a verdict. The judge, it seemed to me, was rather surprised by this, told them to go back again and try a little harder. Another three-quarters of an hour passed and the jury again reported inability to agree on a verdict. On this occasion the judge asked counsel for the prosecution what he had to say. As I understand it, he could have asked for a retrial with another jury. His reply was to throw his papers on his desk and his hands up in the air in desperation, indicating that the Crown would not wish to pursue the matter further. And so the accused was released.

When I asked the foreman why the jury could not agree when the fingerprint evidence was so conclusive, he said that about half the jury were sceptical of so-called 'scientific' evidence, and were not prepared to find the man guilty since he had not been seen and identified by the housewife. 'But,' I exclaimed, 'fingerprint evidence is in any case more conclusive than someone's memory of a face, which can often be so misleading.' He then told me that he was one of those who were suspicious of fingerprint evidence. I argued with him, but after a few moments it became clear to me that we were really not in communication with each other and I gave up.

The attitude of juries to the evidence of expert witnesses called by the Crown was in general one of suspicion. As many of them said to me, 'That's what they are paid for; they are sure to give evidence against the accused.' It was on this kind of view that they tended on the whole to dismiss the evidence of the police surgeon in cases of people prosecuted for being in charge of a motor vehicle while under the influence of alcohol. They persisted in the view that since the police surgeon was a Crown, or, as they put it, a police witness, and was paid, he was bound to say that the accused was drunk, and therefore no reliance could be placed on his evidence. While I had to admit that the police surgeon always gave evidence that the accused *was* drunk—if he had not found him drunk the case would not have been brought—I had no success in persuading fellow jurors that it did not follow from this that his evidence should be dismissed.

The third case, which I call 'The Case of the Aged Opera Lover', was concerned with a man prosecuted for being drunk in charge of a car. The police gave evidence that late at night they observed him driving in a swerving manner, and that when they stopped him and opened the car door he sat there singing at the top of his voice. They asked him to get out of the car, which he did, but could then hardly stand upright. At the police station, where they took him, he was examined by the police surgeon, who gave evidence that in his view the man was quite unfit to drive. The man's own doctor then gave evidence that when he examined the accused (true, about an hour later), in his view he was quite fit to drive. The accused himself gave evidence that he was a great lover of light opera, and that he frequently sang; on the particular occasion in question he was singing something from Gilbert and Sullivan. He admitted that it might seem odd to be singing in his car so loudly, but the reason was simply that he was bursting with joy of life. He seemed to be quite an elderly man; his defending counsel gave his age as seventy-two. One of the most significant things in this case was the way in which defending counsel managed to get the witness to slip out two points in his evidence, although they were quite irrelevant to the charge, and as I understand it ought not to have been mentioned (and so the judge said in his summing up). First, that in his business the man depended on being able to drive a car, and that if his driving licence were taken away from him he would be ruined; second, that he had been driving for thirty years and had never been in trouble before.

The case was absolutely clear, and after a short time the jury brought in a verdict of guilty. The judge then said 'I now have no option under the law but to suspend your driving licence for twelve months (I think it was twelve), but you may apply after a certain time for it to be restored.' I noticed that one of the lady members of the jury tried to rise as if she wished to say something, and she was pulled down to her seat by the man whom I later discovered was the foreman. You see this was another case on which I was not a juryman but observed the proceedings at the back of the court, and discussed the case with some of the jurymen afterwards. When I did so in this case I asked what was the explanation of the smothered incident in the jury box. The juryman I spoke to explained that when the jury discussed the case they were all agreed that the man had obviously been drunk. But the two women members of the jury had said, 'It's a pity for the poor old man; it is the first time he has been in trouble, and he will be ruined if he cannot use his car in his business; let us be merciful and find him not guilty.' The others protested, saying that it was for the jury merely to decide whether the accused was guilty or not. If they were clear on that they must bring in a verdict accordingly. The punishment was for the judge, who would no doubt be sympathetic and probably only impose a small fine. 'All right,' said the two women jurors, 'on the clear understanding that the judge will only fine him and not take away his licence we will agree to a verdict of guilty.' But none of the jurors apparently knew that for an offence of that kind the judge had no option, as indeed he explained, but to suspend the man's licence. When he was delivering sentence to that effect, one of the women jurors apparently wanted to protest that she had been misled and wished no longer to find the accused guilty. She had to be restrained by the foreman; this accounts for the smothered incident which I referred to earlier.

My last case—here I did serve on the jury myself—which I call 'The Case of the Unrepresented Defendant', was a man who was accused of stealing a portable second-hand wireless set from a pawnbroker's shop that had been broken into. One of the important features of this case was that the defendant, notwithstanding advice from the judge, refused to be legally represented and insisted on conducting his own defence. The details of the case were very complicated, for they involved evidence about the time at which the shop had probably been broken into; identification of the wireless set by the man who had pawned it to the shop as the same as the one found in the defendant's possession. There was argument by the Crown, notwithstanding evidence brought by the defendant from friends as to where he had been at various times on that day, that he could have been in the neighbourhood of the pawnbroker's shop at the crucial time. The defendant pleaded that he had bought the wireless set in a pub for three pounds from a stranger whom he did not know and whom he could not now get hold of to bring forward as a witness. I must admit that I do not now remember in detail all the evidence; but I do recall that it was long and complicated, involving a whole series of arguments about times. I also recall that when the judge came to sum up I found it impossible to follow or remember the crucial points because, as I mentioned right at the beginning, we were not in a position to take notes. Towards the end of the evidence the judge said to the defendant, 'Are you quite sure that you have asked all the witnesses all the questions you wish to, and that you have called all the witnesses you wish to call?' At this late stage the accused murmured, 'There are two witnesses who could conclusively support my evidence that I was not at the shop at the relevant time, but it is no use trying to call them.' The judge persisted in explaining to the defendant that if he wanted to call witnesses they would be called. The defendant then made what seemed to me to be the mistake of saying, 'It is no use because they are in Strangeways gaol.' But the case was adjourned and the witnesses were called. Out of the questions that he asked there emerged incidentally the fact that the defendant and these witnesses had been in jail together several times, and from that moment onwards he was clearly regarded as a criminal type by the jury.

The judge summed up the complicated evidence about times and places and told us to ignore the fact that had emerged in the evidence that the defendant had already been in jail for previous offences. When it came to the jury room discussion, we were pretty well at sea, for not having taken any notes, none of us could reliably remember the detailed evidence about times and places. We concentrated on two issues: the plausibility of the accused's evidence that he had bought the wireless set for £3 in a pub, and his criminal record. On the first we asked each other, 'Do people really buy and sell wireless sets in a pub?' None of us went to working-class pubs —here the class composition of the jury was important—and we just did not know whether transactions of this kind were likely to take place there. But we *thought*, and I repeat *thought*, that it was most unlikely. Second, most of the jurymen were influenced by the criminal record of the accused's friends and of the accused himself. And so, I repeat, with practically no consideration of the evidence, we found the man guilty. Perhaps no injustice was done. Certainly when the list of his previous convictions was read out before the judge pronounced sentence, it took quite a long time to get through.

This completes my cases, and the story I have to tell of serving as a juryman in Britain. Do I draw any conclusions? Perhaps I ought not to; except one which I will venture with some assurance. That if the jury is to remain part of the English legal system, it is just as well that its proceedings should remain secret, and that it should be only on very rare and special occasions like this that jurymen should discuss their experience.

[25]
The conference game[1]

Whether in government, business or academic life, modern man has to spend an increasingly large part of his time in conference and committees. This is a heavy and arduous burden, not merely because it steals time from more pleasant pursuits but also because sitting in interminable conference sessions and endless committees exhausts the mind and harrows the soul. There is no ennui like the ennui induced by having to listen to the pompous and obtuse irrelevancies of one's opponents, and even more of one's friends. There are two ways of dealing with this ever-growing problem (I dismiss the possibility of revolutionary action to destroy the conference and committee system as well beyond the capacities of modern man; we must learn to live with it). My solutions are twofold. First, the more scientific; to become a detached observer and use the rich material that is provided by these occasions as a basis for the study of administration. Second, the more artistic and delightful, to play what I have come to call the conference game. Both these solutions are worth trying, but anyone with a true sense of values will recognise the second solution—the conference game—as much to be preferred. Let me explain how the game is played, giving you a real-life example from an international conference that I recently attended.

First I should confess that I am not the inventor of the game. I first came across it when played, in a slightly different variant from the one I use, by a delightful colleague of mine during the war. I then worked as a temporary civil servant in Whitehall, and the department of which I had charge was staffed mainly by academics. Some of these took to bureaucratic life as does modern youth to space travel, but others found it uncongenial and irksome. Such a

[1] From *The Economist*, 4 July 1959, where it appeared under the pseudonym 'Unicorn'.

one was my colleague 'X', now an eminent professor at Oxbridge.[2] He rarely understood what he was expected to do in the department, and even when he did he was incapable of carrying out his task according to the rules of the bureaucratic game. At the weekly staff meeting which I held he had nothing to contribute to our discussions, and wore the air of a completely lost and remote figure. Then one week, to my amazement, I was struck by a strange liveliness in his outlook. He appeared anxious to contribute to the argument and put in a sentence or two—true, not always very relevant—on every conceivable occasion. This went on for two or three weeks before I noticed that at a certain stage in the proceedings his loquacity would stop suddenly, like a road hog meeting a red traffic light, and he would lapse into his more normal silent and remote mood. The following week I watched carefully, for by this time I was sure that some funny business was afoot. Again the same initial ebullience and loquacity for a while, suddenly giving way to misery and silence, just as a clown turns from laughter to tears. But this time I noticed that at the moment of change 'X' smiled and winked to a colleague, who winked in return.

Fascinated, I could hardly wait for next week's meeting. I almost decided to trump up some excuse for holding it early. The same performance again, for I was sure by this time that it *was* a performance. I waited patiently, listening to every word, for the moment of transition, and then at last, to my intense delight and satisfaction, I spotted the secret. In the last sentence he spoke before lapsing into silence, 'X' used the word 'hermaphrodite', and this did not altogether fit in with the flow of the discussion. Now I knew, and as we walked out of the meeting I stopped 'X' and my other colleague and said, 'The game is up; I know the secret.' He admitted, without shame, that through over-confidence as a result of victorious play in earlier weeks he had been reckless and lost. He explained, what I had by now myself realised, that he and his colleague were playing a game to relieve the boredom and monotony of having to attend a weekly staff meeting. An hour or so before the meeting he and his colleague agreed on some word most unlikely to be used in the ordinary course of our discussion, and the game then consisted of seeing which of the two could introduce the word first in

[2] 'X' was in fact David Champernowne, now a Fellow of Trinity College, Cambridge, and earlier Professor of Statistics in the University of Oxford.—*Ed.*

the committee proceedings. It was, of course, a condition of winning that no one else at the meeting should notice what was going on. The word that week was 'hermaphrodite'! What a delightful way of overcoming the ennui of committee life. But he had lost on this occasion and could never play it again at my meetings.

At a recent conference I attended on the application of the social sciences to business management and training, the sessions were so boring, frustrating and irritating that I was reminded of the game. When one evening, in the company of a charming, exuberant Italian and a sensibly sceptical American, I was lamenting the waste of so much effort, I explained to them how my friend 'X' had dealt with a similar situation during the war. The Italian immediately saw the essential beauty and fascination of the game and suggested that we should play a variant of it at the closing session of the conference the following day. He would give me a word and challenge me to introduce it into a speech at the final session without anyone but we three noticing it.

Heady with good local food and drink—it is one of the major compensations of these conferences that the organisers are usually considerate enough to choose a beautiful Continental city—I immediately accepted the challenge. At first, being novices at the game, they chose easy words, such as 'duck' and 'port', and I was able to explain quite quickly how simple it would be to introduce these. Such words would provide no real challenge, and the essential element of distraction and excitement would, therefore, be missing. As the evening wore on, under the exhilarating influence of yet more drink, the Italian with great ingenuity thought of progressively more difficult words and at last hit upon two which I felt were worthy of an advanced player—'unicorn' or 'Tropic of Cancer'. I accepted the challenge of 'unicorn'.

And so we returned to our hotel and our beds. But there was no sleep for me. I tossed and turned till three in the morning, and then in a flash I saw the solution. I earned the reward of peaceful sleep until 7.30, which for me—an insomniac—was a great boon.

The final session came in the afternoon. I ought at this stage to explain that the main work of the conference was conducted in groups, each devoted to one branch of the social sciences. I was chairman of the group on economics, and was by this time maddeningly irritated by having to sit through four sessions listening to pretty idiotic argument about the uses of economics and economic research in business management and training. At the final session a rapporteur was to sum up the proceedings. He was down to speak for forty-five minutes. Considering the rambling and inconsequential nature of the discussion in the groups, he did pretty well, although whether his summary really bore much relation to what went on is another matter. But he went on much too long—well over an hour and a quarter. The conference became restless, and I began to fear that there would be no time for discussion from the floor and that I would not have the opportunity of meeting the challenge I had accepted.

Then at last the rapporteur finished, and the chairman asked, not surprisingly in view of the late hour, in a rather discouraging tone whether anyone wanted to comment. Too obvious if I get up now, I thought, with a sinking sense of loss. But a Dutchman sprang to his feet, said how important it was that social scientists should make themselves understandable and useful to business, etc, etc. What more could I ask for? For on this issue, which had been a recurring theme in most sessions, I felt deeply and passionately. Now was my chance, and indicating my intention to the chairman and interpreters, I spoke as follows.

'Mr Chairman, I had not intended speaking, but in view of the comments of the last speaker I cannot contain myself. I disagree with him fundamentally, and my disagreement has been reinforced by the discussion and argument that I have heard during this conference as chairman of the economics group. If I had to choose a coat of arms for my group it would be a bull rampant, for as economists we have been tossed on the horns of a dilemma. On the one hand, if we deal with problems which we understand in the theoretical forms with which we are familiar, we are accused by business of being remote and unpractical; on the other hand, if we go out into business as economists we are tempted to deceive businessmen into thinking that we have some magic solutions to their problems, and are despised for this by our more honest academic colleagues. Obsession with such dilemmas leads to schizophrenia, and schizophrenia to madness. Why should we be concerned with our usefulness to business? I would much prefer my coat of arms to be a unicorn, and to be impaled, if I must, on the single horn of truth! I agree with the speaker who opened this conference' (a Frenchman) 'that we should follow the example of the natural sciences, but not in the sense in which he argued' (the usual nonsense about the observation of facts and the elaboration and testing of hypotheses). For me the true scientific tradition can best on this occasion be expressed in French, and execrable though my accent may be, I will use the French: "À bas l'utilité, vive la verité".'

Imagine my sense of achievement and exhilaration as I sat down to great applause. I had won, I had said what I wanted to say, and yet got in the word 'unicorn' without anyone, except my two friends privy to the game, noticing. And my victory was confirmed by a note passed to me from the Italian: 'My dear Unicorn, il faut dire la verité et s'immoler. With admiration.'

Just to make sure, we asked one or two conferees whether they had noticed anything odd about my speech, explaining why we were interested, and their replies confirmed my victory. Inevitably, from then on I was known as 'Unicorn'.

I hope I have convinced you what a fascinating game this is, and how it can be played to relieve the boredom of conference and committee life. Do try to play, and if you are successful write to me at ——. If there is enough support we might form a Unicorn Club to codify the rules of the game and adjudicate disputes. Anyone could join, but we might reserve the title of Fellow for those who show evidence of continued success at an advanced level. And if we could get a generous benefactor to give us a little money (I'm sure we could get the Board of Inland Revenue to treat it as a charitable contribution), we could strike a gold medal which would be awarded to the member who successfully played the game at the annual meeting of the society itself.

Index